THE OCCULT EXPLOSION

NAT FREEDLAND

The Occult
Explosion

G. P. Putnam's Sons, New York

For my beloved wife, Mary

Contents

THE OCCULT EXPLOSION

Chapter 1

The Occult Explosion Is Here!

IN Salt Lake City, Utah, an alchemy school—the Paracelsus Research Society, Box 6006, ZIP Code 84106—offers a two-week course on how to turn lead into gold.

From Malvern, Pennsylvania, John M. Hansen (Box 149, ZIP Code 19355) distributes the U.S. edition of *The Waxing Moon,* an Anglo-American newsletter for witches. It was started by Air Force Sergeant Jo B. Wilson, who now publishes from England, writing under the pen name Sean Armstrong.

Astronaut Edgar Mitchell mentally transmitted ESP cards to Chicago engineer Olof Jonsson, and three others during the Apollo 14 moon flight. Chance odds for success would be 20 percent, but Mitchell's earthbound partners picked the correct ESP card order with 25 percent accuracy.

The 1970 Berkeley graduating class included the world's first B.A. in magical studies, Isaac Bonewits, twenty. "Magic is always the last explanation," he says. "I am willing to take fraud, error, hallucination, or anything else first. But you go through all of these things and sooner or later you find a few occurrences that just don't fit in."

The first Festival of the Occult Arts was logged into history April 19, 1970, at the Fillmore East, then Bill Graham's rock concert hall in the East Village. Over three times the expected audience showed up.

About ten miles after Route 69 branches off from Highway 17, the main road north from Phoenix, Arizona, and begins its climb to Jerome, the World's Largest Ghost Town, there is a cluster of trailers and small concrete-block homes. The house

nearest to the road has a banner all along its side: NEW AGE
METAPHYSICAL TRUTH CENTER. A gentleman in Bermuda shorts
and an eyeshade is working on the roof. "Yes, we're developing a
fine little community of metaphysics students here," he says.
"Most of us were in contact through the New Age publications,
and we felt there was a need for a little town away from the
crowds and riots and smog of the cities, a place where people interested in things like Urantia, the Aquarian Gospels, and
UFO's could live together in a spiritual atmosphere."

Eighteen psychic tours of the British Isles were scheduled for
the summer of 1971. The $629 package included visits with some
of England's best-known mediums, a faith-healing treatment,
and haunted castles throughout Britain and Ireland.

The big, big A of the Astroflash Computer Center beckons
commuters hurrying across the great marble arcade of Grand
Central Station. It is open fifteen hours a day and attracts three
hundred daily customers. For $5, the computer will type out a
sixteen-page horoscope in two minutes flat, complete with planetary degrees and configurations, a personality profile, and a six-
month forecast. (I checked mine after the six months were up
and discovered that Astroflash had been at least 75 percent correct in its predictions—particularly with some of the less pleasant ones.)

Or with an annual membership card in Zodiactronics, you can
phone their toll-free number in New York City, read off your
code digits, and within seconds the computer itself will announce your personal horoscope for today. And in Los Angeles,
you can dial a less custom-tailored daily phone horoscope free.
Zodiacphone has different numbers for each of the twelve zodiac
signs, and all you have to give them is thirty seconds of your time
to listen to a commercial before the horoscope comes on. The entire operation is automated and clocks itself as receiving a million calls a month.

Billboards with huge demon heads and questions like, "Is
There Life After Death?" suddenly appeared along the West
Coast during the summer of 1970. "We've never had a client
with quite the same marketing situation," says Don Cunningham, senior vice-president of the Foote, Cone & Belding
advertising agency. London's BPC Publishing Ltd. was spending
$50,000,000 in a two-week saturation campaign to try out four

Western states as the U.S. test market for *Man, Myth & Magic,* a weekly seventy-five-cent magazine which becomes a complete encyclopedia of the occult after one hundred and twelve issues. *Man, Myth & Magic* had already earned hundreds of millions as a best seller in the United Kingdom, Australia, and Canada—far outgrossing the company's magazine-encyclopedias on the two World Wars.

Jonathan Frid was getting 5,000 fan letters weekly while he played Barnabas the Vampire on *Dark Shadows,* the TV gothic soap opera watched five afternoons a week by 15,000,000 people during its seasons on the ABC Network. Frid, who is about forty-five, looks like a hip Sherlock Holmes; he was mostly unemployed as a Shakespearean actor till he showed that a vampire can be a contemporary sex symbol. "I didn't know what a vampire was supposed to be like so I played him as a sex maniac," Frid explains. "At least I'm a lovable and pitiable one. . . Barnabas is looking for a new morality just like the youngsters today."

The Holland House Cafeteria is on one of the flashiest high-rise blocks of the Wilshire Boulevard Miracle Mile in Los Angeles, surrounded by IBM, Equitable Insurance, and the Ambassador Hotel. By six thirty in the evening all the workers have gone, and the whole area looks like a deserted movie set. But every Friday at this time, the check-out line inside the cafeteria is surprisingly busy. And all the diners are carrying their trays downstairs past a half-acre of empty tables to where the arrow points: RESTROOMS—TELEPHONES. There in the basement is a public service meeting room where about one hundred people are handing over their $1 donations to hear the night's speakers of the Jessica Madigan Philosophic Roundtable. Since 1967 the Roundtable has been filling this hall every Friday. A usual program consists of an astrologer or two, a dream analyst, perhaps a slide lecture on Atlantis, and a psychic, medium, or hypnotist. The organizer, perky, middle-aged Jessica Madigan, makes psychic trance predictions through her control spirit, Mei Ling. The audience for all this is cross-section America—young and old, straight and hip, student and businessman, showbiz and secretarial.

One of the night's featured attractions is a deep-trance medium—H. W. "Bud" Riffel from Santa Ana in neighboring Orange County. The barrel-chested, bald Riffel explains, "I was an auto racing mechanic on the Lotus team. Eight years ago during the off-season I started talking in my sleep in some foreign language I didn't know anything about. My wife, Marilyn—a PhD in allergenics—made tapes and brought them to a linguistics professor we know. He said it was a dialect of ancient Arabic." Riffel then goes into a trance, shutting his eyes and grimacing under the neon glare. Standing nearby to help him with the meditation are his harlequin-spectacled, bouffant-haired spouse and Joe G. Evans, a Dupont regional manager who helps the Riffels run their Know Thy Self Fellowship. After a few minutes Bud announces, "I am Paul, born of Arabic descent in the year of four A.D." In a halting, mechanical voice he proceeds to answer audience questions about the Other Side, where he is a teacher at one of the twelve universities that instruct disembodied souls about the mistakes of their past karma (destiny) and prepares them to choose suitable parents for their next reincarnations.

Radio station XERB has a 150,000-watt transmitter on the Mexican border which can blanket the western United States north to Canada when atmospheric conditions are right. Typical of the daytime commercials they used to run is, "It's Madame Stanley for solving your problems with love or money! Madame Stanley, the amazing psychic consultant, can help YOU!! Unveil the secrets of the future with Madame Stanley! Call this number NOW for your appointment!" In 1970 XERB was bought by its leading disk jockey—*Wolfman Jack*.

All of these items are part of the occult explosion in America today. No modern, postindustrial society has ever experienced anything like this occult explosion. For the first time in history, the occult tradition—which began when prehistoric man started scratching star maps into the walls of his caves and speculating on what the gods were signaling with these majestic processions of light across the heavens—is taking on the techniques of advanced technology. Naturally, one of the most visible results is mass marketing of a fashionably commercial occultism. But there are far more important effects too—a remarkable new public understanding of serious occult ideas, and recent scientific breakthroughs that correlate with the occult tradition to a breathtaking degree of accuracy.

Time's "Cult of the Occult" cover story of March 21, 1969,

pointed out that sheer weight of numbers in "the most scientifically sophisticated generation of young adults in history" has turned the occult arts "from a fad into a phenomenon." During 1969 and 1970 *Esquire, McCall's,* and *Harper's Bazaar* had special issues on the occult resurgence, with lengthy articles showing up in such publications as the *Wall Street Journal* and *Newsweek.* Within a two-week period, no less than three TV documentaries on the occult were aired in Los Angeles. Ralph Story's Metromedia Network special claimed in passing that $800,000,000 was spent in 1969 on astrology alone.

In the autumn of 1970 every movie studio still left in Hollywood had at least one film on an occult theme in production, and most had two or three. Surprisingly, the single holdout was Paramount Pictures, which started off the cycle with Roman Polanski's box-office smash, *Rosemary's Baby.*

The greatest common denominator of occultism in the United States is the astrology column. These horoscopes, carried in 1,200 of the nation's 1,750 daily newspapers, have a total potential readership of 40,000,000.

The next largest occult category is the astrology pulp magazines, which sell about 2,000,000 copies monthly. Dell's *Horoscope* leads the field with a circulation of approximately half a million, and *American Astrology,* which originated the genre in 1933, isn't too far behind. The most successful U.S. general-occult magazine, *Fate,* was started in 1947 and now sells 115,000 copies of each issue.

Several European countries have conducted surveys of how widespread occult beliefs are among their citizens. In a 1955 private census published as *Exploring English Character,* one of every six Englishmen queried said they believed in ghosts, 45 percent believed in luck, one-third had been to a fortune-teller, and one in seventeen actually believed that at some time they had seen a ghost. Also in the 1950's the German Institute of Public Opinion found that 29 percent of a nationwide sample believed there was a connection between human fate and the stars.

No such poll has ever been attempted in America. But based on the sales of key occult publications and products here, membership in large occult organizations such as the Rosicrucians AMORC and attendance at occult-related public events, one could reasonably estimate that there is now an occult subculture in the United States of roughly 1,000,000 persons—or one out of every two hundred Americans.

There are, of course, many degrees of activeness within this subculture, but our estimated total of 1,000,000 includes persons involved with the occult explosion to the extent that they seek out specifically occult merchandise and meetings, have perhaps joined occult organizations, and are fairly well informed on occultism.

The sudden visibility of this massive new social group has naturally led to much speculation about its meaning, and any well-known figure in American thought is sought after for quotes.

Harvard University's hip, activist chaplain, Harvey Cox, says unworriedly about the occult explosion, "Our tight, bureaucratic, and instrumental society is fascinated with the slippery stuff that never found a place in it: astrology, madness, witches, drugs, non-Western religions, palmistry, and mysticism, shoddy or serious." But Yale's equally hip, activist chaplain, William Sloane Coffin, fears that America's renewed interest in occultism is "a beautiful example of the lobotomized passivity that results from the alienating influence of modern technological society."

Optimistic as ever about new trends is Marshall McLuhan, the media prophet who pioneered the idea that a culture is whatever it understands itself to be from the tools it develops to extend perception. "The current interest of youth in astrology, clairvoyance, and the occult is no coincidence," he says. "Psychic communal integration, made possible at last by the electronic media, could create the universality of consciousness foreseen by Dante when he predicted that men would continue as no more than broken fragments until they were unified into an inclusive consciousness. Mysticism is just tomorrow's science dreamed today."

Another major technological seer, Buckminster Fuller of Geodesic Dome fame, also agrees that an Age of Telepathy is rapidly approaching. He'd like to prepare for it by linking every American home to a computer voting machine so the public can ballot instantly on important issues.

Alan Watts is one of the most creative interpreters of Oriental philosophy today. He says, "What is constructive and meaningful about the return of occultism is that for the first time, masses of young Americans are learning that life can have a goal of something else besides producing and consuming junk, that life should be directed at spiritual ends. People are bored and disillusioned with the goals of contemporary society, nobody wants a Cadillac or wall-to-wall carpeting anymore. What's pleasurable to thinking persons today are active mind-body disciplines like Yoga or meditation."

The London-born Watts is an ordained Episcopal minister who admits his scholarship in the Hindu-Buddhist tradition started with a childhood addiction to Fu Manchu thrillers. He no longer has any organizational church ties and lives with his wife on a beached ferryboat in Sausalito, a few miles north of the Golden Gate Bridge. Watts considers kimonos the most rational form of male attire and wears them all the time except when he's out lecturing—he dresses in standard suits on the platform so audiences won't be distracted from his message. Lately he has been teaching that Oriental religion is much more like psychotherapy than like the Judeo-Christian concept of theology. He sees Asia's version of reincarnation as a symbolic technique for freeing people of socially induced neuroses, bringing insights which will produce a "reborn" individual who has penetrated past the screen of illusion called maya by occultists, and who can then return to a constructive life "in the world but not of it."

"There's quite a lot of superstitious bunk to the kids' acceptance of this chalk-and-cheese occultism," he says. "Occultism and mysticism are two different things. Occultism without mysticism simply deals with learning how to manipulate the future—it's a power game. But the mystic seeks a basic understanding of the universe and identification with universal realities. This has to be achieved by full involvement with the eternal present. And I can only hope the kids will make this transition to a higher metaphysics."

The occult explosion is largely a youth phenomenon, with the new breed of student-age psychic explorers superseding the former stereotype of occultism as a concern only to uneducated, lonely oldsters desperate for evidence of an afterlife. Tryout college courses on occult topics have been wildly successful, often attracting several hundred registrants.

Professor Robert Ellwood teaches New Religious and Philosophical Movements in Southern California at the USC School of Religion. Ellwood is in his early thirties, a mustachioed occult buff who enjoys dropping in on obscure cult meetings when he has time. He keeps a file box with cards for more than two hundred occult groups he and his students have studied, and he is convinced that American culture has now taken an entirely new psychological orientation. "The unspoken assumption today is that religious reality can be found only in interior exploration, rather than in relationship to any outside God or authority," he says. "It's very characteristic that these movements tend to attract isolated individuals, presumably somewhat alienated from society, while the traditional churches attract mostly families."

Perhaps the most widely recognized social factor of the occult explosion is its relationship to an increasingly accepted use of marijuana and other psychedelic drugs in the United States. Professor Ellwood thinks, "For many younger people, drugs have provided a new sense of transcendence as ecstatic as the traditional heaven or as horrible as the traditional hell. The world of ordinary perception is not all there is, they have learned directly—they have a radical realization that many other states of consciousness really do exist."

But there is something more than drugs and alienation behind the occult explosion. British psychologist Gustav Jahoda's *The Psychology of Superstition* puts it this way, "Scientific thinking involves the ability to suspend judgment until evidence tips the balance. Ordinary thinking (and of course this applies to scientists outside their special fields) is more likely to jump the gap and close the pattern. In our own society in the past, and in traditional sectors of some societies at present, gaps were not even allowed to occur and every phenomenon found its place in a meaningful whole. This served to reduce uncertainty and doubt. . . ."

Another aspect of this idea is expressed in the work of Michael Polanyi, the outstanding European physicist who has become a philosopher of science at the end of his long career. *Humanity always knows far more than it can explain* is Polanyi's concept. For example, science still doesn't know all the facts about the physiological chemistry of respiration—but nevertheless any healthy newborn baby *knows* how to breathe.

A handsome young England-to-California emigré witch, Paul Huson, has a good image for this theme in his book, *Mastering*

Witchcraft. "But if and when the firelight happens to dim in the presence of insurmountable calamity, we know science still completely fails to come to grips with that outer darkness beyond the flickering ring of light which we are pleased to call an enlightened scientific civilization."

What it all adds up to is that the better-informed and more aware a person is today, the more he must realize that although scientific technology has taught us an unprecedented amount about *how* the universe works we still know practically nothing about the deeper level of *why* it works.

True, in any detailed investigation of the occult explosion you can't avoid meeting lots of cranks, kooks, charlatans, ignoramuses and self-deluded neurotics. But the evidence clearly shows that at the center of this unique social phenomenon is a totally sane core of serious, open-minded people who are asking mankind's most important question—What is the meaning of human life and how does it fit into the universal design?

At its higher levels, today's occult explosion is undeniably a quasireligious movement, a heroic attempt to find valid, personal, contemporary proofs of the astonishing paranormal abilities that traditional occultism has always insisted were hidden within the human mind.

Chapter 2

More Than Superstition:
The Case of the Psychic Energy Field

WHAT follows next is an unrevised transcript of the final five minutes of my tape-recorded interview with the best-known psychic in America—Peter Hurkos. I had just taken from my wallet a three-year-old photo of my wife and me in costume, sitting among an afternoon crowd at California's annual outdoors Renaissance Pleasure Faire. And I gave the photograph to Hurkos facedown so he couldn't see it.

"Don't tell me nothing," he began in his Dutch-accented, slightly free-form English. "When you go to psychic, never ask questions. Let him tell you. Don't give me any clue . . . See, I don't look at this picture. It's like a TV in my head if I pick up something. I tell you how I do it, I don't think of nothing. Just nothing. Wait, wait, wait, wait . . . The picture was taken in the afternoon. It was a beautiful day and it was fun. There was a lot of laughing going on. She's wearing a very light dress. I see more people in there. I see really three people. [The camera had caught another girl sitting in the background.] Wait, wait, wait . . . It is sitting position . . . I can see the wife have trouble with her appendix. She had trouble in appendix. And there is three sitting in picture! She went to doctor and she had infection of her appendix."

Everything he said was correct! My wife had an appendectomy within ninety days after this photograph was taken. There is just no way—except by ESP—that Peter Hurkos could have guessed correctly that the undated wallet snapshot was taken at the exact time my wife was about to come down with the illness he specifically named.

One way or another, we have all been taught that the occult is no more than primitive superstition, with nothing worthwhile for a society which can rocket men to the moon. But for many reasons—social turmoil, drugs, rapid technological change—more people than ever before are able to insist on the truth of their own experiences, even when the official view of reality calls these experiences impossible. And the fact is that recent scientific evidence has already substantiated much of occult theory.

To demonstrate this, let's look at what has happened to the idea of the aura in only the past decade.

In the occult tradition, the aura is a border of light that extends for perhaps six inches around the body of a human being —or any living being for that matter. It changes color according to one's physical and emotional health. Most people with psychic gifts claim they can see auras easily. A recommended exercise is to look at your hand against a blank wall in a semidark room. There's even what amounts to a church of the aura in East Hollywood; called the Church of World Messianity in the United States, it is affiliated with the Japanese Johrei sect. Meetings take place in a deconsecrated Protestant tabernacle on San Marino Avenue. Downstairs in the basement gym at almost any time a couple of grimly serious Japanese may be seen moving along a line of seated patients, massaging and "channeling" away the electrochemical disturbances in their auras.

But according to deeper occult thinking, the aura is much more than just a psychic thermometer. It's believed to be the visible edge of the astral body, a nonmaterial wave field that penetrates the entire fleshly body and is the vehicle in which one can travel out of the body to nonmaterial higher levels of being by a process occultists call astral projection.

Centuries before Christian artists began painting haloes, pictures from ancient Egypt, India, Greece, and Rome often showed holy figures with a luminous mist around them. In 1901 two theosophy leaders, Annie Besant and C. W. Leadbeater, collaborated on *Thought-Forms,* a book with sixty-nine illustrations of what the authors saw as shapes and hues of mental energy. Around 1910 Dr. Walter Kilner of London's St. Thomas Hospital claimed the aura could be made visible to normal sight with glasses stained in dicyanine dye, a coal-tar derivative. His book, *The Human Aura,* diagrammed his observations about the patterns associated with various diseases. The occult explosion has brought it back into print after almost fifty years of obscurity, and Kilner goggles are once again a popular item, selling for about $10 at better-stocked occult shops.

Dr. Shafica Karagulla may well be Turkey's first female psychiatrist. However, after filling several important hospital posts in the West, she developed a new interest and established the Higher Sense Perception Foundation in office space contributed by a lady friend with a Beverly Hills market research firm. Her book, *Breakthrough to Creativity*, has had four printings and is a quiet word-of-mouth occult best seller. She writes about her experiences in diagnosing disease with the aid of people who can see and interpret auras, claiming that some of the most effective doctors really make their diagnoses psychically.

Dr. Karagulla, a tiny, dark-haired woman who can't see auras herself, says, "I'm glad I don't see them, it helps me be more objective about my work." Not liking to have the occult word "aura" associated with her work, she prefers to talk of energy fields and believes that the gift of seeing these fields is an aspect of creativity. Unfortunately, she absolutely refuses to give detailed case histories and statistics or to name the names of her aura sensitives. "I couldn't embarrass them by invading their privacy," she insists.

The idea of an aura body which is the real home of the life force is as old as recorded history. The Hindu scriptures called this force prana. Polynesia's Huna sorcerers called it mana. Paracelsus, the alchemist, called it munis. Mesmer, the father of hypnosis, called it animal magnetism and believed he was putting people into trances by waving his hands over their bodies in the direction of the electromagnetic flow. Spiritualists believe it's this energy-wave package that lives on after the body dies. Dowsers call it the etheric force.

From the odic force theory of Baron Von Reichenbach, the inventor of creosote, to Dr. Wilhelm Reich's orgone energy, there have been many speculations about a universal field of psychic energy. However, science could never reliably measure or harness this force so all claims about it were generally ignored. But now a Russian named Semyon Davidovich Kirlian has invented a process that takes photographs of auras or lets you look directly at them through a viewer.

Kirlian photography is done with a high-frequency oscillator that creates a field of electrical waves moving as fast as 200,000 cycles per second. The "bio-luminescent pattern" of any living thing inserted into this field while clamped to a special photographic paper will be reproduced on film.

In 1939 Kirlian was an electrical technician at Krasnodar on the coast of the Black Sea in the south of Russia. While working on some equipment at a local psychiatric institute, he saw a patient getting shock treatment; noticing a tiny flash of light that seemed to exist in the space between the patient's skin and the electrode, he decided to try to photograph the effect. The first experiments gave him third-degree burns as he turned on the current while holding a photographic plate against a metal electrode. But he got pictures that showed not only an aura field but also flares of light coming out of specific areas on the flesh.

All through the forties and fifties Kirlian worked on perfecting his high-frequency photography system, discarding X rays, infrared light, and radioactivity before he found the oscillator principle. He conducted this research on his own time and at his own expense, inventing the entire fourteen-patent process at a cramped workbench in the hallway of his two-room apartment with no assistant but his wife Valentina. By the mid-fifties, delegations of Soviet scientists began crowding into the apartment to see the equipment take aura pictures. Kirlian gradually gained semiofficial recognition, becoming a consultant to the regional agriculture station when his results revealed that plant as well as animal diseases show up in the aura *before* they affect the physical body. Finally, by the early 1960's, Kirlian photography had accumulated such widespread scientific support and major publicity that the conservative Soviet research bureaucracy was forced to act. Suddenly the Kirlians had a government grant, a fully equipped laboratory, and a decent-sized apartment. Kirlian photography is now being investigated at some of the Soviet Union's most advanced research centers and the more its findings appear, the more they verify serious occult theory.

For one thing, those active light flare areas on the body correspond with astonishing exactness to the seven hundred points where for thousands of years Chinese acupuncture healers have been applying their needles. The theory of acupuncture is that "vital energy," which circulates through the body on specific pathways, can be rerouted by long needles in times of illness. Traditionally, a competent acupuncturist was paid only when his clients were healthy because he was supposed to prevent disease. In June, 1971, two of the first American scientists to visit Red China as the Ping-Pong Thaw began, Arthur Galston of Yale and Ethan Signer of MIT, reported seeing acupuncture used as the sole anesthetic in major operations—including open-heart surgery.

The Russians already have an electronic device called the to-biscope which locates these acupuncture points to within a millimeter. It can be used in combination with the EEG and electrocardiograms and was on exhibit at Montreal Expo '67.

Ten sample Kirlian photos have been reprinted in *Psychic Discoveries Behind the Iron Curtain* by Sheila Ostrander and Lynn Schroeder, which also lists fourteen articles about Kirlian's work published in the USSR. These photographs show that if you cut away up to one-third of a leaf or flower, its light-field pattern remains whole. But if more than a third is cut off, the plant dies . . . its lights going out gradually, like a city having a blackout. There are supposed to be Kirlian photos of human aura fields that are still complete, even though the subject has had a limb amputated. This would seem a likely explanation of why amputees often report that they "feel" a missing arm or leg. It also goes along with the findings of Dr. Wilder Penfield, a Canadian neurosurgeon, who noted that many people with large parts of their brains removed in the operating room still function as normally as before. It's one of occultism's more esoteric theories that the mind isn't necessarily all in the brain. There are said to be other thinking centers either within the body or part of the aura field—these would then be the mechanisms that control the paranormal powers of clairvoyance, telepathy, precognition, and psychokinesis which have been demonstrated throughout history by those called sorcerers and are demonstrated today by psychics like Peter Hurkos.

In 1968 a research team from Kirov State University at Alma-Ata published a booklength report, *The Biological Essence of the Kirlian Effect,* describing how a Kirlian viewer hooked up to an extremely high-powered electron microscope revealed that all complex physical organisms have semi-independent "energy bodies" which are complete units in themselves. The Alma-Ata scientists actually observed this energy body nourishing itself on surplus oxygen from the air we breathe. Of course, one of the oldest concepts of Yoga is that daily periods of deep breathing are a must, because it charges the entire body with the vital energies of prana. And there have been promising results from hospital experiments with letting the very ill breathe only ionized (electrically charged) air.

Fortune-tellers and quack physicians who practice in the USSR are generally risking long-term imprisonment in Siberia. But surprisingly, a handful of psychic healers are allowed to function under legal supervision, and they seem to achieve outstanding results. One of the most respected is Alexei Kirovtov, a retired Red Army colonel who shares offices with his physician son in the Georgian city of Tbilisi. He never touches his patients, but they report feeling tremendous heat from his hands—even though the temperature of Kirovtov's hands remains normal. *Psychic Discoveries Behind the Iron Curtain* claims there are Kirlian photos of Colonel Kirovtov during the healing process in which the aura around his fingertips appears to become concentrated into something resembling a laser beam.

Healing by the laying-on of hands has also been reported by Dr. Bernard Grad, a biologist at McGill University Medical School in Montreal. In 1957 a refugee Hungarian who was one of Grad's laboratory technicians claimed that the arthritis in his hip had been helped by another Hungarian emigré whose hobby was natural healing.

Dr. Grad's work always refers to the healer as Colonel E., but the full surname has been printed elsewhere as Estobani. The ex-colonel told Grad he'd discovered his powers while he was a cavalry instructor at the Hungarian Military Academy where he found he could invigorate weary horses during strenuous training rides by rubbing their forelegs. At first he was surprised that none of his students could do the same. When the Communists took over Hungary, they threw Colonel Estobani out of the army. He became a woodchopper in an isolated village where he was often called on to use his healing until he escaped across the border during the 1956 Hungarian Revolt.

"If you're interested in finding out more about this gift you think you have," Dr. Grad told Estobani, "I can't get you any human patients to heal, but I can set up some experiments with animals and plants that might be even more revealing."

So for fifteen minutes twice a day Estobani would hold containers containing eight to ten mice that were fed a low-thyroid diet or had a square inch of their skin cut away. In each series the mice healed much faster than control groups of rodents that didn't get this treatment. These were changes that could be measured and graphed. Dr. Grad has photographs comparing the differences between the two groups of mice at each stage of treatment, and Estobani's mice clearly had smaller goiters and faster-healing wounds than the others. In a later test the mice improved more quickly when treated only with cloth Estobani had held in his hands. But heat lamps set at human-body-temperature didn't speed up the healing.

Barley seeds sprouted bigger and faster with water from a bottle Estobani had held, even if they weren't getting enough water or the water had been salted. Experiments showed that McGill medical students who believed in the possibility of natural healing got better results with the barley plants than a group of confirmed skeptics, but neither group achieved the effects of Estobani. On the other hand, barley plant growth was slowed down with water from a bottle held by a depressed psychotic patient.

Then at Rosary Hill Catholic College in Buffalo, New York, science department chairman Sister Justa Smith measured Colonel Estobani's laying-on of hands healing batches of damaged enzymes—and enzymes are catalytic agents essential to promoting cellular life-processes.

In *Psychic Discoveries Behind the Iron Curtain,* authors Ostrander and Schroeder report witnessing still another Eastern European approach to understanding and harnessing the psychic energy field. Robert Pavlita, a Czechoslovakian in his sixties, who has invented several successful textile manufacturing processes, has used his royalties to develop what seems to be an amazing arsenal of psychic energy amplifiers powered solely by their shapes and the materials they're made of. Ostrander and Schroeder saw many of these devices in action at Pavlita's workshop in a small village near Prague and in a documentary film that hasn't yet been allowed outside Communist Europe.

These psychic generators tend to look like pieces of primitive art, rodlike or circular, rough-hewn or smooth. Pavlita says he studied "very old texts" in working out his ideas but won't go into any more detail. The devices are recharged by holding or stroking them, or sometimes by merely staring at special marks on the surfaces.

Several of Pavlita's psychic generators exert a magnetic pull on nonmagnetic objects and will work through water, glass, cardboard, wood, or any kind of metal shielding. Others will speed up plant growth, clean polluted water, or kill small insects. A few minutes of recharging one device with human touch is said to turn a small electric motor for fifty hours. Pavlita, now working under a Czechoslovakian government grant, claims 100 percent accuracy for a psychic generator that points at the symbol of an ESP card somebody is thinking about in another room.

If this doesn't already sound enough like a science fiction movie, there is more. Pavlita's assistant is his pretty blond daughter, Jana. As a child, her fingers once became temporarily paralyzed when she wandered into the workshop and began playing with the psychic generators.

Still more evidence of a universal psychic energy field has shown up on lie detectors in New York City. Cleve Backster, a slender, intense man who operates the Backster Detector School, has been a specialist in this field for more than twenty years. His zone comparison technique of questioning is the standard method taught at the U.S. Army Polygraph School in Fort Gordon, Georgia, and he's been an expert witness in scores of court cases.

One evening in February, 1966, while watering a philodendron plant at his office, Backster happened to wonder if his equipment could measure any electrical changes in the plant as the water rose from the roots to the leaves. Attaching a pair of electrodes to a leaf with a rubber band, he balanced his dials to show a zero reading on the Wheatstone Resistance Bridge he'd selected as pick-up instrument for the lie detector.

He had expected to see a steady downward line on the chart as the plant absorbed moisture. But instead the line went gradually upward, making occasional little jumps just the way a human heart does when short emotional reaction is being measured. It made Backster wonder what would happen if he made a threat to the plant, similar to the loaded-question technique of triggering emotional responses to people on lie detector tests. He decided to light a match to the hooked-up leaf. The moment he made this conscious decision—while he was neither touching the plant nor making a move to get a match—the stress line on the polygraph zoomed upward. The philodendron had seemingly read his mind.

To get a better idea of what the plant really did, Backster set up a foolproof experiment to show if plants could tell what was happening to other living creatures *without* picking up human mental cues. He assembled a simple motor-timer system that would dump a tray of the live miniature shrimps used as goldfish food into boiling water—and the machine would select a dumping time at random. Three plants were attached to three different lie detectors and all persons were locked out of the school. The plants reacted to the death of shrimps in another room eleven of thirteen times.

By now Backster has reported finding similar telepathic reactions in a wide variety of organic matter: fresh fruit and vegetables, yeast, mold cultures, microorganisms like the amoeba and the paramecium, even in scrapings from the roof of a human mouth. Metal shielding won't cut off the effect. Plants can pick up thoughts from a considerable distance if they have previously been in contact with the sender. They registered a reaction to Backster from fifteen miles away when, at a preset time, he concentrated on returning to the office and burning a leaf.

Other researchers have been able to duplicate Backster's results, according to reports in publications such as *Medical World News* and the *International Journal of Parapsychology*. Even two high school students in Pleasanton, California, Jack Hagerty and Patrick Stack, were able to record electrochemical reactions in plants that were being yelled at or witnessing fruits or vegetables destroyed in their presence or even hearing the names of people who had yelled at them earlier.

Cleve Backster now argues that there is a primary ESP capability in all living matter at the cell level and it doesn't depend on any kind of nervous system. But that's very close to what the occult tradition has been saying all along!

Chapter 3

Toward a Scientific Occult Theory

THE massive pink stucco slab of the Philosophical Research Society dominates the hill where Las Feliz Boulevard swoops down to LA's Griffith Park. Manly Palmer Hall began the PRS in 1936, seven years after he published—at the age of twenty-seven—*Secret Teachings of All Ages: An Encyclopedic Outline of Masonic, Hermetic Qabbalistic and Rosicrucian Symbolical Philosophy.* One of the most ornate books produced in the twentieth century, the original edition was the size of a library atlas with leather binding, gold leaf, and many elaborate color plates. It is now a collector's item worth over $100. The book itself is still in print but in a reduced scale, photocopy edition minus the color illustrations and other frills. Its two-column pages of gothic typography really do constitute an occult encyclopedia, an evocative mystic's-eye-view of just about all the information we have today on primary occult traditions.

Now in his early seventies, Manly Hall still leads the Philosophical Research Society. He has written thirty-five books and hundreds of articles and has delivered some seven thousand lectures. Hall is a spell-binding public speaker who never uses written notes, although his talks may last up to two hours. Extremely heavy—he must weigh well over three hundred pounds —he comes onstage and seats himself in a big armchair. Then, with never a pause or false start, he begins speaking in a deep, mellow voice as if he were reading the words from an invisible teleprompter.

Hall's PRS is dedicated to developing a unified contemporary approach to occult metaphysics, combining Eastern religions, esoteric tradition, astrology, reincarnation, and ceremonial magic. The society's reputation is strong enough to attract major speakers such as Gardner Murphy, the psychology pioneer and psychic researcher; comparative religion professor Marcus Bach; Gerald Heard, the influential metaphysical essayist; and Zoroastrian teacher Framroze Bode. "I consider myself a rebel educator teaching that materialism is a dead failure," says Hall. "One of the most important things I've worked on is building bridges between the East and the West. The Philosophical Research Society doesn't offer a magic key, but we can help people to a better balance and greater life abilities."

Since 1963 Laurence O. Anderson has been following his own road to what he calls the Unified Multiple Approach to the Unknown, at his Anderson Research Center. The center is located in an old Spanish-style house at 3968 Ingraham Street, a quiet residential block in East Hollywood. "I was a counselor at Dr. Paul Popenoe's Institute of Family Relations for years," says Anderson. "My primary interests are psychodrama and general semantics." He admits that his own family has never quite understood why he would leave a respectable career as a marriage counselor to delve into the occult. "I guess nobody's a prophet at home," he says ruefully. About fifty, neat, and birdspry, Anderson still has to arrange the chairs and sweep up between daily sessions himself.

The converted livingroom-lecture hall of the Anderson Research Center regularly holds audiences of over a hundred people for metaphysical discussions that have been led by practitioners of Subud, body awareness, T'ai Chi Ch'uan, nudist group therapy, psychism, automatic painting, and just about everything else on the borderlands of knowledge. "I'm less interested in any particular method than I am in the remarkable way they all relate to each other. Any speaker will be invited here if he seems to have even the germ of something valuable."

Manly Hall and Laurence Anderson are only two of the contemporary explorers attempting to incorporate occult traditions into a unified, rational theory. Everywhere in the occult explosion there is a new awareness that ritual and esoteric dogma should no longer be blindly accepted but must be thoroughly reexamined in the light of our present knowledge of social science and technology.

The church [Christian] needs to do the same, but based on the Bible.

Actually, the very word "occult" is used only by the general public today. Occultists themselves reject the superstitious connotations of the term and always say they are students of metaphysics—the branch of philosophy concerned with the ultimate answers to universal questions. A single scientific theory of occult phenomena is still in the future, but many of the vital elements of such a theory are already taking shape.

To the committed occultist, the accepted version of man's upward climb through history is laughably incomplete and shot through with error. Occult literature maintains that ancient civilizations discovered all sorts of secret powers completely lost today, a lost body of superknowledge usually called something like the Ageless Wisdom. The occult offers several different theories to explain its historical viewpoint. The one that does least violence to established ideas is that civilizations whose existence we know of—such as ancient Egypt or the Incas—learned ways of tapping universal forces by methods modern man has forgotten. Another occult speculation is that civilizations we now mistakenly believe to be mythical, such as Atlantis or Mu, were actually populated by superhuman beings—demigods or fallen angels—who intermarried with humans and passed along their superior learning. The most recent variation is that these lost superhuman races of the past were really space beings, time travelers or mutants—which leads to the unsettling implication that these vanished cultures destroyed themselves in nuclear holocausts our own society is only now able to duplicate.

Until very recently it was no trouble at all to pooh-pooh claims for the existence of an Ageless Wisdom. All over the world the forces of technologically advanced nations were pushing into contact with primitive societies that believed devoutly in magic powers. Nowhere is there any record of a witch doctor able to beat off soldiers with guns.

Only now has anthropology collected enough data on the social behavior of primitive societies so that we can begin to understand how irrelevant things like competition and technical progress are to their world outlook. And at the same time, our sophisticated technological culture has come to a demonstrable dead end in satisfying the needs of its citizens to feel they are leading meaningful lives.

Some evidence of lost Ageless Wisdom already exists. An excellent example is the development of tranquilizing drugs, which were discovered during an investigation into the chemistry of a plant Europeans named *Rauwolfia,* which had been used by Hindu folk healers to calm nervous patients in India for centuries.

In *The Savage Mind,* French anthropologist Claude Levi-Strauss attempts a complete analysis of the differences between our way of thinking and that of the primitive world which, by definition, still believes in magic. He begins by pointing out that many primitive cultures have an astonishingly expert knowledge of their environments. Any youngster in the tribe might know hundreds of species of plants and animals and whatever practical uses one could make of them and would be able to identify a tree from a tiny wood chip.

Levi-Strauss writes, "It was in neolithic times that man's mastery of the great arts of civilization—of pottery, weaving, agriculture and the domestication of animals—became firmly established. No one today would any longer think of attributing these enormous advances to the fortuitous accumulation of a series of chance discoveries. . . . Each of these techniques assumes centuries of active and methodical observation, of bold hypothesis tested by endlessly repeated experiments. There is no doubt that all these achievements required a genuinely scientific attitude, sustained and watchful interest and a desire for knowledge for its own sake." Levi-Strauss compares the difference between primitive science and today's science to the difference between a handyman who makes do with the tools in his kit . . . and an engineer.

One of the main arguments of those who want to prove there was really an Ageless Wisdom is the remarkable massive cities of stone in Central and South America, the Mayans' Chichén Itzá, and the Incas' Machu Picchu, and also the Egyptian pyramids. How could these architectural wonders have been built with only crude tools? How did they cut twelve-ton blocks of granite to exact size? Is the standard explanation of hordes of slaves sliding the giant blocks on roller logs from the quarry sufficient? Then how about the fifty-ton stone statues standing on sparsely populated Easter Island?

There is apparently a rediscoverable secret of easily cutting and moving huge stones. In Homestead, Florida, just south of

Miami on U.S. 1, is an awesome structure called the Coral Castle. It was built of rock slabs weighing up to thirty-five tons by a one-hundred-pound Latvian immigrant named Ed Leedskalnin who worked entirely by himself for thirty years. Leedskalnin created his eccentric masterpiece hoping it would win him world acclaim and regain the love of a Latvian beauty who jilted him at the age of sixteen. He was sixty-four when he died in 1951 without revealing his secrets. His equipment was no more than chains, cables, jacks, winches, and pulleys, most of which he scrounged from junkyards. He made log tripod supports of some sort. Apparently he quarried the rocks by a method combining sawing with cables and hammer-driven wedges.

The wall around Coral Castle is entered through a three-ton door of coral balanced so precisely a child can push it open with one finger. The castle itself is a two-story tower estimated to weigh two hundred and thirty-five tons. The castle garden is full of more massive stone wonders: rocking chairs of genuine rock, a solid fifteen-foot coral table carved in the shape of Florida, an obelisk that at twenty-seven feet is higher than any of the Stonehenge pillars, a year-round sundial that's never more than two minutes off, a twenty-five-foot telescope that has a crosswire which lines up exactly on the North Star.

No occult theorist has ever had more fun punching holes into the comfortable assumption that we live in a coherent universe than Charles Fort, an important transitional figure in the modern development of psychic research. Fort lived on a small inheritance in a Bronx apartment, and from about 1910 till his death in 1932 he collected verifiable reports about events and facts that simply couldn't fit into the established structure of science. *There was a rain of frogs in Birmingham on June 30, 1892. . . . Winged beings were spotted in the sky above Pallermo on November 30, 1880. . . . A flying iceberg broke up over Rouen on July 5, 1853.* He collected about 25,000 similar impossibilities and then wrote four books that gleefully accused science of existing only through massive lies. Fort's final step was to suggest horrendous alternatives to accepted scientific outlooks —such as our being controlled by outer-space monsters—catastrophes he imagined with the greatest gusto and relish.

Surprisingly, classic occult theory has never attached much significance to ghosts. They are supposed to be merely low-level

spirits who have probably died by violence and are too trauma-
tized to realize they can now ascend to higher dimensions. A true
occultist believes ghosts are to be pitied and helped instead of
feared. Usually a seance with a sympathetic medium is sufficient
to make the ghost aware it is now time to leave the earthly plane.
Exorcism rituals of banishment are only necessary for mean,
stubborn ghosts who cling to their haunts in a misguided lust for
vengeance.

The most influential modern theory about ghosts was put forward in 1942 by veteran psychic researcher G. N. M. Tyrell in
his book *Apparitions.* "Apparitions are the sensory expression of
dramatic constructs," he wrote, "created in regions of the personality outside the field of normal consciousness."

But such hallucinations can produce observable effects in the
real world. Poltergeists are defined as mischievous ghosts who
make their presence known by throwing physical objects about.
Poltergeist reports go back hundreds of years, and Charles Fort
assembled scores of dazzlingly bizarre ones. Since the advent of
psychiatry, it has become strongly suspected that the phenomenon of poltergeists is somehow triggered by family tensions—
especially when the group includes a youngster with repressed
aggressions and sexual hostilities. Dr. Hans Bender, a German
MD and psychologist at the University of Freiburg, actually
made a videotape of poltergeist activity in 1967.

The videotape shows a painting in a heavy frame rotating in a
one-hundred-and-twenty-degree arc on the wall of a lawyer's
office in the Bavarian town of Rosenheim. Annemarie Schaberl,
a plain-looking girl of nineteen, hated her secretarial job at the
law firm. Her fiancé had just broken off their engagement because on eight consecutive bowling dates the electronic pin spot-
ters went haywire. At the same time, all the electrical systems in
the office began acting berserk. Light bulbs and fuses exploded.
Late in the afternoon, as quitting time approached, the lawyer's
phone would register hundreds of calls to the number for time
announcements. Before Dr. Bender was called in, the electric
company checked out the entire building's wiring system with a
voltage recorder that charted impossible peaks in power consumption. Even when an emergency generator was installed, the
law office's lights still kept shorting out.

Dr. Bender, who was elected president of the professional ESP researchers' Parapsychology Association in 1970, has studied other young poltergeist generators besides Annemarie. In 1965 a China shop in Bremen had the bad luck to hire Heiner Schultz, then fifteen. Hundreds of dollars worth of dishes were broken before Dr. Bender was brought in and isolated Heiner as the cause.

Although Sigmund Freud, the father of psychoanalysis, dealt gingerly with the subject of psychic phenomena, he wrote several sympathetic essays on the possibility of extrasensory perception . . . though he did suspect most ESP episodes of being powerful hallucinations associated with Oedipal childhood sex tensions. However, not long before he died in 1938 he wrote a letter to an old acquaintance, the pioneer British psychic investigator Hereward Carrington, in which he made the astonishing statement, "If I had my life to live over again I should devote myself to psychical research rather than psychoanalysis."

But it was Freud's early associate, the great Swiss psychiatrist Carl G. Jung, who did more than any other twentieth-century thinker to make occult theorizing respectable. Profound Jungian interpretations seem to emerge everywhere in a serious study of contemporary occult philosophy.

Jung conducted one of the first polls attempting to establish a statistical basis for astrology. He had the horoscopes of four hundred and eighty-three married couples analyzed and found at least some tendency—though nothing mathematically significant —toward certain planetary patterns in lasting marriage partnerships. At his Zurich clinic he had horoscopes charted for every new patient. He said he found the charts useful as a preliminary diagram of the forces operating within a patient's total personality—at the very least it provided something to talk about during the tension-filled opening sessions of psychotherapy.

Volume 14 of Jung's collected works, his last book before dying in 1961, is about the psychological symbolism he saw in alchemy. He spent thirteen years working on this project. For Jung, it didn't matter if lead could really be turned into gold. He believed that the alchemists of the Middle Ages were stumbling through the darkness in search of the principles of nuclear physics. And as they experimented, their creative subconscious gave off classic psychological projections that were, in effect, maps of a universal mind pattern. Jung believed that the entire alchemical process was a symbolic diagram for the isolation and eventual synthesis of opposing personality traits. He called the legendary philosophers' stone which was supposed to turn lead into gold a disguised symbol for the Christ figure or man's potential for self-perfectibility.

"Jung understood that the alchemist's gold was really a symbol for the highest state of mind," says San Francisco artist Wilfried Satty, whose eerie metaphysical collages have illustrated occult reports in *McCall's, Holiday,* and *Man, Myth & Magic.* Satty calls himself a visual alchemist. "A visual poetry is what I want, so I'm an alchemist in the same sense as William Blake or Bacon. I use the symbols and color theory of classical alchemy in my work, and some of the laboratory processes have been helpful in mixing new colors for my poster reproductions." Now in his early thirties, the German-born artist says he was raised in an occult environment, even living for most of his teen years in an old castle. His current quarters are spectacularly arcane. Beneath his storefront studio one block from Fisherman's Wharf is a candle-lit grotto filled with comfortably bizarre antiques. "My alchemy circle meets here regularly," he says. "We have about six other artists and a psychiatrist who are interested in the Jungian approach to the occult and how this can be applied to artistic techniques."

Much of Jung's deepest occult thinking went into his extremely ambitious prefaces for the first Western translations of the *I Ching,* China's ancient method of divining psychic trends and directions integral to a present situation; *The Secret of the Golden Flower,* the Chinese Taoist method of meditation; and the *Tibetan Book of the Dead,* which he saw as using reincarnation to symbolize "an initiation process whose purpose it is to restore to the soul the divinity it lost at birth."

Over and over again, Jung returned to the idea that the ancient occult thinkers were presenting the best information their times had to offer about depth psychology, using the only available tools—observation and imaginative, symbolic myth-making. Jung's prefaces also related these occult classics to his own little-understood concepts of the "collective unconscious" and "synchronicity." As yet, there is no way of proving either idea to be more than theory, but if they are ultimately found to be true they would explain a wide spectrum of paranormal phenomena.

Jung envisioned the collective unconscious as the level of mind where mystical illumination and ESP communication occur. It is a kind of psychic linkage between men, made possible by the archetypes of thought we share as a species. "Just as the human body shows a common anatomy over and above all racial differences," he wrote, "so too the psyche possesses a common substratum transcending all differences in culture and consciousness." This collective unconscious "consists of latent dispositions toward identical reaction" which he called archetypes of thought and behavior that trace back to a common heritage of psychological development. "It means we have common instincts of imagination and of action . . . This explains the analogy or even identity between various myths and symbols."

Synchronicity was Jung's idea that "the coincidence of events in space and time . . . is something more than mere chance." Meaningful coincidences are the result of a cause-and-effect relationship not yet understood by science. Jung elucidates this by stating, "Whatever happens in a given moment possesses inevitably the quality peculiar to that moment . . . There are certain connoisseurs who can tell you merely from the appearance, taste and behavior of a wine the site of its vineyard and the year of its origin. There are antiquarians who with almost uncanny accuracy will name the time and place of origin and the maker of an objet d'art or piece of furniture with no more then merely looking at it. And there are even astrologers who can tell you, without any previous knowledge of your nativity, what the position of the Sun and Moon was and what zodiacal sign rose above the horizon in the moment of your birth. In the face of such facts, it must be admitted that moments can leave long-lasting traces." *or they are revealed by a familiar spirit.*

But the most ambitious, far-ranging occult theorist of the twentieth century was George I. Gurdjieff, who died at the age of seventy-three in 1949. Stocky and bald, with a flamboyant handlebar mustache, Gurdjieff was a Greek born at Russia's distant Persian border in 1877. His early years are a mystery, though he claimed to have traveled through central Asia and found isolated mystery schools and seers whose secrets he learned. His first book, *Meetings with Remarkable Men,* offers tantalizing glimpses of this period and the kind of personalities it involved.

Gurdjieff gave his disciples a series of astonishing metaphysical fragments which he hinted would be revealed as elements of the Universal Answer to those who gained enough wisdom to understand him fully. His central concept was that every man who does not train himself to be fully "awake" is literally sleepwalking through life. He stressed such self-awareness exercises as looking at the minute hand of a watch while concentrating on the thought: My name is —— and I am *here* right *now!* This is not easy. As in any kind of concentration technique, the mind encounters a constant stream of distractions.

Gurdjieff first attracted attention in Moscow on the eve of the Communist Revolution. Since his whole teaching method was based on the mind's being kept in a continuous state of imbalance, he often seemed to be—or perhaps really was—acting erratically.

Fortunately for Gurdjieff, at the start of his career in 1915 he met P. D. Ouspensky, a highly successful journalist who'd become obsessed with finding the ultimate truths he sensed were hidden behind the symbols of occult tradition. Just before being introduced to Gurdjieff, Ouspensky had taken a long trip from Egypt to India searching for schools of esoteric wisdom. Despite his romantic lust for ideal knowledge, Ouspensky was more like a Prussian than a Russian. Rigid and severe, bespectacled and crew-cut, he was the kind of man who inspired respect rather than affection. He was, however, a brilliant logician, and his book about the years he spent as Gurdjieff's pupil, *In Search of the Miraculous,* is the best systematic presentation of Gurdjieff's thought. The two men were such complete opposites in personality that it was inevitable they should part. "There began to take place in me a separation between G. himself and his ideas," Ouspensky wrote (he always referred to Gurdjieff as G.). The break came after a bafflingly weird experience in which Gurdjieff spent six weeks, day and night, revealing the most profound aspects of his thought to a hand-picked group of disciples in Essentuki, an obscure Caucasian village to which they had fled after the 1917 Bolshevik uprising. After insisting the group would have to study with him for ten years before they truly understood what he had to teach them, he suddenly announced that he'd changed his mind and was leaving immediately for the Black Sea. He wouldn't stop any of the group from following him, but all work was over!

In many ways, Gurdjieff's philosophic *style* was as important as the ideas themselves. For the first time, concepts as profound as anything in the history of occultism were being taught with absolutely no overlay of dogmatic superstition. He called achievement of a transcendent consciousness "the work" or "working on yourself." He never claimed to be anything more divinely exalted than a teacher. Nonetheless, Gurdjieff's ideas have an eerie way of sounding like occult approaches to the most avant-garde speculations in physics and neurology. Certainly they go beyond an exercise program to awake the mind from its robotized state.

Gurdjieff expanded on the Yoga chakra tradition that there may be several "minds" attached to the body. He sketched a system of centers for activities of the intellect, emotion, sexuality, instinct, and learned physical response. Any of these centers may predominate in a personality regularly or at different times. There is, of course, no physical evidence yet for these beliefs, but Gurdjieff's detailed descriptions of how these different centers work can explain many of the mysteries of the relationship between the body and the mind. He also explained brilliantly some crucial differences between man's culturally induced personality and his "essence," or self.

Dr. Jack Haer, a Los Angeles clinical psychologist and sociologist who has participated in Gurdjieff groups says, "I found the classes very much like a therapeutic community. The whole approach reminded me of Gestalt psychotherapy in its emphasis on the fullest awareness of here and now. Gurdjieff's whole idea of an army of subselves in conflict within every human mind is certainly in line with modern psychology. And my own personal experiences make me agree with the idea that there are people on a higher level of awareness who do have certain powers." Haer teaches a course at San Fernando Valley State College titled The Social Psychology of Esoteric Communication and believes "Ritual is a way of enhancing consciousness and very useful if you don't get hung up on the drama of occult ceremonials. It's the hardest thing in the world to be fully aware of what's going on at any given moment, and Gurdjieff was definitely on the right track in teaching that nothing can happen to get you into a psychically altered state without tremendous amounts of consciousness."

Gurdjieff's idea about the true nature of the universe was that all matter and space is made up of vibrations ascending and descending like the octaves of a musical scale. He postulated systematic laws of action and reaction that pictured the galaxies as living, growing creatures in close contact with the highest realm of absolute being—which religion calls God.

For unexplained reasons of his own, Gurdjieff chose to emphasize the toil and mental strain involved in his awakening techniques, rather than the mystical illumination which was their goal. Perhaps it was for this reason that his movement never became a mass organization, although several great artists, including architect Frank Lloyd Wright and writer Katherine Mansfield, became deeply interested in his work. Miss Mansfield even chose to spend her last days, as she was dying of tuberculosis, at Gurdjieff's briefly attempted International Study Colony outside Paris. The occult explosion has revived a great deal of interest in Gurdjieff. Books about him now sell well at the occult shops after having been out of print for twenty years.

After his death, Gurdjieff's penchant for being mysterious led his followers to make a fetish of secrecy. One must be practically an FBI infiltrator to locate and be accepted into one of today's surviving Gurdjieff groups. The most official Gurdjieff study group in Southern California is led by a Hollywood housewife named Norma Flynn, who does not "feel the time is right" to talk to journalists but is always willing to meet with serious students . . . if they can find her. Similar conditions exist in most of America's larger cities.

Gurdjieff was not, however, consistently secretive in his lifetime, occasionally going so far as to stage publicly advertised ballets with his students. He said that the dance exercises came from his Asian mystery schools and contained metaphysical formulas. For the dancers, the ballet steps were practice at achieving the excruciating self-awareness of the waking state, requiring efforts such as counting off constantly changing rhythm cycles while waving their arms in opposing circles.

As for the success of Gurdjieff's awakening techniques, Ouspensky wrote that in August, 1916, he "observed facts that entirely transcended the sphere of what we consider possible." For several weeks he was able to maintain telepathic contact with Gurdjieff, sometimes over considerable distances. "It all started with my beginning to *hear his* thoughts. We were sitting in a small room . . . And suddenly I noticed that among the words which he was saying to us all there were 'thoughts' which were intended for me. I caught one of these thoughts and replied to it, speaking aloud in the ordinary way. G. nodded to me and stopped speaking . . . After a while I heard his voice inside me as if it were in the chest near the heart . . . *I replied mentally.*"

"This is what you wanted, make use of it," Gurdjieff said to him. *"You are not asleep at this moment."*

Chapter 4

Occultism and the Altered State of Consciousness

THE first profound modern examination of the mystical illumination, that legendary transcendent "high" so often described by occult thinkers, was made by Dr. Richard Bucke, a Canadian MD in charge of a large mental hospital at London, Ontario, and a pioneer in medical psychology. After an adventurous youth in the California Gold Rush, he returned to school, raised a family, and began a distinguished career in medicine. For him, the turning point of his adult life came in 1868 when he first read the metaphysical poetry of Walt Whitman. The two men didn't meet until nine years later, but when they did they became great friends, and Whitman named the doctor as his literary executor.

In 1872 Bucke had a classic mystical illumination. During a visit to England he'd spent a late evening reading poetry aloud with a group of friends. While returning to his lodgings in a hansom cab, he felt "a moment of indescribable splendor."

In his third-person account, Bucke wrote of finding himself wrapped around "by a flame-colored cloud . . . without warning of any kind." After an instant he knew that the light was within himself. "Directly after there came upon him a sense of exultation, of immense joyousness, accompanied or immediately followed by an intellectual illumination quite impossible to describe. Into his brain streamed one momentary lightning-flash of the Brahmic Splendor which ever since lightened his life. Upon his heart fell one drop of the Brahmic Bliss, leaving thenceforward for always an aftertaste of Heaven." Later he added that a prime characteristic of this experience is "a consciousness of the life and order of the universe. . . . It is like being on a new plane of existence . . . elevated, exalted, joyous and morally upright."

In 1901, a year before his accidental death at sixty-five (he went out to look at the stars and slipped on his icy porch), Dr. Bucke published Cosmic Consciousness, a mental state he described as a relatively permanent and complete illumination that could come after exhaustive preparations or else simply appear without any advance notice. This overpowering sense of being at one with an endless flow of life through the universe is what science now calls an altered state of consciousness.

Bucke argued that an ability to function in an altered state of consciousness *as well as* in a normal waking state was necessary for humanity's evolution to a higher level. He said Walt Whitman and other mystical poets such as Dante and William Blake, along with Jesus, Buddha, and Muhammad, were really experimental mutants whose teachings—inspired by their cosmic consciousness—were helping mankind climb to its next phase.

The psychedelic awareness possible through drugs is obviously one of today's most widespread approaches to the altered state of consciousness. And nothing better has ever been written about the crucial relationship of psychedelics, the altered state of consciousness, and the occult quest than Carlos Castaneda's *The Teachings of Don Juan: A Yaqui Way of Knowledge.*

Castaneda is a young South American teaching anthropology at UCLA, and his Don Juan is not the legendary seducer but a wise and tough old Indian of the Yaqui tribe in northern Mexico. The *Teachings* records in excruciating detail the mind-trips that Don Juan put Castaneda on in an attempt to show him the vanishing brujo methods of "passing through the crack that leads to the other world" with the aid of drugs—peyote, magic mushrooms, and the even more powerful and dangerous datura (locoweed). To Don Juan, the importance of these hallucinogenic plants was their capacity to create different stages of perception. And Castaneda reports very convincingly, in the logical, factladen language of a trained field anthropologist, that he experienced both the heights of mystical transcendence and the horrific depths of demonic possession.

The Human Potential Movement, centered at Esalen Institute in Big Sur, has been developing a wide range of contemporary nondrug exercises aimed at reaching this mystical illumination. Body awareness, sensitivity group marathons, and Gestalt therapy are some of its better-known techniques. The underlying premise of Human Potential is the scientific consensus that human beings ordinarily never use more than 10 percent of their brain cells—the corollary being that 90 percent of mankind's potential is never realized.

A landmark of Human Potential theory is psychology professor Abraham Maslow's book, *Toward a Psychology of Being,* which explains his concept of the "self-actualized man." Maslow, having concluded that there was no real data about what constitutes a mentally healthy adult personality, spent almost twenty years making depth tests and case histories of people who were leading demonstrably successful and creative lives.

"All my subjects were relatively more spontaneous and expressive than average people," Maslow wrote. "They were more *natural.* They had the ability to express their ideas without fear of ridicule, like the child who saw the emperor was not wearing any clothes." Or like the Yoga or Zen adept who has freed himself from the maya screen of cultural illusions. — *the social "filter"*

Maslow also found that among his self-actualized individuals nearly all had at one time or another what he labeled a "peak experience." And this peak experience is simply a new psychological definition of Bucke's cosmic consciousness or occultism's mystical illumination.

"The person in the peak experience usually feels himself to be at the peak of his powers, using all his capacities at their best and fullest," wrote Maslow. "What takes effort, straining and struggling at other times is now done without any sense of striving. Afterwards there is a reverent awe in remembering the experience."

A little-known but very relevant Esalen experiment was "Symbo," a living group-mind that six of the resident fellows tried to keep up for three days under the leadership of Edward Maupin, a youthful psychologist from UCLA whose PhD thesis was the first U.S. meditation experiment. The idea of Symbo was to discover what new areas of empathy a group could think and feel its way into together, perhaps the way future interplanetary spaceship crews will have to react on long voyages.

"Symbo had a profound, mysterious quality for us," says Maupin. "It was as if the intuitive interplay of a jazz group were transposed into many different activities. We could listen, really listen to each other. The movement of people from one place to another in the room seemed like a dance. Symbo could generate a party—a wonderful fete in which music, the dancing, the conversation seemed to me real communication. What began happening was a kind of listening into the center of the group. We focused on what we were experiencing together at that moment, and often it seemed as if we *were* parts of an emerging organism."

"Normal men have killed perhaps 100,000,000 of their fellow men in the last fifty years," says R. D. Laing, the English psychiatrist. "The condition of alienation, of being asleep, of being unconscious, of being out of one's mind is the condition of normal man. Society highly values its normal men. It educates children to lose themselves and to become absurd, and thus to be normal."

Laing's most popular book, *The Politics of Experience,* states flatly that insanity can be the altered state of consciousness. "Transcendental experiences sometimes break through in psychosis, to those experiences of the divine that are the living fount of all religion. Madness may be breakthrough as well as breakdown," his argument goes. He points out that a madman's confusions often seem to move his experience center "from real time to the eternal . . . In a painful way it gets past the ancient veil of the ego's illusion. . . . If a person is mad, he may either be ill or having a transcendental experience by an unearthly light of illumination . . . as the inner world overwhelms our structured ego images." In modern psychiatric terms, R. D. Laing restates the symbolism of the *Tibetan Book of the Dead*—a death of the ego smothered in social illusion and rebirth of a psyche in touch with reality.

Religious ecstasy can bring on the altered state of consciousness—and obviously did for most major prophets and saints. The Vatican has always kept complete records of its admirably thorough investigations into alleged miracles and so we can be as sure as we are about anything else happening three hundred years ago that Joseph of Copertino could fly! This historical Flying Monk was a shoemaker's apprentice who entered the Copertino monastery at seventeen and was expelled eight months later for extreme dull-wittedness. But his deep piety brought him acceptance by another order, and at twenty-five he became an ordained priest. Presiding over his first Christmas Eve Mass in 1627 at the village church of Grotella, Joseph of Copertino was witnessed by the entire congregation as he ". . . gave a sob, then a great cry and at the same time was raised in the air."

Brought before an ecclesiastical court on charges of black magic and blasphemy 400 years ago, Joseph won acquittal by flying before Pope Urban VIII. There were at least one hundred reliably eyewitnessed levitations by the Flying Monk, and among the thousands who saw him fly were several cardinals, Princess Marie of Savoy, and the Great Admiral of Castille.

Descriptions of Joseph's flights were usually given in terms such as, "He flew through the air at a height of about four feet from the ground and up into an almond tree some thirty yards distant" or "He flew like a bird from the middle of the church onto the high altar, a distance of forty yards." Dozens of these statements went into the report ordered by the Vatican as soon as Joseph of Copertino died in 1663. Even the Flying Monk's deathbed physician reported that Joseph "raised about a palm's width above his bed" and could not be pushed down until the abbot of the monastery ordered him to stop levitating.

Hypnosis was the first controlled modern method of altering states of consciousness.

One of its early advocates was Franz Anton Mesmer, a German physician of the eighteenth century who spent most of his career in Paris. He believed that he could control the flow of an "invisible fluid" which he called animal magnetism by passing his hands slowly above the subject's reclining body from head to foot. Reversing the direction of the hand-passes would remove the subject from his trance. Having adopted these premises, Mesmer was able to produce some remarkable hypnotic effects before reliable witnesses.

Even before Mesmer died in 1815 at the age of eighty-two, other early nineteenth-century hypnotists believed their work had nothing to do with animal magnetism. They found they were able to produce trance states without hand-passes simply by telling the subject he felt relaxed, drowsy, and sleepy. In the intervening years, periods of great interest in the promise of hypnosis have alternated with periods of neglect and suspicion. By now, hypnotism is pretty firmly accepted as a valid scientific phenomenon, but on the whole it's still relegated to occasional use as a medical or research gimmick. And to date, there is practically nothing known about the physiology of hypnosis and how it works.

Nonetheless, in the nineteenth century there were some remarkably audacious experiments in hypnotism that deserve to be studied instead of simply written off as too unbelievable to be taken seriously. Mesmer and his followers maintained they could perform telepathic hypnosis and put their subjects into trances over long distances. A number of people in Europe and America, once hypnotized, displayed prophetic and healing powers. Most astonishing of all were the nineteenth-century claims that hypnosis could create "traveling clairvoyance," another term for occultism's astral projection. Among those who reported being able to produce this state were Freud's teachers, Richet and Janet, and two highly respected English Society for Psychical Research members, Gurney and Podmore.

The oldest recognized altered state of consciousness is sleep. From earliest times man has felt that dreams were a key to the unknown, but until the past twenty years or so practically nothing was known about the one-third of man's life that he spends sleeping. The electroencephalograph (EEG) machine, with electrodes that can be hooked up to measure most body changes, made sleep research possible for the first time.

One of the earliest EEG sleep discoveries was that the physical sign of dreams going on is always rapid eye movement (REM). It is quite literally as if you're *watching* the action in your dreams. If a dreamer is wakened as soon as the REM lines cease to show on the EEG graph, he can more accurately report what he dreamed than he could the next morning—and go right back into deep sleep. A normal night's sleep has five or six REM periods, and dreaming is necessary to the human mind! When experimenters suppressed dreams of lab sleepers for several nights by disturbing them as REM started, the subjects became noticeably tense and edgy during the daytime and started exhibiting neurotic confusions.

A special research project, started with private foundation grants in 1962 under Dr. Montague Ullman's psychiatry department at Maimonides Medical Center in Brooklyn, is called the

Dream Laboratory, which tries to produce measurable ESP dreams. A volunteer dreamer comes in by 11 P.M., has the EEG electrodes attached with paste, and goes off to bed, just as in any other sleep lab. Meanwhile, in another room one hundred feet away, this night's telepathy sender has chosen at random some pictures from the laboratory's large collection. The senders concentrate on their pictures, and when the sleeper goes into REM, he is awakened and recounts his dream. Then three men not connected with the Dream Laboratory try to match the pictures transmitted that night with the transcripts of the dreams. Results are tabulated as statistically significant or random on a one-hundred-point scale. Some of the correspondences under these test conditions have been startling, and overall the data has been useful for charting the common distortions of telepathic dreams (presumably applicable to *all* psychic transmissions) in classic Freudian patterns of fragmentation, dissociation, and transformation.

For example, a typically brooding Orozco painting, "Zapatistas," with expressionistically slanted Mexican guerrillas marching before a darkling sky, has evoked in the dreamer, "A storm, rainstorm. It reminds me of traveling. I get a feeling of New Mexico when I lived there . . . Santa Fe during the Fiesta, a great many of the Indians came in with their wares." Dali's open-lit, ambiguous "Sacrament of the Last Supper" prompted a dream about "small size fishing boats. My associations are to the fish and the loaf, perhaps some sort of Biblical times." George Bellows' realistic Americana painting of the Dempsey and Firpo fight induced in a young cabdriver a dream of, "Something about posts . . . Ah, something about Madison Square Garden and a boxing match."

Gradually, the EEG researchers were able to isolate four basic brain wave patterns: Alpha rhythm, associated with a relaxed, eyes-closed waking state; Beta, normal waking consciousness; Delta, the rhythm of sleep and passive psychosis; Theta, associated with emotional reverie. Each of these rhythms looks very different as the electrodes feed it onto the EEG chart. Beta gives jagged sawtoothed lines. Theta is a gentle ripple. Delta is long waves. Alpha is about halfway between Beta and Theta.

In 1966 Japanese physiologists wired veteran Zen masters to

the EEG and found that during meditation, even with their eyes open, their brain wave rhythms were predominantly Alpha. The implication was clear—Alpha waves are the key to reaching the Zen enlightenment called Satori or are at least the sign of achieving a deep tranquillity by willpower.

This discovery opened the way for new uses of EEG technology. The Bio Feedback Research Society had its first convention in 1970. President of the organization of three hundred scientists is Barbara Brown, a petite, salty physiologist on a long-term federal research grant at Sepulveda Veterans' Hospital in LA's San Fernando Valley where she has a basement laboratory and a complement of young, long-haired graduate assistants.

"My system teaches voluntary control of Alpha waves—with the eyes open—in forty-five minutes," says Barbara. "In three sessions half our trainees have learned to control all four brain wave patterns."

Barbara Brown calls bio feedback "a technique of externalizing physiological symbols." Human life will literally be revolutionized as we learn more about consciously controlling "involuntary" body functions.

Research is also being conducted on medical projects, such as teaching cardiac patients to control their heartbeat in order to prevent seizures. At the Colorado Medical Center people suffering from tension headaches have been taught to relax their muscles and cut down attacks.

In bio feedback, signal devices—different-colored lights or various sounds—are attached to the EEG as cues to show the person wearing the electrodes when he has achieved whatever brain wave or body function is being tested. The trainee then tries to put himself into emotional states that will make the light shine or the bell ring. Barbara Brown uses a colored light for each of the four brain wave cycles and considers the experiment a success when the trainee is able to register Alpha waves on the EEG at will, even when the cue light is no longer connected.

At this writing, Swami Rama, former dean of one of India's largest Yoga ashrams, was to come to the Menninger Clinic in Topeka, Kansas, for several months of testing by the husband-wife bio feedback research team of Louise and Elmer Green. At a demonstration session in 1969, while the forty-five-year-old yogi was visiting the United States, the Greens measured Swami Rama making the left side of one hand hotter than the right side and stopping his heart for seventeen seconds.

The public is becoming increasingly fascinated with bio feed-back as an approach to the deeper mind within the reach of everybody, and simplified Alpha wave teaching devices are now on the market. The Aquarian Alphaphone is manufactured by a hippie corporation at Mendocino on California's north coast. This self-contained Alpha teacher is a set of earphones with electrodes and two little black circuit boxes attached to the headpiece. The earphones emit a low buzz when Alpha is on and users report feeling a mild high.

The first research center exploring the entire spectrum of mind-expanding techniques that can lead to an altered state of consciousness is the Foundation for Mind Research, started in 1967 by R. E. L. Masters and his wife, Jean Houston. Although Bob Masters never received a college degree, he became a highly original author and researcher in historical social psychology. His books are *The Cradle of Erotica,* a study of Afro-Asian sexual expression, and the occult best seller *Eros and Evil,* about the sexual psychopathology behind the witch burnings of the Middle Ages. Jean Houston was an actress and an NYC Drama Critics Award-winning playwright. She published a widely used guide to the Stanislavski method and is now a philosophy professor at Marymount, a Catholic girls' college on the Hudson. In 1969, she and Masters collaborated on *The Varieties of Psychedelic Experience.* All their experience is going into their current project, *New Ways of Being,* a book about their techniques of achieving the altered state of consciousness without drugs.

They keep two Manhattan apartments in an East Side high rise on Eighty-sixth Street. One apartment they live in with their art collection and cats. The other apartment is the Mind Research Foundation's experimental psychology laboratory. The equipment they've adapted for it is simple but wonderfully effective. Most of one room is taken up by a cork-lined box, a sensory deprivation chamber. Behind its double doors there is total darkness and silence. For those who tend toward claustrophobia, it can be a horrendous nightmare. For others, after an hour or so, it seems like free-floating in the womb, very good for meditation.

They also have a strobe-light box that you put your forehead against with eyes shut and sense the constant flicker of light by heat variations. It's supposed to put the mind in a free-spin meditation, but for one of every five who try it, the machine brings on a headache.

A brilliant adaptation of an occult artifact is their version of the witches' cradle. The traditional medieval witches' cradle, used for producing visions at a black sabbath, was made by wrapping a witch in a sack and dangling her from a tree branch. Masters and Houston's cradle is like a playground swing you stand up in with your eyes shut, and for full meditation sessions they strap you in and blindfold you with sleep goggles. The metal-tubing swing is actually swaying only a few inches above the floor, but after a minute or two of sightless flight you've lost all sense of being earthbound since the balancing mechanism of the inner ear goes out of kilter without sensory clues.

Their sensory overload room is a superb light show, designed and built by Don Snyder, one of the psychedelic artists they began working with when they were doing research with LSD. Aside from painting and assembling the beautiful graphics, Snyder coordinated the effects of two slide projectors, a color wheel, a strobe, stereo earphones, and a circuit box that controls the whole program. The images are rear-projected on a curved fabric screen which surrounds the audience with visions. Of the several shows prepared, one is a space exploration fantasy à la *2001,* and another evokes ancient Egypt with pyramids and artworks.

The basic light show is an assemblage of Snyder's abstract slides. Most of it seems like relaxingly eerie moonscape mountains, but the final phase becomes pop-geometric and causes far more jolting reactions. Masters and Houston have tried sending this light show as a telepathic dream across the fourteen miles to the Maimonides Hospital Dream Laboratory, with some promising results reported.

"All our work at the Foundation for Mind Research is directed at finding new ways to allow the 'old mind' to break through fully," says Bob Masters. "This old mind—the reticular stem at the base of the brain—was the earliest portion of the brain to develop in prehistoric man, and we believe it is the old mind that's in touch with Jung's collective unconscious, our psychic and creative wellspring."

The most daring modern altered state of consciousness experiment of them all was performed around 1964 by Dr. Bart Hujes, a Dutch MD known as Dr. Bart. He was a major influence on the Provo movement (now known as the Kabouters), the constructive, organized group of hippies who have even won seats on the Amsterdam city council.

Dr. Bart became convinced one factor brings adults down from the natural high of childhood—the final hardening of the skull, which takes place between the ages of eighteen and twenty, cutting off brain tissue from direct oxygen intake through the head. Deciding the third eye tradition was meant to be taken literally, he opened a neat little hole in his forehead with a dentist's drill, performing the operation himself with a local anesthetic since he couldn't get any other physician to help him . . . even though he claims a number of them informally agreed that his theory is sound. This third eye went only through the bone in his skull, causing no damage to the tissue underneath which contains the cerebrospinal fluid and protects the actual brain. He had to wear a bandage for about eight months, starting with a mini-turban and working down to a mere patch. Afterward the skin over his hole healed and he looked just like anybody else.

Dr. Bart now claims he's high all the time. His own description is, "I feel always like a fourteen-year-old going out to play." Occasionally the Underground Press carries rumors of other young men who have had their heads drilled with reportedly similar benefits, but the number is certainly small.

Chapter 5

Meditation: An Occult Journey for Everyone

"TRANSCENDENTAL meditation is as mystical as the working of a clock is to a child," says Jerry Jarvis, a businesslike gentleman in his early forties, who is director of SIMS, the Students International Meditation Society, which gave Maharishi Mahesh Yogi his first solid organizational base in the United States.

Jarvis was a landscape gardener when he heard Maharishi on his second visit to America. He and his wife became instant enthusiasts and began spending their evenings teaching transcendental meditation in any living room they could get invited to. After several years they realized that the teen-age children of their hosts were far more enthusiastic about what they were saying than were the adults. "The kids at El Camino Junior College in Manhattan Beach saw how one boy who'd never smiled was smiling all the time once he started TM," says Jarvis. "So they asked me to give a program for twenty students and it went from there."

SIMS headquarters is a converted medical-dental building in Westwood, UCLA's campus community. The offices are a continual bustle of long-haired-but-clean-cut young people, many of whom had been strung out on drugs or the general tensions of adolescence before adopting transcendental meditation. One of the earliest to enroll in SIMS was Robert Keith Wallace, who was about to drop out of school with a variety of personal problems. Wallace has now received a PhD in physiology from Harvard and has published a scientific paper showing that fifteen students experienced at transcendental meditation averaged a

20 percent cut in oxygen consumption and a significantly above-normal output of Alpha brain waves in an EEG test.

But *many* methods of meditation are now being taught in the United States. Roy Masters, a bouncy forty-two-year-old with a curly Liberace mane and one of the world's more charming smiles, lectures at his Foundation of Human Understanding. "Anger at others only hurts us," is the gist of Masters' message. "People can only annoy us if we allow them to." His solutions can be learned from his record album, *Your Mind Can Keep You Well,* priced at $7.95. "We'll give you the record free if you tell the girl at the desk you can't afford it," insists Masters. "There's a donation basket out there, but nobody is going to pass it around. We don't want to see you here week after week. Take home the record or the $2.95 book that covers the same things. You don't need anything else. If a problem comes up, phone our radio show." The show, sponsored by Masters himself, is broadcast every day at 1 P.M. over KTYM in Los Angeles, and Masters spends his time talking to people who phone in about his psychocatalysis meditation method. The one-hour program is transmitted to the radio station from Masters' private studio in his storefront foundation at 624 South Western Avenue, just north of Wilshire Boulevard.

Masters teaches self-hypnosis as part of his meditation. One should sit in a chair with either arm dangling down and imagine that the motionless hand is being raised till it touches the forehead. A relaxed, tingly feeling is likely to result. Simultaneously the recorded Roy Masters voice goes on with instructions to keep calm at all times because your anger hurts nobody more than you.

"We've distributed twenty thousand records, giving away maybe ten percent of them," says Masters. "It's still a miracle how we survive—it takes eight thousand dollars a month to keep everything going. I became a diamond cutter when I arrived in the United States from London in 1949 and I used to travel around giving lecture-demonstrations. Finally I settled with my wife and five kids in Houston and was able to start something I'd always wanted to—making a career of my lifelong interest in hypnosis. Soon I had the busiest office in town and was heartily hated by all the psychiatrists and psychologists. But I gradually realized hypnosis was only giving my clients temporary relief and not really helping them solve their own problems. I moved the family to Los Angeles in 1962, where we lived in a house trailer, and I started the whole thing with a thousand books and records I made up to explain my new system."

Yoga is an old Sanskrit word meaning yoke and at least three hundred years before Christ, the sages of India developed Yoga as a system of mastering the mind and body so that man could be yoked in union to his highest potential. Meditation is the primary technique of Yoga and of its Buddhist counterpart, Zen.

The first yogi to teach in America was Swami Vivekananda, who created a sensation at the World Parliament of Religions held as part of the 1893 Chicago Exposition. He was a disciple of Sri Ramakrishna, India's greatest nineteenth-century religious thinker. Vivekananda founded the Vedanta Society in the United States, basing his teachings on Ramakrishna's interpretation of the Vedas, the earliest Hindu scriptures. Many members of the emigré European colony that gathered around Los Angeles during the late 1930's joined the society. Aldous and Laura Huxley, Christopher Isherwood, and Gerald Heard were all Vedantists.

Parmahansa Yogananda arrived at Boston in 1921 for another international religious conference and spent the next thirty years establishing the Self-Realization Fellowship in America. When he died in 1952, the SRF owned a nunnery-monastery complex on a mountainside near the Rose Bowl, a beach colony north of San Diego, a meditation park where Sunset Boulevard meets the Pacific Ocean, and a Hollywood temple with a locally famous vegetarian restaurant. A child prodigy yogi, Yogananda had his own school in central India by the time he was twenty-four. He was a fine-looking man with long, flowing curls, the fourth in a succession of gurus who taught Kriya Yoga, meditation on the living presence of God by concentrating on inspirational texts. SRF offers correspondence courses for $2 a month and is staffed by renunciants who have vowed poverty and chastity.

The mortuary director of Forest Lawn Cemetery, where Yogananda is buried, wrote to the SRF, "The absence of any visual signs of decay in the dead body of Parmahansa Yogananda (observed through the glass lid of his casket) offers the most extraordinary case in my experience. No physical disintegration was visible even twenty days after death. This state of perfect preservation of a body is unparalleled in mortuary annals. Yogananda's body was apparently in a phenomenal state of immutability. No odor of decay emanated from his body at any time. And when the bronze cover was put into position, he looked as fresh and unravaged by decay as he had on the night of his death."

The U.S. headquarters of Meher Baba's movement still stands at Myrtle Beach, South Carolina, but interest in this sage has dwindled since he died in January, 1969, without giving the momentous message his followers were expecting through forty-four years of silence. Since 1925 Meher Baba had communicated only by gestures and an alphabet board.

Baba Ram Das used to be Timothy Leary's associate Richard Alpert during the Harvard LSD days and afterward went into Human Potential sensitivity group leadership around San Francisco. Then he decided to go to India to find a guru. He's an excellent teacher of Yoga and has the advantage of being able to express his new philosophy in terms of the psychedelic experience and humanistic psychology.

The fastest-rising new yogi is Sai Baba, whom his followers claim to be not only a teacher but a miracle-worker. Disciples say they have observed him walking along a beach with prayer beads forming miraculously in each footprint. Even as a child he was able to make candy materialize from his school bag. He still produces holy items at will, anything from sandalwood idols to books of Hindu scripture. His most remarkable feat is the reputed manifestation of a sacred ash called bivhuthi on pictures of himself, Jesus, or other deities over distances of hundreds of miles. His astral body, accompanied by the odor of a special incense, reputedly calls on disciples anywhere in the world who need help. He explains his powers as "visiting cards to instill faith in God" and maintain long-distance contact with his devotees. "You may call these miracles, but for me they are just my way. For me they are no mystery. They are part of my essential miraculousness."

But the guru most responsible for publicizing meditation-consciousness is undeniably Maharishi Mahesh Yogi, who won short-lived followers among such pop superstars as the Beatles and Mia Farrow. Born in 1911, he graduated from Allahabad University as a physics major when he was thirty-one. His interest in Yoga and the Vedas began while he was working in a factory. His growing spiritual awareness led him to spend thirteen years at a Himalayan foothill retreat with his own guru, Swami Brahmananda Saraswati of Jyotirmath. After originating a new method of transcendental meditation, he started teaching in the South India city of Madras and made his first swing through the West in 1959, establishing the first International Meditation Society in a London apartment. "New ideas get better acceptance in technologically developed countries," he says.

Maharishi's original plan was to spend the 1960's turning transcendental meditation into a worldwide mass movement and then to withdraw to a cottage on his fifty-eight-acre school at Rishikesh to concentrate on writing and supervising an advanced instructors' course. There are now about 50,000 people following Maharishi's method of meditation, and the number almost doubles every year. Since the Rishikesh academy in the secluded highlands where India borders Tibet isn't equipped to turn out enough teachers, Maharishi is now on a demanding international schedule of six-week seminars to meet the need for more instructors.

On his travels many paranormal experiences have occurred, his followers report. Even before he began flying in a private jet, Maharishi never missed a connection although he was always running late. Charles Lutes, a steel and concrete salesman who is prominent in the transcendental meditation movement, says, "We had to make a ferry one time through the sleet and snow up on Mount Rainier. I told him we would have to drive over one hundred miles an hour to get to this boat. We had a lecture that night on Vancouver Island and this was the only ferry going across in time. He stood there for a minute with his eyes closed and then said, 'You drive.' We were coming down a long grade at about one hundred and five miles an hour toward a crossroad with trees hiding it. I told Maharishi that if anything came out of there we would be out of luck. He closed his eyes a minute again and said, 'No car will come out.' So down we went. When we got to the town it was still another fifteen minutes to reach the dock, and the ferry was due to leave that very second. He closed his eyes and said, 'The ship will be there when you get there. That's all.' So I drove onto the ramp just as it went up. The purser came down and said, 'This is your lucky day. The old man's been on this run for about eighteen years and he's never missed leaving the dock on time. But today he was standing on the bridge as if he were in trance.' "

The two introductory lectures to the beginners' transcendental meditation course teach that "the natural tendency of the mind is to seek ever greater happiness and thus bliss consciousness." This is attained by experiencing the "subtle states of thought" which are explained with a diagram of ever-larger bubbles of thought rising from the mental level where thought begins. Normally, we don't notice these bubbles till they get fairly large, but learning to comprehend the smaller primary bubbles will expand the range of consciousness and lead inevitably to the ultimate state of bliss consciousness.

The practice of transcendental meditation is presented as a simple answer to the ills of the world. It would "neutralize the power of war for thousands of years" if 10 percent of the population was taught to achieve bliss consciousness. Unfortunately, the only way to learn the method is by personal oral instruction, for Maharishi insists the written word alone is not sufficient.

Tuition for a fifteen-minute initiation ceremony with unlimited refresher sessions for those who have trouble currently costs $35 for students, $70 for housewives, and a week's salary for the employed. Fruit and flowers are brought in a white handkerchief to be burned as a symbolic sacrifice. The teacher has learned from Maharishi the secret of observing from the student's appearance and actions which is the proper Sanskrit sound to be assigned as a meditation mantra. This mantra is never supposed to, be spoken aloud to anybody else because doing so will make it seem less personally meaningful. No one is certain exactly how many mantras there are, but Maharishi has stated that he doesn't recommend use of the most widely known mantra sound, Om (Aum), because he feels it encourages withdrawal from life. Esoteric Yoga tradition has held that Aum—a Sanskrit word for God —is a primal occult symbol. The sound Aaa is said to represent material reality, Ooo stands for the psychic state, and Mmm is believed to symbolize a higher state of consciousness leading to the perfect world of stillness.

What one does with the mantra sound obtained from a transcendental meditation teacher is to silently think it over and over again while sitting or lying comfortably for fifteen minutes twice a day. A blond coed named Toni credits transcendental meditation with getting her through an unhappy period as a counselor at Ventura Girls Reformatory in Southern California. "I only went on TM for the hell of it," she says. "I really figured I was throwing away $35. But all at once as I was practicing it along with my teacher for the first time, I started to feel something—flashes of different visions. I thought, 'I'll be damned. It really works.' Meditating every night really helps when I'm blue, but usually I do it a couple of times a week. I think of meditation as a psychological technique for relaxing yourself and sometimes making you feel a little high. I imagine if you repeated any sound over and over in your head you'd get results."

The know-nothing wing of the meditation movement consists of a pair of chanting disciplines which appeal to those who seek One Simple Answer. The more middle-class organization is Nichiren Shoshu, the international arm of Japan's militantly puritanical Sokagakkai Buddhism. Members are assured if they chant faithfully for six months, they will get their heart's desire. The chanting is to be done morning and evening in front of the Gohonzon, a wooden altar box with a scroll in Japanese. At regularly scheduled Shakubuku meetings, group chanting aims at producing an ecstatic state. The society's literature is full of endorsements from converts whose dreams really did come true . . . "I can walk again!" . . . "Now, skin allergy gone!"

Swami A. C. Bhaktivedanta's International Society for Krishna Consciousness, better known as the Hare Krishna Movement, came to the United States in 1965. It teaches that one realizes God by chanting his names in proper order for hours on end —"Hare Krishna, Hare Krishna, Krishna Krishna, Hare Hare, Hare Rama, Hare Rama, Rama Rama." Members must also shave their heads and wear saris, give up sex except for the purpose of procreating children in marriage, and accept the principle that men are superior to women. By now most larger cities have a central street on which Hare Krishna disciples appear chanting, begging, and selling a magazine titled *Back to Godhead,* which tells the complex convolutions of Hindu mythology in a comic strip.

Little helpful literature has been written about meditation. Many books do no more than give lists of profound thoughts to concentrate on. But passages in Tibetan lama Chögyam Trungpa's *Meditation in Action,* published by Berkeley's Shambala

Bookshop, offer specific advice. The method described is simply: Sit comfortably with "the back straight so there is no strain on the breathing" and try "to become one with the feeling of breath . . . It is not a matter of concentrating . . . One should feel quite natural and spontaneous, and simply try to identify oneself with the breath. That is all there is to it." The Chinese Taoist meditation method given in Richard Wilhelm's translation of *The Secret of the Golden Flower* corroborates this technique, but adds that one should close the eyes and pretend to be looking at a bump halfway down the nose. Since many people may find this produces a distracting eyestrain, a more comfortable alternative is to shut the eyes and imagine seeing through a third eye approximately at the center of the forehead—this will become a viewing screen for whatever visions arrive.

Alan Watts wrote in the March, 1971, *Earth* magazine, "There is an art of meditation, known in the Orient by such names as Yoga and Zen, which consists of the temporary stopping of words and notions in the head, of being aware quite simply of what *is*, here and now . . . In this clear and silent state of mind, much that one takes for reality just vanishes. The past and the future are nowhere to be found. There is no feeling of separation between oneself and the world outside . . . Later on it may well occur to you that the world as experienced in meditation may be much more real than the world as conceived in thinking. If so, many of the most distressing human problems may be nothing more than futile efforts to grapple with illusions."

It is no accident that the goal of ancient Eastern meditation brings us to still another description of the occult's mystical illumination, which modern science studies as the altered state of consciousness.

Chapter 6

The Occult History of America—
From Salem to the Space Age

SALEM, Massachusetts, today is a quite ordinary factory town on the coast just north of Boston. But over each main intersection hangs a cute sign with a silhouetted witch riding a broomstick, and the local Parker Brothers plant—which turns out most of America's *Scrabble* and *Monopoly* sets—attaches a MADE IN WITCH CITY USA label to all the Ouija boards and occult-theme games manufactured there. For years, the city fathers have been arguing over how much emphasis the community should put on Salem's being the only town on the North American continent to have brought to trial and executed people accused of witchcraft.

With the advent of the occult explosion, Salem's history is drawing more interest than ever. *Bewitched,* the long-running TV situation-comedy series about a mixed marriage between a witch and a human, filmed five shows on location at Salem for the 1970 season, and Louise Huebner, the "Official Witch of Los Angeles County," was given a key to the city when she visited there.

Few witch-hunt landmarks remain in Salem. Gallows Hill is now a children's playground, and the phone company tore down Old Witch Jail to use the site for their central switchboards. Old Witch House, where preliminary hearings were held, is still standing, but it has become so run-down it's unsafe to enter. Actually, the only colonial monument of Salem kept up today is the House of Seven Gables, the inspiration for Hawthorne's novel.

Less than three-quarters of a century after the Pilgrims landed at Plymouth Rock, Increase Mather, the president of Harvard

University, and his clergyman son, Cotton, earned themselves a place in the history of fanatical demagoguery by inaugurating a short reign of terror. Opinion began to turn against them only when they overreached themselves and accused the governor's wife of witchcraft.

The Salem Witch-Hunt was the only truly memorable event of occult significance in prerevolutionary America. This is understandable, because the hard struggle to settle the new colonies left little leisure for metaphysical speculations. But by the second quarter of the nineteenth century, the northeastern seaboard of the United States was a secure society with many urban centers. And an unprecedented combination of factors existed which would make 1800's America the most fruitful environment of modern times for metaphysical exploration—prior to today's occult explosion.

The foundation of a new kind of democratic government created something like a metaphysical euphoria in the young, growing nation. There was a feeling in this new America that now that the oppressive shackles of Europe's rigid social structure had been thrown off at last there was time to experiment with new philosophies which dealt more honestly with the reality of human experience.

The early U.S. commitment to compulsory education had created a wide reading audience, and even the smallest township had its Lyceum, a meeting hall where touring lecturers—who provided one of the most practical forms of live entertainment— could be heard.

A Frenchman named Charles Poyen began giving demonstrations of Mesmer's form of hypnotism on the Lyceum circuit in the 1830's. The whole country became fascinated by dramatic new evidence that a form of mind-expansion was possible and there were ways to experience the world which arose marvelously different from ordinary waking consciousness. The effect of Mesmerism's instant popularity in the United States was not unlike changes of mental attitude brought about by the drug culture of the 1960's.

America's most influential lecturer was Ralph Waldo Emerson, the ex-Unitarian minister whose writings on his philosophy of Transcendentalism made him the darling of the Boston intelligentsia, the unchallenged cultural leaders of the United States.

Emerson taught that man has an "over-soul" which enables him to transcend his senses using knowledge that comes from a divine spark within him. This version of the mystical illumination or altered state of consciousness was presented by Emerson as a way to replace worn-out dogmas with a metaphysical self-reliance and was very much in tune with what America wanted to hear. Emerson and his Transcendentalism reflected the highest spiritual aspirations of the American Dream. His diverse sources were Plato, Oriental religious thought, the works of Swedenborg, and the German idealist philosophers as interpreted by England's Romantic writers.

Emmanuel Swedenborg, whose religious movement still exists today, was another important influence on nineteenth-century American occultism. Swedenborg was the greatest scientific genius of Sweden during the eighteenth century. He was an inventor, engineer, chemist, physicist, anatomist, a member of Parliament, astronomer, zoologist, financier, poet. In 1744 at the age of fifty-six he proclaimed that God had opened his eyes and allowed him to enter the realm of spirits and angels. From then on, he devoted himself to writing some twelve books about his continuing visions and founded the Swedenborgian church. Several reliable witnesses were present during his clairvoyant vision of the Great Fire of Stockholm as it swept toward his house. He was at the time three hundred miles away in Gothenburg. It is important to the development of American occultism that he was the first world leader in modern times to insist he had direct contact with the dead and with non-physical higher dimensions. Several of the main trends of contemporary occult metaphysics can be traced directly to this insistence.

Andrew Jackson Davis, the "Seer of Poughkeepsie," is almost completely forgotten today. But some of his many books were reprinted annually for thirty years. Davis combined practically all the occult elements which were extant in the 1840's in the United States. He was able to go into deep hypnotic trances in which human bodies appeared transparent to him enabling him to diagnose disease with high accuracy. Then in 1844 he wandered off overnight in a posthypnotic trance and returned saying he had learned the true secrets of the universe from a trio of spirits, one of whom he later reported was Swedenborg. He began turning out book after book, all dictated while he was in trance. (Eventually he was able to will himself into what he called his "superior condition" without hypnosis.) He acquired a socialite wife, an influential following, and a publishing company which issued his own magazines. Davis' first book, *The Principles of Nature, Her Divine Revelations and a Voice to Mankind*, predicted that the truth of spiritual communication with the dead would be revealed "ere long," and this soon proved to be a widely repeated prophecy.

Andrew Jackson Davis was neither the first nor the only American to produce a directly revealed gospel in the nineteenth century. Others also felt the time and place seemed right for starting over with God. The earliest of these new scriptures is the one that had the most lasting effect. It was the *Book of Mormon*, revealed to Joseph Smith by the angel Moroni in upstate New York in 1827, which is still the gospel of the Church of Jesus Christ of the Latter-Day Saints, more popularly known as the Mormon church.

The rest of the nineteenth-century gospels are kept alive today only by tiny cults, within the occult subculture. *Oahspe: A New Bible,* was revealed to Dr. John B. Newbrough in 1881 through automatic writing on the typewriter then still a novelty. He found after ten years of "purification" that he could turn himself over to a higher power in the hour before dawn. His God democratically called himself the chief executive of the world rather than its creator.

Another turn-of-the-century revealed bible is *The Urantia Book*. This work discloses that Earth's true name is Urantia and we are part of the local universe of Nebadon which in turn is part of a superuniverse called Orvonton from whose capitol, Uversa, came the committee that dictated the book. Seven superuniverses circle the eternal center universe of Havona which contains the stationary isle of Paradise, where God dwells at the geographic center of infinity.

The *Aquarian Age Gospel of Jesus Christ* by Levi (Levi H. Dowling) claimed to reveal the akashic records—imperishable impressions of all events since the beginning of time stored in light waves and sound waves somewhere out in space. The concept of akashic records seems to be derived from early Yoga writings, but over the centuries they have been the key to many occult systems.

Phineas Quimby was as well known in nineteenth-century America as Jeane Dixon is today. A New England clockmaker, with only six weeks of schooling in his whole life, Quimby began practicing as a hypnotist, inspired by seeing one of Charles Poyen's demonstrations of mesmerism. By 1840, after only two years of working with hypnosis, Quimby emerged as a hero of the lecture circuit. He found a happy-go-lucky nineteen-year-old named Lucius Burkmar who was able to go into very deep hypnotic trance. And once Burkmar was under hypnosis he became a clairvoyant psychic who repeatedly obtained excellent results at treating illness.

But in 1859 Quimby felt he could now consciously will clairvoyance in himself. He came to the conclusion that what he had thought was telepathic medical treatment was really a self-fulfilling belief by the patient that the healer was making a cure. So, if the mind itself could cure physical disease, Quimby felt, then disease was actually no more than a mental error. Until his death in 1866, he carried on a busy faith-healing practice in Portland, Maine. Patients came from all over the country for his help. The most famous was Mary Baker Eddy, who had been an invalid for twenty-five years before Phineas Quimby cured her. She went on to found the Christian Science Church—whose teachings concerning mental healing owe a great deal to Quimby.

All of these early American metaphysical trends led to a dramatic event in March, 1848—one year after Andrew Jackson Davis' offhand prediction about the truth of spirit communication being revealed ere long.

On the night of March 31, the three little Fox sisters of Hydesville in northern New York began to experience "spirit raps" from a ghost who eventually identified himself as a murdered peddler named Charles B. Rosma. Bones were later found in the Fox cellar where Rosma said his body had been hidden. Thus was founded modern spiritualism.

True, communication with dead relatives or powerful spirits is an almost universal factor in primitive pagan religions. But it had generally been used in the past as a sorcerer-priest's technique for divining the future, not as a primary part of theological belief. Certainly in the major religions of Asia and the West, personal communication with the dead occupied a very minor role or was forbidden completely. Spiritualism was the first movement in any civilized society to be based entirely on the idea that communication with the spirits of the dead can be achieved by anybody, given a "medium" possessing the necessary psychic talents. Spiritualism is a social invention as completely American as jazz.

The Fox family had moved into a reputedly haunted house at Hydesville on December 11, 1847, and the knocks and bumps soon started, gradually getting more annoying. On March 31, the banging was ferocious. The young sisters, Margaret, then fifteen, and Kate, twelve, playfully started to clap their hands in reply to the invisible noisemaker and found that they were answered by the same number of taps. Next they began asking spoken questions and requesting simple signals in reply.

That very night neighbors were called in to witness this remarkable dialogue. Thereafter, as many as three hundred visitors would crowd into the little wooden house for the nightly rappings. The sisters—including the youngest one, Leah, who soon also began calling forth spirit raps—were sent off to various relatives to escape the crowds, but they were able to make these noises happen wherever they went. Next, the family moved to the nearest large city—Rochester—where by local demand the first spiritualist meeting took place on November 14, 1849, at Corinthian Hall. The word spread like wildfire and not all of it was favorable. The girls were almost lynched at least once, and angry fundamentalist mobs were sure to turn up wherever the Foxes made an appearance around the country. Before they left Rochester two skeptical committees were appointed to test the genuineness of the raps. Neither one could find any evidence of fraud, the rappings continuing even when the girls were standing on pillows with their legs tied together. But then three professors from the University of Buffalo claimed to have discovered in 1850 how it was possible to duplicate spirit raps by "cracking the joints of the knees and toes." A Harvard committee of 1857 refused to endorse the Fox sisters or the several other mediums who appeared before them. It never issued a final report but let it be known that it had not seen what it considered genuine phenomena.

Even as the Fox family was moving out of Hydesville other mediums were claiming they could contact the spirits. Voice mediumship, materialized ghosts, and flying furniture were all familiar events at seances in only a year or two. By 1854, 15,000 convinced American spiritualists sent a petition to Congress demanding an official commission to investigate and verify the new revelation.

The second spiritualistic stars were the Koons family of Millfield, Ohio. Farmer Jonathan Koons discovered that all his eight children were mediums and under spirit direction he built a log cabin on his land, where night after night unprecedented happenings took place in the darkness. Lights flashed, spirit hands played musical instruments, and furniture floated in the air. By 1857 the majority of western Ohio's population were said to be spiritualists, and for some years the orthodox churches stood empty each Sunday.

There were many prominent converts to spiritualism—colonels, judges and governors, the fiery abolitionist orator William Lloyd Garrison, writers James Fenimore Cooper and William Cullen Bryant, journalist Horace ("Go West, young man") Greeley. Two antispiritualism lecturers of the 1850's, Leo Miller and the Reverend C. H. Harvey, had fits in the middle of speaking engagements and declared themselves instant converts.

There is a great deal of intriguing evidence that Abraham Lincoln believed in spiritualism. It seems that after the death of Lincoln's young son, Todd, Mrs. Mary Lincoln became interested in spiritualism and held seances in the White House during the Civil War, which the President attended with gradually increasing enthusiasm. Lincoln is even supposed to have slipped unnoticed into public seances while visiting New York. In 1891 a book, *Was Abraham Lincoln a Spiritualist?* by Mrs. Nettie Maynard, claimed that the authoress had been one of the White House mediums and that psychic messages played a key role in erasing the President's doubts about issuing the Emancipation Proclamation. The first story about Lincoln's interest in spiritualism appeared in the *Cleveland Plain Dealer* while the President was still alive, and he never publicly denied it.

But a reaction against spiritualism was already beginning. The chaos of the Civil War had not advanced spiritualism's cause, and the occurrence of increasingly spectacular miracles seemed to be more rare. All these marvelous spirit communications hadn't really changed the problems of everyday living. But the main factor that reduced American spiritualism to the status of a minor cult by the start of the 1890's was the exposure of a great number of phony mediums. Several early-modern stage magicians found it profitable to insist they were tapping spirit power. A popular trick was spirit slate writing. Two slates would be tied together and handed to a member of the audience to hold. When opened, the center slates revealed a spirit message. Of course, this was done by using false slate panels that could be switched from one frame to the other by pressing a hidden catch. The Davenport Brothers, Ira and William, had an apparently undetectable escape routine involving spiritualism, in which they were bound and placed in a portable closet. Hidden behind the doors, they were instantly untied by the spirits and started playing invisible noisemakers. They toured the world for more than twenty years as stars of vaudeville, and in that time nobody was ever able conclusively to catch them cheating.

In 1884 a wealthy Philadelphia spiritualist named Henry Seybert willed $60,000 to the University of Pennsylvania for an impartial investigation of spiritualism. A commission of professors was appointed to do the job. In 1887 its report branded the whole thing a fraud. Henry Slade the top slate medium of the time, was easily caught cheating, and Margaret Fox's toes were observed to be flexing inside the shoes when her spirit taps were heard.

The real deathblow to the first heyday of American spiritualism came in 1888 when Margaret Fox, by now a much-married poverty-stricken alcoholic, sold the newspapers a story that the whole thing was a sham and even appeared at the New York Academy of Music to demonstrate how it *was* done by cracking her knees and toes. Other reformed mediums were soon making a good thing of confessing their fakery on the lecture circuit, and it would have been logical to expect spiritualism to fade away completely.

But no such thing happened. There was too large a core of committed spiritualists who would never change their minds about what they were convinced had been genuine psychic experiences. No matter how much of the spirit communications were proven false, it didn't automatically follow that *everything* was fake. Also, Margaret Fox recanted her confession a year later, blaming it on a desperate need for money and a disturbed mental state. She died in 1893, the last of the three Fox sisters. A nonspiritualist physician, Dr. Mellen, attended at her deathbed and reported that knocks were heard all over the place, although Margaret was too weak to move a muscle.

The entire development toward a rational unification of traditional occult knowledge can be traced from spiritualism. It was at the spectacular Vermont seances of the Eddy Brothers in 1874 that the incredible Madame Helena Petrovna Blavatsky—shortly to become the founder of theosophy—burst on the scene and enraptured her first influential supporter, Colonel Henry Olcott. Calling herself Countess Blavatsky, "a passionate devotee of spiritualism for fifteen years," she made an attempt to carve out for herself a starring role as a medium before moving on to her true role in occultism. Also, just before her arrival in America, she had tried to create a "Société Spirite" in Cairo, Egypt, which never evolved.

Madame Blavatsky was the daughter of a wealthy Russian artillery officer. At seventeen she married an old general, on what seems to have been a petulant whim, and shortly afterward took off for twenty-five years of wandering around Europe and the Middle East. She later claimed to have spent seven years studying with the sages of Tibet during a period when she was actually having an illegitimate child by an operatic basso named Metrovich. She was forty-two, overweight, and destitute when she sailed over to New York in steerage and moved into a Home for Working Women. But even her worst enemies couldn't help admitting she had a most hypnotic personality, and three years after she had arrived in America penniless, her Theosophical Society was an important international organization. Madame Blavatsky said she was teaching the central "Wisdom Religion" which was the original source of all religious revelations but had been revealed in different versions to suit the specific needs of past times. What she really accomplished was to combine for the first time Oriental and Western occultism in a well-organized modern context. She had all the elements for a cohesive occult system: the immortal soul, ancient lost races with secret knowledge of the universal plan, auras, the psychic energy field, higher planes of existence, control of psychic powers, and karma. This last is a Hindu term for the working out of the ultimate perfection of the soul. Karma is destiny, and in some interpretations it is supposed to involve paying for the sin's of one's past lives before the soul can progress.

Madame Blavatsky also claimed to possess the "Secret Doctrine," an esoteric teaching underlying this Wisdom Religion, which would give those who could master it the key to the universe and all sorts of superhuman powers. And finally she insisted that this Secret Doctrine had been practiced since the lost, ancient super-civilizations by an unbroken succession of semi-immortal "adepts" who lived at secret cities in the mountains of Tibet and had chosen *her* as their sole ambassador to the later nineteenth century.

This convenient bestowal of authority by invisible superhumans unfortunately became a very popular claim by the imitative occult organizations which sprang up around the turn of the century after Theosophy became so successful. There is, of course, no evidence whatsoever for the existence of hidden cities —in Tibet or anywhere else—inhabited by occult masters who seem to have different names and different messages for every self-proclaimed prophet that contacts them.

Madame Blavatsky herself faced a devastating exposure in 1884 when two assistants at the international Theosophic headquarters she had established at Adyar, India, revealed that Madame forged her numerous letters from the masters and had them slipped through secret panels behind the organization's most important shrine. It took all of Madame Blavatsky's formidable persuasive gifts to keep Theosophy alive after this, but by the time she died in 1891 the society was once again flourishing.

There are still many students of the occult who are searching for the kind of sensible, wide-ranging metaphysical system Madame Blavatsky tried to teach, and several competing branches of the Theosophical Society are still very much in existence. But in the twentieth century no leader has appeared strong enough to unify the entire movement, and the story of organized Theosophy after Madame Blavatsky's passing becomes as complicated as that of a Sicilian blood feud. The Theosophical Society in America, located in the Chicago suburb of Wheaton, survived all the labyrinthine power struggles to remain the official U.S. affiliate of Adyar's international center. The United Lodge of Theosophists is a kind of back-to-Blavatsky movement that began during the 1920's as a protest against all the unpleasant struggles for power then taking place.

San Diego's Point Loma Theosophical Community was an independent feifdom established by an energetic lady named Katherine Tingley. The experimental gardens at Point Loma played a major role in establishing the avocado as a southwestern crop. This self-supporting community had the first outdoor Greek-style amphitheater in America and a superb amateur symphony orchestra. More than 2,500 children grew up and went to school in the kibbutz-like atmosphere of Point Loma between 1897 and 1942—when the property was sold to become the campus of California Western University. The remnants of the community—its numbers yearly reduced by death—settled till 1951 at a former prep school east of Los Angeles and are now scattered in a few houses around Pasadena.

The most impressive piece of Theosophical real estate left in America is the Krotona Institute on one hundred and eighteen acres of wooded hills tucked in the mountain town of Ojai, between Los Angeles and Santa Barbara. Founded in 1924 and named after the school founded by Pythagoras, the father of mathematics, at Crotona, Italy, the institute has a colony of some forty homes nestled around a tremendous El Rancho Grande mansion where classes and services take place. Krotona's school is open for several ten-week semesters each year, and about one hundred students show up and pay tuition fees of seventy-five cents per class. Most of the instructors are retired PhD's and the average age of the Krotona residents is at least sixty-five. The Krotona Institute is "associated" with the Theosophical Society in America but does not really come under its jurisdiction. . . . This lends some credence to what I heard from a former Theosophy leader who is now the North American president of another metaphysical organization. He said that Krotona is really the world headquarters of the Esoteric Section—a special in-group to which Madame Blavatsky taught her most arcane secrets shortly before she died.

Occultism in the Laboratory

The entire development of research into psychic phenomena and parapsychology can be traced back to spiritualism. By 1852 spiritualism had crossed the Atlantic to London with touring American mediums. England's spiritualist movement had a growth less flashy but more solid than that of the United States parent branch. The Spiritualist National Union, with some 20,000 members, is today the United Kingdom's biggest organization in the field, and the Spiritualist Association of Great Britain, which has daily seances, classes, and lectures at its cavernous London building, is the largest single spiritualist club in the world. Since the mid-1950's, England has even had trade unions for both spiritualist mediums and spiritual healers.

From the first, the English spiritualists formed a number of committees to study what was going on in seances. These committees exposed their share of fakers but also built up an impressive body of reports on paranormal events witnessed by thoroughly reputable observers. Interest in the entire range of psychic phenomena began to spread in Victorian England. In 1882 Britain's Society for Psychical Research was organized to investigate both the claims of the spiritualists and spontaneous psychic experiences. The founders were all eminent members of England's scholarly establishment, and three years later their example led to the foundation of the American Society for Psychical Research.

In early team-efforts like *Phantasms of the Living*, the English SPR invented the technique of cross-checking separate witnesses to psychic phenomena. SPR founder F. W. H. Myers' *Human Personality and its Survival of Bodily Death* was a classic of psychic research that laid the groundwork for modern ESP theory by inventing such terms as telepathy, subliminal and supernormal. Myers' one-thousand-page book investigated scores of verifiable psychic experiences in an attempt to prove that a soul exists which is capable of leaving the physical body and which goes on to future stages of life in the higher dimensions. Frederick Myers, the son of a country minister, gave up his career as a classics teacher and promising minor poet to spend a lifetime in psychic research when his great love—the wife of one of his cousins—died suddenly after a passionate but chaste three-year romance during which they spent a great deal of time walking in the country and holding hands. He began going to seances and eventually received communications which satisfied him that his beloved still existed on the other side.

Another active SPR member was the great physicist, Sir Oliver Lodge, whose book, *Raymond,* reported in painstaking detail the sessions with mediums that convinced him his son was communicating from the beyond after his death in World War I.

Today it is a matter of record that the early SPR investigators were sometimes taken in. Even so famous a man as Sir Arthur Conan Doyle, the creator of Sherlock Holmes, could come out in support of something as seemingly farfetched as the book of "fairy photographs" snapped by Elsie Wright, sixteen, and Frances Wright, ten, and developed by their electrician father, Arthur, which was published in 1920. The fairies look like awkward Walt Disney sketches. But Sir Arthur admittedly thought of himself less as a researcher than as a missionary preaching the truth of psychic phenomena. And it seems absurd to suggest that all the truly eminent Englishmen involved in the early stages of the SPR could have been wrong all the time—the work of F. W. H. Myers and Sir Oliver Lodge is in itself enough to prove otherwise.

The main force behind the founding of the American Society for Psychical Research in 1885 was William James; redoubtable philosopher, psychologist, educational theorist, man of letters, experimenter with laughing gas, Harvard professor, and brother of novelist Henry James. William James had many characteristically pithy things to say about the start of systematic psychic research and his most memorable metaphor was, "To upset the conclusion that all crows are black, there is no need to seek demonstration that no crow is black; it is sufficient to produce one white crow."

The white crow William James believed he had produced was Mrs. Leonore Piper of Boston, probably the greatest turn-of-the-century medium and certainly the only great medium of the period who was never found guilty of even the slightest hint of faking. James wrote of his first sitting with the well-to-do Boston housewife, "Mrs. P. was either possessed of supernormal powers or knew the members of my wife's family by sight and had by some lucky coincidence become acquainted with such a multitude of their domestic circumstances as to produce the startling impression which she did."

Mrs. Piper was also the most thoroughly tested medium of her time. For nearly fifteen years she was observed and checked by

Richard Hodgson, an English lawyer brought over by the ASPR especially to work with Mrs. Piper. Hodgson was the bloodhound of early psychic research. It was he who conducted the SPR investigation of Madame Blavatsky's India headquarters and uncovered the forgeries and secret panels used for communications from Theosophy's "masters." He also caught Euspasia Palladino, a renowned Italian medium, slipping out of her shoes and using her bare toes to "fly" objects around darkened seance rooms. Before Hodgson began with Mrs. Piper he was, in fact, convinced that all professional mediums were "a gang of vulgar tricksters." But he never found anything the least suspicious about Mrs. Piper's mediumship, even though his investigations included the hiring of private detectives to follow her around, forbidding her to read newspapers for months on end, and selecting her clients at random so Mrs. Piper couldn't have any advance knowledge of them.

From the start of the twentieth century, attempts were made to expand the field investigation methods of the Society for Psychical Research into a systematic laboratory technique. Isolated experiments were tried, with some impressive results. But there was no long-range experimental program to follow up on this newest evidence of psychic phenomena.

The true father of contemporary psychic research is Dr. Joseph Banks Rhine. Surprisingly, Rhine's PhD was in botany. During his smalltown Midwestern boyhood, he fully intended to become a Protestant minister. But gradually he turned from religious orthodoxy to scientific empiricism, though his underlying interest was still in the larger questions of metaphysics. He and his wife Louisa, also a botanist with a PhD, were introduced to psychic investigation by a lecture by Sir Arthur Conan Doyle during the early twenties when they were both young teachers. They began reading SPR literature and at Harvard in 1926 met the important psychologist William McDougall, who had made some of the early attempts to test psychic phenomena under laboratory conditions. In 1927 when McDougall went to Duke University at Durham, North Carolina, to found a psychology department, the Rhines came along as his associates for psychic research.

Although Rhine's ESP studies have generally been associated with Duke, the university never felt too comfortable about having him there. As soon as McDougall retired, the psychologists at Duke ousted both Rhines from the department. Dr. Rhine coined the word "parapsychology" to stand for the psychology of paranormal mental powers and opened a separate Parapsychology Laboratory. It was considered part of Duke University because he had achieved tenure there, but basically Rhine had to raise his own research funds. And when he and Louisa reached retirement age they moved off-campus to an independent Institute for Parapsychology.

Rhine decided his most important job was to develop a reliable method of measuring psychic phenomena. He wanted large amounts of test cases which would stand up statistically. His most creative period of work was during the early 1930's. It was then he invented the terminology and testing approach which for the first time made ESP laboratory research systematic. As a beginning, he developed the concept of extrasensory perception itself, and later he applied the more neutral Greek letter psi to symbolize the range of faculties he was testing for: telepathy (thought transference), clairvoyance (knowledge of distant events not transmitted through the five senses or telepathically), precognition (seeing into the future), and psychokinesis (moving physical objects by mind power). Then he developed tests using the now-famous ESP cards, a deck alternating five symbols: circle, square, cross, star, and wavy lines. The statistical math would follow easily since chance odds for a right guess are one in five.

Rhine and his associates began casually testing whatever students or staff were handy, and when they kept finding good scores, they gradually tightened up the test conditions to conform to the most exigent scientific standards. In 1933 the Duke team made what they considered their first "foolproof" experiment with one of their best subjects, a Divinity School student named Hubert Pearce. He was guessing the cards from a room in another building one hundred yards away, and his results were a fraction less than *twice* what chance would allow.

In 1934 Rhine's first book, *Extrasensory Perception,* was published. Rhine writes that he had no idea his preliminary academic studies would cause such a furor. But obviously, any work claiming to set aside the established scientific structure of the world would get an electrifying response. By the tail end of the thirties, debunking criticisms of ESP were much more frequent in the scholarly journals than actual reports of parapsychology research. Rhine's work was attacked for its statistics, for cheating, for the possibility of cheating, for unconsciously biased errors in marking scores, in fact for everything under the sun. It is to Rhine's greatest credit that he was always willing to cooperate in opening his lab and records to any serious critic. He more than anyone wanted to root out the mistakes in his experimental techniques, and his later work was never charged with the same errors.

Despite all brickbats, Rhine's work was not exploded. Year after year, he and others working along his lines came up with thousands of group tests that showed statistically impossible results. Rhine's approach produced for the first time a mass of experimental evidence (not proof, but at least evidence!) that the supernormal psychic abilities claimed by the occult tradition since the dawn of history really might exist. . . .

Early Twentieth-Century Occultism

There was a great deal of organized occult activity in America during the first half of the twentieth century, but most of it tended to be rather commercial and fundamentalist. The really important insights into occult mechanisms were being made in the ESP laboratories. Movements like Psychiana and the I Am sect attracted good-sized and enthusiastic followings during the twenties and thirties but soon fizzled out. Fake swamis often did well until they were exposed. Joveddah de Rajah, for instance, received serious attention until his real name was revealed to be Joe Dawkins.

The days of the Great American melting pot brought in a leavening of occult beliefs from all over the world, but nothing that really lasted into the native-born generations beyond the level of superstition. We learned of Irish leprechauns, English faerie-folk, German trolls, East European werewolves and vampires. The Italian—Sicilian, really—tradition of witchcraft best known for the technique of warding off the evil eye (*malocchio*) by "making the horns" with thumb and little finger, was brought to the United States by a generation of old-country grandmothers.

The Latin culture has some ornate occult folkways. There are all sorts of specialized psychics for Spanish-speaking Americans. The spiritista communicates with dead relatives and friends like any other medium. For more uplifting messages there is the sanctista, who contacts only saints. Or if demons are needed to do a black magic job, the man to see is the satanista. Not much is known about the Espiritismo cult, but it's apparently active from coast to coast in Chicano ghettos. There is no central organization for the storefront churches or the tenement apartment mediums who charge $2 to $5 for their water-bowl gazing, palmistry, and seances. Most of the customers are women with worries, seeking advice on health, love, children in trouble, or the number to play that week.

The American Negro's independent occult tradition is popularly known as Voodoo. African magic traditions first took on the distinctive Voodoo style in Haiti, the Caribbean island-nation which was the earliest Afro-slave society to battle its way to independence. Haitian Voodoo is a genuine Dionysian religion, its ceremonies specifically directed at arousing the participants into a frenzied state of "possession by the gods."

From French-speaking Haiti, Voodoo traveled to the North American mainland via New Orleans. There it blended with the magic practices of the U.S. slaves. In the old days, when a white person's interest in any point of black culture was regarded as an honor by the Negro, there was a certain amount of first-hand reportage of U.S. Voodoo ceremonies. But now, with black militancy finally making it possible for the Negro to express his real feelings, the white man is barred. Ben Harris of the Timeless Occult Shop on Sunset Strip knows the major Voodoo shop in Los Angeles and occasionally goes there with a white astrologer friend who's a long-time customer, but he feels himself in physical danger every time.

It would take a very persistent black investigator to put together a full picture of American Voodoo today. What we do know about it is that it's very decentralized with no chief Voodoo church. Compared to the Haitian original, American Voodoo is pretty low-level stuff, less an organized ceremony than a front for commercial magicians who sell elixirs supposed to solve everyday problems.

In Houston, Texas, Bichon's Voodoo Store sells Master Gambling Oil for anointing the armpits in order to win games of chance, and Essence of Bendover to conquer the minds of friends and family. In New Orleans many downtown druggists find that their customers demand they keep a stock of items like Gamblers' Lucky Oil and the Black Wash That Kills. Harlem Voodoo shops tend to be somewhat furtive even with their own customers. The Negro ones are called Botanical Gardens and the Latin ones Botanicas. A client has to really insist he wants something like a red skull candle before the proprietor will fish it out from behind the counter.

There are a few sanitized interracial Voodoo variations here and there. In Denver a black man named Reverend John Wilson leads a good-sized one. A Jamaican version of Voodoo is Pocomania, which practices leaping about and singing in order to over-oxygenize the system and thus produce ecstasy. The high priest of this in the United States is Mallico Kapo Reynolds, about sixty-five. He got a fair amount of publicity a few years back, and Pocomania may still have some scattered followers.

Perhaps the best place to observe what Voodoo is all about these days is Africa itself. Correspondents stationed in Africa can satisfy their editors with a magic round-up when news is slow, and they often come up with interesting dispatches.

In Rhodesia the white coach of an African soccer team, Des Lawler, lost his job because the players listened to their witch doctor more than to him. Soccer spells were selling for $14.

An Irish missionary who reached Rome on the last plane out of Biafra said witch doctors were deciding military strategy for the Twelfth Biafran Division—they lost!

South Africa has an anti-magic law, and in 1955 Ghana found it necessary to amend its election code to make it illegal for any person to "purport to cast any spell and relate such act . . . with the voting or refraining from voting by any person at any election."

When Ghana gained independence and started a five-year industrialization plan, veteran British civil servant James Neal was hired as Chief of Security to try to cut down thievery on the construction projects. As he closed in on one of the major robber gangs, they hired a witch doctor to put a death curse on him. Neal thought this was a big joke until he found himself in the hospital with a bloodstream virus the doctors had never seen before. For the rest of his stay in Ghana, he writes in his book, *Jungle Magic,* he hired the most powerful Voodoo magician he could find to ward off the curses.

Until the occult explosion, twentieth-century amateur psychic experiments tended to be an obscure pastime of the intellectual elite, and it is remarkable what big names were involved. Thomas Edison was working on a machine to communicate with spirits when he died in 1931. Edison's close friend, Luther Burbank, claimed to have had telepathic communication with his sister and visions of his dead mother and was a supporter of Parmahansa Yogananda. But it was considered Burbank's wildest eccentricity that he insisted his plants would make better hybrids if he talked to them nicely and projected only loving thoughts, a notion which no longer seems so farfetched in view of Cleve Backster's lie-detector recordings of plant emotion.

Author Upton Sinclair's *Mental Radio* was published in 1930. The introduction to the German edition was written by none other than Albert Einstein, who is said to have accompanied Sinclair to seances now and then. The book records a series of experiments with Mrs. Sinclair, attempts to duplicate telepathically two hundred and ninety simple drawings Upton made under various conditions during a period of several months. According to the novelist, his wife succeeded with sixty-five of the drawings, was partly right one hundred and fifty-five times, and failed on only seventy tries.

Every once in a while in the early part of the century some inexplicable event would occur to pique America's interest in occultism temporarily. Starting in 1913, Mrs. Pearl Lenore Curran of St. Louis began spelling out—first on the Ouija board and later orally—poems, novels, short stories, and essays purportedly by a witty seventeenth-century English spinster named Patience Worth. A number of these books were good enough to publish on their literary qualities and seemed genuine in their archaic language and command of centuries-old minutiae. Mrs. Curran was twenty-one years old at the time this process began, not particularly well educated and apparently uninterested in historical scholarship. She always picked up the letter-by-letter dictation of quite complicated stories exactly where she left off at the previous session. Similar public interest was set off by the "Darby and Joan" seances of Ruth Finley, transcribed by her husband, Emmet, in *Our Unseen Guest,* and Betty and Stewart White's *The Betty Book* and *The Unobstructed Universe.*

After World War II, many rumors circulated about Adolf Hitler's alleged occult proclivities. At the very least, there seems no arguing the fact that Hitler did have astrologers casting his horoscope during most of the war. Since British Intelligence was aware of this, they assigned their own astrologer to report on what the stars would cause Hitler's astrologer to advise. The best compendium of occult Hitlerian speculation is in *Morning of the Magicians,* a book by Frenchmen Louis Pauwels and Jacques Bergier which presents the flashiest available evidence for the existence of a lost Ageless Wisdom, in typically suave Gallic prose. According to the authors, Hitler was a psychic and perhaps a medium too, and he certainly acted as if possessed by demonic powers. He came from a part of Austria known for its psychics and even had the same wet nurse as a famous spiritualist medium. If Hitler was not actually a member of certain occult secret societies, then it seems fairly certain that many of his early key advisers were. It is even suggested that Hitler lost the war with the suicidal second-front advance into Russia because he was convinced his demon helpers would turn back the freezing winter weather.

Seeds of the Occult Explosion

When the war was over, Dr. Rhine's ESP research had been around long enough to be reasonably respectable, and the American public was in an unprecedentedly open-minded mood. We had become used to believing in all sorts of surprising new technological developments which would not have seemed possible a few years before . . . jet aircraft and supersonic jets, atomic bombs and hydrogen bombs, electronic computers, television, polio vaccine, heart transplants, the space program. One effect of the early phase of this process was to make a big pop-intellectual cult of science fiction—the genre seemed to translate the confusions of rapid technological change into a romance within human dimensions. And science fiction was the breeding ground for some far-reaching occult-related movements.

In 1950 science fiction writer L. Ron Hubbard published *Di-*

anetics, the book that eventually led him to the founding of Scientology. A Dianetics article in *Astounding Science Fiction* magazine started the book selling briskly among SF devotees. Hubbard pictures the mind as a master computer which can function perfectly if all mistaken information is erased—the familiar altered state of consciousness theory with an overlay of computer engineering jargon. Scientology is not occultism, but it competes in the metaphysical marketplace for the Groovy Culture's losers who are seeking desperately for One Simple Answer. Scientology puts itself forward as a rational, updated version of the occult tradition's self-perfection techniques, and the approach has been successful enough to claim a growing worldwide membership of 15,000,000 and a weekly gross income of $1.4 million in the United States alone.

It was June 24, 1947, when salesman Kenneth Arnold saw America's first flying saucers while piloting his private plane near Mount Rainier in Washington state. He told of encountering a formation of nine circular objects moving at fantastic speed which "flew like a saucer would if you skipped it across the water." The tale might well have been buried as just another silly season item for the wire services if it wasn't for a true American original, Raymond A. Palmer.

Palmer edited the science fiction magazines *Amazing Stories* and *Fantastic Adventures* during their most popular years. But this sort of thing was too tame for him, and from 1944 to 1948 his magazines printed a seemingly endless series, the *Great Shaver Mystery*. Pennsylvania welder Richard Shaver claimed to have developed a racial memory of man's saga in the lost continents of Atlantis and Lemuria, and he revealed that all the troubles of the world are caused by Deros—evil Detrimental Robots created by the power-crazed Atlanteans. These Deros survived the sinking of Atlantis and now skulk about in underground caverns hatching their nefarious plots.

Palmer's refusal to quit running those installments of the *Great Shaver Mystery* more or less forced him to get out of science fiction. He founded *Fate Magazine,* and the first issue's lead story was *I DID See the Flying Disks* by Kenneth Arnold—with extensive ghost-writing by Ray Palmer. This article and its follow-ups were the source of the idea that flying saucers are spaceships and that the Air Force is guilty of a conspiracy of silence about it and thus they created the whole style of the flying saucer movement.

A strong, well-researched body of evidence for the reality of Unidentified Flying Object (UFO) sightings was assembled for *True* magazine in 1950 by Major Donald Keyhoe, a former Marine pilot. "The Flying Saucers Are Real" had a tremendous public impact. But unfortunately, what followed were a rash of absurd books like George Adamski's *Inside the Space Ships* and Howard Menger's report of his marriage to a beautiful Venusian. Purported flying saucer sightings synchronized with the needs of the low-level One Simple Answer school of occultism. A University of California social psychologist, H. Taylor Buckner, made a three-year study of sects that claimed contacts with UFO outer-space creatures and called the movement a flying Rorschach blot. As for Ray Palmer, he sold *Fate* to Margaret and Curtis Fuller, who have made it a much more solid and responsible occult magazine. He and Richard Shaver now live on neighboring Wisconsin dairy farms and Palmer publishes Amherst Books and a 10,000-circulation magazine, *Search,* which propagates his latest theory that flying saucers come through a polar opening from the hollow-Earth core where the Deros live.

But although the kooks on the fringe of the flying saucer movement made the whole thing seem silly by the early 1950's, there has been a great deal of serious investigation of UFO phenomena and many sightings seem thoroughly authenticated. George Van Tassel's annual flying saucer conventions at his 640-acre Giant Rock desert park north of Palm Springs have been attracting hundreds of fans since 1954 and feature a convincing array of UFO photographs and movies. In the autumn of 1965 author John Fuller and many other residents of Exeter, New Hampshire, were seeing strange orange glows around the town. Fuller collected the best eyewitness reports in his book, *Incident at Exeter.* He later followed it with *The Interrupted Journey,* the story of Mr. and Mrs. Barney Hill of Portsmouth, New Hampshire, who are embarrassed but absolutely insistent about their claim that they were picked up by a flying saucer which followed their car down a dark, deserted road in 1961. The Hills' only memory was of blanking out for about two hours. Then their growing nervousness about the incident sent them to psychiatrist Benjamin Simon, who hypnotized them and so obtained their story about being taken aboard a UFO and examined by manlike creatures before being released back to their everyday lives. As Dr. Simon points out, a hallucination shared by two persons and capable of standing up under hypnosis is unheard of in the history of psychotherapy.

America is by no means the only country to have experienced UFO sightings. France has had a very active flying saucer movement since about 1954. And Dr. Felix U. Ziegel of the Moscow Aviation Institute was quoted in *Psychic Discoveries Behind the Iron Curtain* as saying, "In truth, Soviet radar has picked up unidentified flying objects for twenty years. We have well-documented sightings from every corner of the USSR. It's hard to believe that all are optical illusions. Illusions don't register clearly on photographic plates and radar." Russians have never lost their interest in the 1909 Tunguska "meteorite" which knocked down most of an isolated Siberian forest and left behind a great deal of radioactive debris after having been observed by local woodchoppers to be circling around like a crippled aircraft searching for a safe place to land.

Even more than the UFO sightings, the Bridey Murphy craze showed clearly that the American psyche was ready for an occult explosion. In 1952 millionaire Colorado heir Morey Bernstein whose hobby was hypnotism decided that he should try to regress somebody back to a past life. He needed a subject who could be put into deep trance and the best one he knew was a pretty, brunette, twenty-nine-year-old mother of two named Virginia Burns Tighe, who had been hypnotized easily by Bernstein at several country-club parties. Virginia's husband disapproved of the project and the lady herself was not overly enthusiastic, but Morey Bernstein was politely persistent and she cooperated for six tape-recorded sessions before she began a third pregnancy and refused to continue. Bernstein's book, *The Search for Bridey Murphy,* came out in 1956 and was the best seller of the year. In the most simple everyday terms, the tape-recording transcript claimed to give what was nothing less than conclusive proof of human immortality.

Bernstein had first guided a hypnotized Virginia back through her earliest childhood memories and then he instructed her to try to recall even earlier events. Suddenly she began talking in a brogue and describing her life as Bridey Murphy, born in Cork, Ireland, in 1798. Bridey was married at twenty to a law clerk named Sean Brian Joseph McCarthy and died childless in Belfast at the age of sixty-six. There were several small-scale attempts to find proof of Bridey's existence by the Denver *Post,* the Chicago *Daily News,* and Doubleday and Company. Census records just weren't being kept in Ireland some one hundred and seventy-five years ago, but a number of extremely obscure details Bridey mentioned in passing have been verified. A good example is her naming of Farr's and John Carrigan as the Belfast grocers—the names were verified from a rare 1865 city directory, and they were probably the town's only big food stores.

However, the bubble was supposedly burst with a 1956 *Chicago American* series that found all kinds of parallels between Virginia's actual childhood in the Windy City and her Bridey Murphy memories. Suspiciously, most of the eyewitnesses the newspaper quoted were anonymous, purportedly to protect their privacy. And Virginia Tighe insisted to her hometown paper, the Denver *Post,* that the exposé was made up of out-and-out lies, but her list of faked points never got the wide attention it deserved.

For example, Virginia did remember a Mrs. Corkell living on her street but claims she never even spoke to her and had no idea her first name was Bridie. Later, the Denver *Post* was unable to verify that Bridie Corkell's real maiden name *was* Bridie Murphy. Even more revealing was the Denver *Post*'s interview with Mrs. Harry G. Saulnier, identified in the Chicago series as "Mrs. H. S. M." who taught Virginia to memorize stage-Irish monologues. Mrs. Saulnier says she vaguely remembered Virginia as a mediocre student in her elocution classes, but she never taught any Irish dialect. There are many other such samples, like the Irish aunt who supposedly regaled her with tales of the old sod. Virginia says this coleen was born in New York and didn't know any more details of Ireland than the average Scotch-Irish American. Perhaps the most blatant of all was the original *Chicago American* claim that Bridey, like Virginia, had a little brother who died. Virginia Tighe pointed out that she never had a brother.

The East and West coasts both had late-night radio talk shows which played important parts in preparing the way for the occult explosion. Long John Nebel's midnight show was the first to bring the occult subculture before a general radio audience and has been heard in New York since the early sixties. Long John was a carnival barker and a store pitchman and generally led a checkered career in fast-talk jobs which included traveling with a hotel room mind-reading "act." He was discovered by a perceptive executive from station WOR while running an auction shed in New Jersey. To launch his show with maximum notoriety, Long John used to specialize in interviewing people like the Brooklyn dentist who had been to Venus with the flying saucer people. He extracted a good deal of entertainment from these poor unfortunates and gradually built up a panel of erudite people to help him demolish their pretensions. As the show caught on, he phased out the wilder guests, but he still continues to hold round-table discussions on metaphysical controversies.

In Southern California during 1967 and 1968, psychedelics and Love-Ins were heralding the breakthrough of the new youth counterculture. And the forum for the occult elements in this social phenomenon was a remarkable 11 P.M.–1 A.M. program called *Radio Free Oz,* broadcast over KPFK-FM, the Pacifica Foundation listener-sponsored station in Los Angeles. Hosted by the "Wizard of Oz," every guest was a "mystery guest" and only in the course of three-way conversations with the audience phoning in was it gradually revealed what occult activist was on-mike. The Wizard was a prematurely egg-bald young man in his mid-twenties named Peter Bergman, who unfortunately soon tired of being an electronic seer at the subsistence wages of listener-supported radio and joined an improvisational comedy group, the *Firesign Theater,* which has recorded for Columbia Records.

The occult explosion seems to have followed a classic social-trend pattern of beginning as an interest of the intellectual avant-garde, then spreading through the bohemian subculture—except that in this case there was available the wider scope of the hippie youth culture, the world's first mass bohemia.

Certainly no single astrologer can be credited with popularizing the idea that we are entering the Age of Aquarius—when art, science, and religion will be one and a golden era of peace is to reign. But during the later sixties when Haight-Ashbury was in full hippie flower, the only San Francisco astrologer with a strong influence among the counterculture's young leadership was a distinguished-looking septuagenarian named Gavin Arthur, whose explanations of Age of Aquarius theory were quoted a great deal in the *Oracle,* the beautifully designed 100,000-circulation pioneer of psychedelic journalism. Five years ago, Gavin Arthur was the only San Francisco astrologer well enough known to receive regular invitations to join local talk shows, but he was ekeing out a living doing $15 horoscopes when his health permitted and living with a lot of transient male roomers in a squalid duplex flat over a Japanese luncheonette. Gavin had changed his name from Chester Alan Arthur III, so his grandfather the President and the rest of his aristocratic family wouldn't be disgraced by their black sheep. Gavin's busy social whirl has left him time to write one small book, *The Wheel of Life,* which uses the zodiac as a pattern to diagram mankind's sexual types—he gave the place of honor to Julius Caesar, "husband to every wife, wife to every husband."

American journalists have not been educated to understand the occult implications of contemporary news events and so rumor plays a far more important part in the occult explosion than it does in most other areas of life today. The great numbers of young people whose interest is really responsible for the occult explosion do not pick up their metaphysical news from the press or in the classroom—they hear it from friends on the street.

The contemporary occult rumor par excellence was the Great California Earthquake of April 16, 1969, that didn't happen. The media didn't begin to cover this story until near quake deadline, when a sizable portion of the state was worried stiff. The seed of all the gossip seems to have been a December, 1968, announcement by the CalTech Seismological Laboratory—the most authoritative earthquake study center—that some creep could be expected along the San Andreas Fault during the first eight days of April.

Creep happens to be the comedy-relief of earthquake phenomena. About the worst damage it does is buckling a few sidewalks and winery floors in the Salinas Valley. Unlike real earthquakes, creep can now be predicted fairly accurately. And it has a very helpful function, in that it seems to remove some of the strain on the San Andreas Fault.

But just at the time of the CalTech announcement, Curt Gentry's fantasy, *The Last Days of the Late Great State of California*, was published and its gimmick of a monstrous earthquake which removes California from the world in April, 1969, seemed to have a sort of Orson Welles *War of the Worlds* effect. Also, the occult explosion brought back mass interest in the prophecies of psychic Edgar Cayce, who had predicted during trances in the twenties and thirties that both New York and California would be under water by the end of the century. But Cayce didn't specify any year for this to happen, and his record on geological predictions has not been perfect anyhow.

In San Francisco, where the earthquake rumors began, a cute, blond, Dutch-born housewife named Elisabeth Steen was regularly getting into the local papers with stories on the earthquake visions she'd been having since 1964. Mrs. Steen's predictions were taken seriously because she'd had well-witnessed, verifiable psychic flashes that came true. She foresaw Holland's big 1952 flood and also the assassination of Martin Luther King—off by only two days. The resultant publicity caused Mrs. Steen to be invited to take an ESP test with Dr. Charles Tart, a young parapsychologist who teaches at the University of California at Davis. She insisted that one of the sealed envelopes with human hair she'd been given really contained a black cat's hair. Even Dr. Tart didn't know until afterward that a lab assistant had tricked him by sneaking in the cat hair.

The earthquake rumors leaped down to Los Angeles. Mama Cass made a hit record titled "California Earthquake." Ministers of four apostolic churches moved their congregations to Missouri, Georgia, and Tennessee—arriving just in time for the first major earthquake along the Mississippi Basin in one hundred and fifty years. A choice of different earthquake dates in April, 1969, became available. Amateur astrologers charted April 4 at 3:13 P.M., and numerology students preferred Good Friday, the anniversary of the big 1964 Alaska earthquake. One of the Instant Hippie Leaders who kept popping up in Haight-Ashbury around this time, Beau Maverick, claimed that his hippie computer programmers had worked out the date to exactly April 19 at 8:19 P.M. He sent an open letter to Pocatello, Idaho, warning the city fathers to get ready to shelter 10,000 refugee hippies at the new seashore. Every major professional psychic and astrologer—from Jeane Dixon to Sydney Omarr—pooh-poohed the earthquake scare, but it didn't help much.

Elisabeth Steen's husband quit his job with the San Francisco electric company, and the family moved to Washington state. And the weirdest thing of all about the Great Earthquake Rumor was that Mrs. Steen was really right in forseeing death and calamity for some time around April, 1969. The only trouble was that she greatly overestimated the scope of the disaster. Elisabeth died suddenly and mysteriously in a Spokane hospital on March 28, 1969, at the age of twenty-nine.

Dr. Stanley Krippner is the director of the Maimonides Hospital Dream Laboratory in Brooklyn, but since 1967 he's been taking periods off from his ESP dream studies to look into psychic phenomena in the new Youth Communes. "Belief in the paranormal is virtually an act of faith on the communes," he says. "Use of the I Ching, the Tarot cards, the Ouija board, and astrology is a common element in their lives. The notion that mental vibrations can influence crops, the weather, animals, and people is taken for granted." At one New Mexico commune, the residents coolly told Krippner they were expecting his visit because a girl there had had a vision about it the week before.

"Extended use of consciousness-expanding psychedelics tends to decondition users from their past beliefs and bring them closer to their own genuine reactions," Krippner believes. "Ego-boundaries are weakened and there's a we-are-all-one group mind feeling with a loosening of space-time concepts. Even the communes that have switched from drugs to meditation retain the members' strong but unproven conviction they are psychic."

The psychologist admits he never actually observed any psychic happenings at any of the eighteen communes he visited, but he feels that a culture so much more open to the psychic than the standard one is a very important environment for ESP testing.

And some astonishing results were recorded during two visits to the Maimonides Dream Laboratory by members of the Colorado mountaintop artistic commune, Libre.

The Libre colony includes a published novelist and a successful painter. It runs a school for teen-age dropouts in Gardner, the nearest town, and tours regularly with group concerts and lectures about the commune life plan, which includes daily rituals celebrating the paranormal. They try to have childbirth outdoors with the entire group around for a welcoming chant. Children are encouraged to submit their dreams for interpretation—a common practice in primitive tribes. One mother claims she has such a strong ESP bond with her child that she can call her telepathically. The commune hunter, known as Peter Rabbit, provides the bulk of Libre's meat supply by a kind of mystical poaching. He says he places a salt block at a streamside drinking place and telepathically asks the herd of deer that show up to sacrifice one of its number for a constructive purpose. Every time, claims Peter Rabbit, a lone deer will come over and stand quietly as he shoots it.

Six adults and two children from Libre were locked in a soundproof room at the Maimonides Dream Laboratory and a staff assistant concentrated for five minutes on sending an image from another room down the hall. He picked a desktop calculating machine that happened to be handy. When the Libre group was asked what they thought the message was, they said they'd held a group discussion and decided it was a "machine with buttons." The next time, one Libre member concentrated on a picture of a bridge, and six receivers from the colony were questioned separately. Two said they thought it was a bridge and another used the words, "suspension bridge."

Chapter 7

The Occult Business

BY the start of the 1970's, occultism had become a big business in America—and commercializing on occultism was an even bigger business. Merchandisers found that a touch of occult packaging helps sell almost any kind of product. A national gasoline company saturated TV prime time with commercials to announce it was giving away free zodiac cups with every fill-up. The Armour Meat Company offered a copy of Sydney Omarr's *Cooking with Astrology* to anyone who tried their bacon.

The Associated Press polled 850 manufacturers at the 1970 Toy Fair and concluded that occult games are the industry's big hope to boost sales in the next decade. A typical new item was the $5 *Mystery Zodiac,* featuring a spinning plastic wizard with a magnetic wand. Department stores and Five and Ten Cent outlets carry a seemingly endless array of astrological glasses, napkins, stationery, makeup, and clothing.

Visible as all this is, it has little to do with genuine occultism. At best, it may help keep the general public aware of the occult explosion and serve as a first step to real occult studies. But like as not, it just causes an oversimplified, confused misinterpretation of what the occult tradition is all about.

But there also exists an occult commerce directed at filling actual needs of the metaphysics subculture.

"Business has tripled in the past couple of years, more kids than ever before are buying actively in this field," says Don Weiser, who has run the forty-year-old Samuel Weiser Bookshop since his father retired in 1965. Located at 734 Broadway, just south of Eighth Street in Greenwich Village, Weiser's is America's best occult bookshop, and its only serious rival in the English-speaking world is Stewart & Watkins of London. The store's astonishing bulletin board gives the fastest introduction to what is going on in occult circles in New York. On a certain afternoon, the notices included the fiftieth anniversary of the Parapsychology Forum at 64 West Ninth Street; the first annual Tri-Metro New Age Weekend Seminar at the Trenton, New Jersey, War Memorial Building, and Kundalini Yoga classes on a barge in the Hudson River. "A lot of people are just looking for quick answers," says the stocky, bearded Don Weiser. "I can only hope many of them turn into true occultists, searching seriously for the purpose of life and not content with being led blindly."

Occult equipment is now sold along with psychedelic accessories at most head shops, those rebel retailers to the youth culture. And suddenly occult shops that sell full-fledged lines of magical goods are popping up in the unlikeliest places.

Eleanore Person's Hermetic Workshop is across from the Los Angeles Farmers Market and CBS Television City at 123 Fairfax Avenue. At first glance, the inside of the place looks like a typical bric-a-brac shop with stacks of Made-in-Hong-Kong painted porcelain figurines and brassy costume jewelry. The first indication that the shop is something more is a neatly hand-lettered sign on the wall, SHOPLIFTING PLAYS HELL WITH YOUR KARMA.

Miss Person is a hefty, colorfully dressed lady who has told reporters she is a ninth-generation white witch. She presides over a coven whose membership consists of professionals like doctors and engineers. Her two racks of herb shelves are arranged in precise rows of little brown bags placed alphabetically from absinthe to yohimbé, which both happen to be extremely powerful and tricky drugs, though legal. Absinthe is used to spike wine making the drink which drove Toulouse-Lautrec crazy. Yohimbé is a genuine aphrodisiac from the Amazon River that William Burroughs tested on his expedition to find the yage drug medicine men.

Next comes the rack of aerosol spray incenses packaged with bilingual labels in English and Spanish. There's aerosol Frankincense & Myrrh Spray, aerosol High John the Conqueror

Bath Spray, even aerosol Tannis Root, the substance with which they revive the mummy in all those horror films. The cans sell for about $1.50 apiece.

The Hermetic Workshop also carries two brands of tiki voodoo dolls for sticking pins into. A bronze Goat of Mendes statuette (the horned God of magic) costs $125, but in metallic-looking wax mold it's only $10.

Tucked in a secluded glass case are little open boxes of dried bat hearts and jellied cats' eyes for $2.50 apiece, and there's a bargain $2 price for swallows' hearts and guaranteed black cat bones.

Ben Harris, a friendly and articulate under-thirty native Chicagoan, now operates the Timeless Occult Shop & Bell Bottom Jeans $4.95 in a bungalow court at the eastern border of Sunset Strip, just below the classic old-Hollywood Chateau Marmont Hotel. He carries the usual multicolored witchcraft candles, some shaped like cats, skulls, or devils; oils and incenses for every magic purpose and various talismans. Top of the line is a Brain Wave Synchronizer Self-Hypnosis Machine that is supposed to give an electronic high by flashing a light in rhythm with brain oscillations. It sells for over $200. Ben's small store has been visited by every big name in contemporary occultism who passes through Hollywood. But when he put in a mod clothing section, he was thinking of phasing out his entire occult business to go into health foods. "Right when Sharon Tate got murdered and Charlie Manson was busted, all these bad-news black magic types started coming around and trying to buy potions that would kill people and all that," says Ben. "It was a big drag. But since Manson was soon discredited as a genuine occultist, I think the trend is back to white magic and the higher metaphysics—my own real interest."

Even the chummiest black magic store somehow gives off negative vibrations compared to a metaphysical oasis like the unique Bodhi Tree on the Melrose Avenue antique-dealer row in Los Angeles. The Bodhi Tree is in a soft-lit little cottage, with home-made beanbag sofas for browsers in every room. The place was totally renovated by four young partners who have a total of twenty-six years of higher education among them. They met while working as aerospace engineers at McDonnell Douglas.

"We used to eat lunch together at the company cafeteria and try to figure how we could get on a more spiritual trip that would still be constructive instead of escapist," says Dan Morris. He works fulltime at the store for a subsistence salary underwritten by the other three partners who continue to punch the clock at McDonnell Douglas until the Bodhi Tree is self-supporting. The store's stock—mostly books—concentrates on Asian religion and the high road to metaphysics.

Dan Morris is in his thirties and divorced. He'd been earning $20,000 a year, had teen-age children, and a big house in a chic canyon. "Acid got me to where I could dig the trip," he says. "It showed me the possibilities. I had a groovy guide who put me on very spiritual sessions. He would read to me from the great books; the ideas came alive in a state of consciousness that opened up the universe. I admit drugs are scary, but they did turn on many serious people if they were treated with reverence. I was ready to understand how the holy men really can teach you how to float around the room if you are ready, and they do these little things to show they could do it.

"About five years ago the four of us—who didn't know each other then—started reading about Eastern religions," says Dan. "My first guru was Maharishi; I was at his big Squaw Valley seminar. Then after a while I felt there ought to be a deeper approach, though I certainly don't put down transcendental meditation. I believe that Maharishi thinks of his work as a good way to get people on the trip. He's cool. I've seen him rapping about physics with a roomful of PhD's. But my partners and I studied with a lot of different Zen and Yoga gurus. As a matter of fact, we made up our minds about this store—even decided to name it for the tree Buddha sat under when he attained his illumination —during a retreat at Malibu with Krishnamurti."

James Bolen was a debonair San Francisco public relations man who gradually developed more and more of an interest in occult studies the way one does these days and decided to do something constructive about it. His wife, Japanese-American psychiatrist Jean Shinoda Bolen, agreed and in 1969 they put their savings plus a bit of borrowed cash into what was to be a slick-format publication which would report the occult and psychic phenomena from a rational, contemporary viewpoint.

Most of the many things that can go wrong with a new magazine went wrong on *Psychic,* but within a year after the first bimonthly issue circulation was 35,000 copies. This is practically the break-even point as long as Bolen keeps putting in fourteen-hour workdays at the head of his two-and-a-half-man staff and continues to find quality articles for the $75–$100 he can afford to pay. But as soon as he reaches his first circulation goal of 100,000 copies he can keep up a more ordinary production budget. To this end, Bolen has been switching distributors in hopes of finally overcoming the usual new-publication newsstand logjam.

Even before the occult explosion came, books on occultism were profitable, bought by a steady public. And because the subject is so wide and complex, a reader guidance service of occult book clubs made good business sense too. The Universe Book Club, owned by Doubleday and Company, is the newest active club. The Mystic Arts Book Club—recently bought by the aggressive publishing firm of Lyle Stuart (*The Sensuous Woman*) —features the works of its sister company, University Books, which has become the standard reference line of occult classics in English. The only comparable occult publishing specialist in the United States is Weiser Press, an offshoot of the Manhattan bookshop, which has brought back a number of important out-of-print works in magic and metaphysics. Don Weiser is able to produce very small editions profitably by printing photo offset copies of the original books.

The pop recording industry prides itself on being the communications medium most responsive to changes in public taste. So it's not surprising that the occult record shelf is growing rapidly. But as yet nobody has found the right combination of ingredients to record an occult smash hit. There have been instructional spoken-word record albums like the *Signs of the Zodiac* series on Herb Alpert's A&M label; Louise Huebner's *Seduction Through Witchcraft*—one of the album cuts is titled "Orgies: Tool of Witchcraft"; and a twin-record package with Vincent Price called *Witchcraft and Demonology.* Astrology columnists Carroll Righter and Sydney Omarr are also represented on disks.

There have been occasional hit songs with occult overtones like "Got My Mojo Working" or "I Put a Spell on You." And a few attempts have been made to create a genre of occult rock.

Mercury Records put a good amount of push behind a trio called Coven, whose first and only album was titled *Witchcraft* and had the slogan "Destroys Minds and Reaps Souls." The record jacket was an unusually deluxe double foldout . . . The center spread showed the lovely blond lead singer serving as nude altar for a black sabbath. But the album sold only 20,000 copies, a barely respectable total. Its evil freakiness was clearly too contrived for the funky spontaneity of the mass teen audience . . . all those lyrics about eating babies and drinking blood en route to eternal torment in hell just didn't make it.

There are other rock groups called Electric Lucifer and Black Sabbath—this last being an English quartet that changed its name from the ecologically minded "Earth." But from both an artistic and sales standpoint, the only successful occult rock record is Dr. John the Night Tripper's *Gris-Gris*. During his early publicity, Dr. John was presented as John Creaux, an authentic New Orleans Voodoo convert out of Sister Caterine's Temple of the Innocent Blood and a disciple of Perfesser Longhair, last of the great bayou rent-party pianists.

However, he soon proved to be a front-rank Hollywood studio pianist in his early thirties named Mac Rebbenack, who was indeed raised in New Orleans but had little else in common with the flamboyant legend. Rebbenack has gotten excellent response to his occasional stage shows, which are masterpieces of campy grotesquerie complete with eerie lights, incense, and robed musicians. Dr. John's costumes run to snakeskin, fish-net, and huge turbans topped with three-foot-high feathers. He also paints his bearded face in day-glo designs.

By now, Rebbenack has cut three interesting Dr. John albums, but nothing that equaled the impact and 50,000-album sales of his *Gris-Gris*, an evocative Voodoo pastiche that describes Dr. John and his methods. A trio of weirdly piping black girls intone an ersatz hoodoo curse "Gris-gris, gumbo ya-ya" over and over again while the band wails threateningly on cane flutes, a gourd mandolin, and oil-can drums. In a sort of bayou Brooklynese dialect, Rebbenack sings, "They call me Dr. John, known as the Night Tripper/ Got my satchel of gris-gris in my hand." His remedies include "Get-Together Drops" if you have a bad woman, "War Water" for neighbors putting your troubles in the street, and for the overworked, "Boss-Fix Jam."

Mail-Order Metaphysics

To most of the public—and for good reason—the commercial occult consists of mail-order mystery schools that claim to sell the Secrets of the Universe on the installment plan.

Anybody who's read an American magazine since the early 1930's has probably seen one of the full-page ads of the Rosicrucians' AMORC (Ancient Mystical Order Rosae Crucis)—the world's greatest occult mail-order house. AMORC's annual postage bill is $250,000; they send out 6,000,000 envelopes a year, and if all the paper they mail was laid end to end, it would stretch the 1,236 miles from New York to Kansas City. The organization claims 110,000 members who have paid a $10 initiation fee and $4 a month for lessons in "the mysteries of time and space, the nature of matter and important discoveries in Rosicrucian chemistry and physics." Half the membership is overseas in the sixty-six nations with AMORC charters. It takes only a bit of simple arithmetic to conclude that annual Rosicrucian gross income is at least $5,000,000.

The Rosicrucianism responsible for four decades of those "What Secrets Did They Possess?" advertisements featuring pictures of Benjamin Franklin, Isaac Newton, and Francis Bacon, is located in San Jose, a commuter suburb south of San Francisco. Rosicrucian Park is a square block of reduced-scale concrete models of ancient Egyptiana—a sphinx, an obelisk, shrines, and mosaic murals. The new administration building is a copy of the Great Temple of Ramses II. To keep up its benevolent local image, AMORC serves the community with a good Egyptian museum, a planetarium, and a Sunday-painter art gallery—they are also charter members of the city's Chamber of Commerce.

Rosicrucians' AMORC calls itself a nonprofit incorporated fraternity—not a religion but a system of metaphysics intended to awaken the latent faculties of the individual so he can lead a happier and more useful life . . . "A livable philosophy that unites metaphysical idealism with the practical sciences."

The first verifiable record of Rosicrucianism's start is a pamphlet dated 1614 with a long Latin title beginning *Fama Fraternatis* which popped up mysteriously in Cassel, Germany. It was the purported history of a magical prodigy named Christian Rosenkreutz who had plumbed the deepest secrets of Asiatic wizardry on a pilgrimage to the hidden desert cities of the magi and then returned to his Teutonic homeland to spread the word among a chosen few. But AMORC claims its metaphysical pedigree extends back to the Mystery Schools of Ancient Egypt where it was first discovered that man really had an immortal psychic energy body about which the masses were not yet ready to be taught.

The overwhelming impact of the inescapable Rosicrucians' AMORC advertising has by now pretty well obscured the fact that anybody could start an organization which includes Rosicrucian in the title. There are at least three other Rosicrucian rivals to AMORC in the United States alone. During the 1930's, the Rosicrucian Fraternity of R. Swinburne Clymer at Beverly Hall in Quakertown, Pennsylvania, gave AMORC serious competition. H. Spencer Lewis, the metaphysical merchandising genius who guided AMORC's remarkable success, came up with a proclamation from some European convention of mystery schools which gave his group exclusive jurisdiction over North American Rosicrucianism. The best Clymer could counter with was an accusation that some of AMORC's symbolism was disguised black magic. His son, Emerson Clymer, still carries on the fraternity from its Pennsylvania headquarters, claiming 19,000 members who have paid a $50 lifetime initiation and $12 for a set of books which contain the secret knowledge of the Egyptian Age, the Age of Christ, and today's Age of Man.

The Society of Rosicrucians in New York at 321 West One-hundredth Street claims a worldwide membership of 10,000. Its founder, the late G. E. S. DeWitow, was a well-regarded esoteric thinker, particularly for his book, *The Temple in the Clouds*. The society is being carried on by his widow.

The most viable rival to AMORC is the Rosicrucian Fellowship—at Oceanside, the community across El Toro Marine Base from President Nixon's San Clemente hideaway. Founder Max Heindel's brand of Rosicrucianism combined fundamentalist and mystical Christianity with liberal helpings of astrology, reincarnation, and the occult tradition.

Mount Ecclesia, the Oceanside Rosicrucian headquarters, is one of the earliest big private landholdings along the coast between Los Angeles and San Diego. The property, worth millions, is kept up very nicely with cute stucco temples all over the place. There is a department of healing where believers pray over the mail. The main temple is almost absurdly majestic atop a precipitous bluff with a panoramic view. The fellowship maintains a really fine low-price vegetarian restaurant and has an unusually tolerant attitude toward the new breed of long-haired young occultists who are always around the grounds.

Max Heindel got his version of Rosicrucianism from the "Beings" of the thirteenth century lesser mystery school near the German-Bohemian border, an ethereal temple disguised by the shell of an ordinary-looking house. He was sought out to spread the word after he came ashore from his career as ship's engineer on Cunard liners and passed through Theosophy. Under astral orders, he wrote *The Rosicrucian Cosmo-Conception* in 1908. His astrological textbooks and tables are still in fairly wide use today.

Heindel died in 1919 and his widow, Augusta Foss Heindel, died in 1938. But there was a fifty-year lawsuit over the Mount Ecclesia property by feuding factions of the Rosicrucian Fellowship that wasn't settled till 1956. The only reason both sides came together then and began running the operation in partnership was that everybody in the original suit had died, and the next generation was finally able to bury the hatchet.

For a Universal Brotherhood of Wisdom, Rosicrucians tend to sue each other a lot. In the mid thirties the widow of one of the AMORC cofounders, Mrs. Thor Kiimalehto, sued surviving Imperator H. Spencer Lewis to get a piece of the action, claiming she had been frozen out and there were millions of dollars involved. H. Spencer Lewis died in 1939, and his son, Ralph Maxwell Lewis, is now second-generation Imperator. He was sued during the forties by a lady named Jeanette Scott Seymour Young, who said she was a former concert pianist and that AMORC agents had railroaded her into an insane asylum and had her sterilized when she wanted back a large sum of money she had given them.

The tremendous economic success of Rosicrucians' AMORC has inspired dozens of other mail-order occult lesson enterprises. Many of them claim direct authority from those mysterious superhuman beings who travel from their hidden lairs by astral projection—one of Madame Blavatsky's more unfortunate legacies to occultism. Madame's favorite "Mahatma" from the mountain fastnesses of Tibet was named Koot Hoomi, and quite a few other ambitious sect-founders have claimed to be on an exclusive psychic pipeline to this great adept. As our century became more cynical, the pronouncements of these masters slackened off considerably. But Koot Hoomi and his cohorts are by no means in complete retirement.

Robert and Earlyne Chaney didn't start the Astara Foundation till 1951, but they managed to find two previously untapped masters, Rama and Zoser, as well as the ubiquitous Koot Hoomi. The Chaneys met at Camp Chesterfield, Indiana, which is just outside Indianapolis and the biggest spiritualist summer camp in the world. Robert was a fast-rising young medium, and Earlyne was delving into New Age religions after a promising career as a Hollywood actress that included an appearance in Shirley Temple's *Kiss and Tell*. Her fiance, an Air Force captain, died in a plane crash, and Earlyne recalled how a friendly father-image spirit used to appear to her out beside the woodpile during her lonely Texas childhood to prophesy that her life would change after she lost a dear one, which would inspire her true mission of solving the mystery of the afterlife. It was only later that she realized her ethereal childhood visitor was none other than Koot Hoomi!

Robert and Earlyne are still in the process of initiation into ever higher realms of the spirit. One of the most recent astral promotions took place inside Mount Shasta in Northern California, which is widely believed to be a holy mountain of the Indians. The Chaneys report that inside Shasta is a magnificent cathedral where they met Koot, Rama, and Zoser, and saw Jesus on a magic mirror from his home in the higher planes. According to the Astara theory, twelve Lords of the Flame from Venus came to Shambala, the magic city in the Gobi Desert (formerly the Gobi Sea), and Jesus is one of four of these Kumaras who sacrificed himself in an earthly incarnation. Rama was the direct disciple of Christ, and Robert Chaney was picked to succeed Rama.

One can become an Astarian for $5 and ascend the many degrees of Lama Yoga at $2 a lesson. Membership also includes a sheaf of postcard forms to fill out when you're sick; the cards are stored in a special carved box, and Earlyne prays over the box in the Astara Temple at Mariposa and Third in midtown Los Angeles.

The late Alice Bailey had *her* meeting with Koot Hoomi in 1895 as a fifteen-year-old who had tried to kill herself three times because her wealthy family in Manchester, England, kept her secluded with private tutors. She said she assumed the tall stranger in a turban was Jesus until she joined Theosophy and saw Koot's pictures. By 1919, after being driven to a nervous breakdown by her fire-and-brimstone efforts as a YWCA missionary, she and her second husband, Foster Bailey, had become national officers in U.S. Theosophy. Then a new master who introduced himself as the Tibetan spoke to her on a hillside and requested that she take down a few books that he would dictate to her astrally from the Himalayas. With the approval of Koot Hoomi, she published the opening chapters in the *Theosophist,* which she was editing. By the next year she and Foster were denounced as heretics and kicked out of the organization.

They moved to New York, teaching classes in pure Blavatskianism and beginning to publish the Tibetan's books. The response was so great that they were able to found the Arcane School, which is still sending out correspondence courses from a building right down the street from the United Nations. At its height during the early forties, the Arcane School employed one hundred and forty secretaries to service 30,000 students. The Tibetan, who eventually revealed that his name was Djawhal Khul, made Mrs. Bailey transcribe a three-foot shelf of blue-bound books for him. This output is kept in print by the Lucis Trust Fund. The gist of the Tibetan's message is that all spiritual paths lead to God and the return of Christ is imminent. From 1923 to 1956 donations to the Arcane School totalled $1,527,380.

Alice Bailey followers still hold meditation ceremonies at the full moon that are supposed to harness lunar vibrations to help speed up the Second Coming. The biggest Arcana turnout is in Los Angeles where Mrs. Marguerite Rompage of the Beverly Hills Arcana Workshop has for years had well-attended Wesak Festivals—the three main full-moon ceremonies—at the rococo old Wilshire Ebell Theater.

There's a brand-new occult school in the making if a gentleman better known as Ophiel than by his real name of Edward C. Peach has his way. In 1961 Ophiel received a $1,100 accident settlement and had a thousand copies of his manuscript, *The Art and Practice of Astral Projection,* printed in Hong Kong. The slender hard-cover books in their colorful psychedelic jackets sold briskly, and Carl Weschke of Llewellyn Publishing in St. Paul made a deal to be his distributor through their Gnostic Institute subsidiary. Ophiel has published five occult books under this arrangement, all selling about 20,000 each at $4.95.

A couple of years ago, Ophiel's mother died, and he was able to leave San Francisco for the warmer climate he prefers. He now lives upstairs in a small Hollywood apartment complex he owns. He says that he obtained this property by following the method he explained in his *The Art of Getting Material Things by Creative Visualization.* He says, "You must keep expanding your sphere of availability by pasting a picture of what you want on your subconscious mind. It won't work if you have three dollars and want a million; you must do it by gradual degrees." To make sure he didn't lose track of any friends by moving to Hollywood, Ophiel had his new address and phone listing printed on the final page of his more recent books.

Ophiel is a large, heavy man in his sixties. His door seems permanently open, and the apartment bustles with male friends and young men visiting from the street. "I chose my pen name from an occult dictionary just because I liked the look of it," he says after seeking out a quiet corner. "Ophiel is an archangel associated with Mercury, the messenger god, so it's a rather appropriate choice . . . don't you think?"

Llewellyn sends him a big box with his fan mail every month. "All occultism is a blind," he says as he goes through the pile. "It means the opposite of what it says. After studying for thirty years through all sorts of misfortunes in my life, I know that most occultists are running around in a circle. They would give a great deal to go someplace and get a sensible system without loose ends, as I believe mine is. For example, I show that astral projection is the transfer of consciousness to the inner planes of the mind."

Attempting to compile a complete list of today's mail-order mystery schools is a research task roughly equal to the battle of Hercules with the Hydra that kept growing two heads for each one chopped off. At each interview with leaders of esoteric organizations, three or four obscure groups were mentioned.

There's Al G. Manning's ESP Laboratory at a little shopping arcade in Hollywood, which is by no means as scientific as its title would suggest. A choice is offered of either Green, Blue, or White Light mail-in prayer proxies as well as a Divine Companionship Altar for the lonely. Manning is both a spiritual counselor and a CPA, who accepts Bank Americard or Master Charge for his services.

A 1956 best seller in England was *The Third Eye,* in which T. Lobsang Rampa narrated his remarkable experiences as a lama in Tibet—including a meeting with an Abominable Snowman. When it was revealed that Lobang Rampa was really an Englishman named Cyril Hoskin who had never been to Tibet, he explained that a blow on the head in 1949 brought back full memory of his former life as a lama. Rampa has since published four other books and is selling a Meditation Kit for $37.50, which contains a robe, incense and burner, and an LP record of chanting.

Sri Paul Twitchell's church of astral projection called Eckankar makes its earthly home at Box 5325, Las Vegas 89102. Twitchell's books tell about his out-of-body tours of the Seven Temples of Golden Wisdom with Tibetan master Rebazar Tarzs and have sold widely in paperback.

Edwin J. Dingle was renamed Ding Le Mei by the Tibetan lamas who taught him their innermost secrets so he could go back to downtown Los Angeles and start the Mentalphysics Institute ($8 initiation, $1 per correspondence lesson). One of his secret chant goes, "I am whole. I am strong. I am powerful. I am young. I am harmonious. I am happy."

Anthony Norvell has been lecturing on occult Positive Thinking at Carnegie Hall for some twenty-five years now. "There is a magnetic core of cosmic power within the higher mind centers which can be stirred into creative action," he says in his latest book, *Cosmic Magnetism.* "This center of dynamic power can be charged, just like a battery, with Cosmic Magnetism . . . a magnetic field, which is capable of attracting into the reader's orbit of daily experience the money he wants, the love he desires, the friendship he wants, the right type of work, and the mental, material, and spiritual treasures longed for."

Chartered at Florida in 1956, the Prosperos have now ascended to a National Servers' Center Headquarters which used to be the Hollywood Hills mansion of Sammy Davis and Mai Britt, and before that belonged to Judy Garland and Vincente Minnelli. The man behind the Prosperos is Thane Walker, a silver-haired Shakespearean actor type who refers to his organization as a Fourth Way mystery school. This is a Gurdjieff term which means, among other things, a stress on the superiority of oral teaching over written lessons. Accordingly, the Prospero method of teaching full use of the mind consists of three closed classes which apparently can be described as a type of occult sensitivity group marathon. The basic course lasts fourteen hours over a weekend and costs $110—but the fee includes unlimited return privileges and it is claimed that the seminar yields new insights with every repetition. The Prosperos are, of course, named after the wizard in Shakespeare's *Tempest* and according to the group's interpretation, they too are teaching control of the beast subconscious Caliban with the fully developed intelligence symbolized by Prospero and the help of the ethereal-spirit Ariel. The Prospero organization has been notably successful at attracting metaphysics-hungry young people, and membership now stands at around 1,000.

The most intimate of all the correspondence mystery schools I found is the Brotherhood and Order of the Pleroma. It is pledged to quit recruiting after the membership reaches seven hundred so that the founder, Australian-born metaphysician Richard Duc de Palatine can keep up his personal coaching of the brothers. At the moment, there are about three hundred openings left. Palatine is a professorial-looking divorced businessman who enjoys jokes, cigars, and brandy when he's not on the speaker's platform—he feels that he is in a state of inspiration when he lectures and always speaks ad lib without any notes. He travels every year from Pleroma's London center to the chapters in America and throughout the British Commonwealth. Since dues for the Pleroma correspondence course are $2 a month, nobody is planning to get rich from the eventual seven hundred members.

The West Coast center for Pleroma is a little duplex apartment belonging to Stephen Hoeller which has a big, pretentious illuminated sign out front, at 4758 Melrose next to Hollywood's only Chilean restaurant. Hoeller is embarrassed by the flashing neon on his doorstep. "We have a member in the electric sign business, and he thought it would be a good idea to give me one. I suppose it helps keep members from getting lost when they come a long distance for meetings."

Hoeller is a native Hungarian who came to this country in the mid fifties after studying for the Catholic priesthood at a seminary in Austria. There he was assigned to help an old priest research a book about occult history, and he's been looking into the field ever since. When he first came to the United States he became active in LA Theosophy circles until he heard Palatine speak and decided that the Pleroma's emphasis on the Western mystery school tradition was more practical than Theosophy's Orientalist style. Stocky and curly-haired in typical Middle European style, the recently divorced Hoeller comes across as the best kind of contemporary serious-minded occultist. He is a scholarly man who spent two and a half years as the multilingual researcher for Irving Stone's new novel about Freud.

"The Pleroma is a Neo-Gnostic movement," he says. "It began just prior to the birth of Christ in the Middle East, Greece, and Rome. We feel that Christ's authentic teachings were a lot closer to Gnosticism than what is considered Christianity today—a church structure that wasn't laid down till 325 A.D. at the Council of Nicea. The central concept of Gnosticism is that God is inside all of us, not someplace out there, and it's possible to learn to unite yourself to the godlike core inside you. This is what all the great illuminated mystics of the past were striving for, whether they called it Raja Yoga, the Middle Path of Buddhism, the Way of the Cross, the Philosophers' Stone of Alchemy, the Lost Word of Freemasonry, or the Great Labor of the Rosicrucians. 'Gnossis' was a Greek word for knowledge, and they use it as a very special form of knowledge—the highest state of consciousness which the esoteric tradition calls illumination. 'Pleroma' is Greek for completeness, and it was a term used a lot in Gnostic writings to refer to this state of complete mystical unity with the universe."

Originally it was planned to call Pleroma the Order of Illuminati, but the change turned out to be fortunate. "The John Birch Society and the crank right wing has a mythical whipping boy they call the Illuminati," says Hoeller. "It's supposed to be a powerful black magic society that loves doing evil. Sure enough, in the Winter 1969 issue of *American Mercury* there was a scare story about the mysterious chiefs of the Illuminati, naming us and how we're going to take over the world with our four hundred members. I assure you, I'm not a black magician or a Communist by any stretch of the imagination. I left Hungary because I like the Reds about as much as I like an invasion of cockroaches."

If you're looking for an occult bargain, there probably isn't a better deal than from this spiritual medium who advertises occasionally in the *Canyon Crier,* a weekly newspaper of the predominantly artsy Hollywood Hills. She'll help you in love, marriage, and business—for the price of one Blue Chip Stamp Book.

Chapter 8

The Trouble with Astrology

THE trouble with astrology is that although the theory behind it doesn't fit in with current scientific concepts, it works—not 100 percent but with amazing flashes of accuracy.

My very first occult reporting assignment was to interview a lady who had come to town to publicize her book for a small publishing house. *Linda Goodman's Sun Signs* was priced at $7.50 and contained five hundred and fifty pages about the personality patterns associated with the twelve signs of the zodiac—a subject which had already been dealt with in millions of words. Things didn't look very promising for the book, but since 1968 it has become Taplinger's biggest seller ever and a sure-fire promotional item for the occult book clubs.

Instead of the old vapid generalities (Leo the Lion is proud, boastful, and generous), Linda Goodman put everything in down-to-earth contemporary terms. "There's one thing the Leo woman owns that you won't like. A scrapbook of pictures and mementos from all her old boyfriends. It's no use trying to get her to burn it, because the lioness is sentimental. She's not a wallflower. She's a sunflower." With the surprise success of her book, the imitations came piling off the presses. Some of these also had spurts of insight, but none managed to equal Linda's touch all the way through. What the Goodman book really did was to re-popularize the idea that the twelve zodiacal sun signs are really overall character indicators, not meant to be used only for short-term horoscope predictions. Linda believes that the sun sign is the key to about 80 percent of one's personality and the rest of the planetary influences complete the picture.

The day I went to see Linda Goodman, she was holding forth at a suite in the Hollywood Roosevelt Hotel. The publisher's Western salesmen were present, and one happened to be the twin brother of President Kennedy's colorful press secretary Pierre Salinger. "Typical Gemini," she muttered about the brothers Salinger. For starters, she was guessing the sign of everybody who came in; I never saw her miss. She didn't guess as soon as the person walked in the door; she would observe him in conversation for as long as she needed to be sure. For example, one slender, horn-rimmed, scholarly looking man who was as un-bullish as could be, she spotted as a Taurus. "Taurus ears are set very close against the head," she explained.

Linda is an attractive, forceful lady—married, young children —with an energetic nonstop astrological rap. ("Don't mind me; it's just Aries ego," she apologizes.) She was dredging up all sorts of exotic details from the past of another visitor, a very tall young Englishman named Vivian who was functioning as leg-man for David Frost on what was to be a book about people all over the world who claimed to have The Big Answer. Earlier she had done a more complete horoscope on the Taplinger senior salesman and told him he'd been in on the founding of an important artistic endeavor whose original head-man committed suicide after a painful staff crisis—which was exactly the case when he'd helped start the Pacifica listener-sponsored FM station in Los Angeles a number of years ago.

Then Linda looked up a few planetary tables on my wife's birth date and told her, "When you were five, you had a very dangerous mastoid operation." Now this is not exactly a vague tall-dark-man-in-your-future fortune-teller ploy. As it happens, Mary had to catch up on her first-grade work home in bed, and the only reason she survived the mastoiditis infection was that penicillin had recently come into use.

It was this particular interview that made me aware there was something more to occult astrology than I'd had reason to believe before. One of the next places I went to find out more is a unique Los Angeles institution, First Temple of Astrology at 733 South Burlington Street between Hollywood and downtown.

Despite its tax-exempting title, location in a deconsecrated church building, and a creed that astrology reflects the Divine Will, the First Temple is purely a school . . . probably the most complete school of astrology in the Western world. None of the teachers are paid—they volunteer out of gratitude for having learned their own astrology at the school—and so the place is open only on Tuesdays. They don't advertise or sell correspondence courses; there aren't any other branches. Near the door is a big sign, STAFF MEMBERS ARE NOT ALLOWED TO SOLICIT HOROSCOPE FEES. It costs $5 to register as a Temple student and then $10 for each six-month semester. For this fee, anybody able to sit through all that trigonometry and logarithms could take classes from ten in the morning to nine at night. The math involved in courses like *Rectification, Radix System,* and *Prenatal Mathematics* is not kid stuff, and the school recommends taking two years to complete the three levels of courses and try the certification exam.

"The First Temple was founded in 1907 by Mrs. Harriet Banes, a truly dedicated astrology teacher, and it's been open every Tuesday since," says Lila Gregory, a perky retired nurse who's been a member since 1927. She now gets driven in each Tuesday by her husband, 260 miles round-trip from Yucca Valley. "We're open even if there's a big storm or Christmas comes out on Tuesday," Mrs. Banes said. "We must always be open on the regular day in case somebody needs our help."

The First Temple is quite sparsely furnished inside, the classrooms bare except for blackboards and school chairs. There are offices and a large book counter, usually presided over by the Temple's current director, grandfatherly Charles Kay Hewes, a retired Richfield Oil chemist who became interested in astrology only twelve years ago. "It's fascinating what a chart can show about people's lives," he says. "I've never studied anything as interesting as astrology."

The first time I came around, it was Nixon-Humphrey Election Day and the lady teaching the class had their charts up. She was leaning over backwards to be neutral about what nice men the stars showed them both to be. But it was obvious the zodiac showed Richard Nixon winning; his horoscope indicated triumph after early setbacks while Hubert Humphrey's chart just fizzled out.

Temple board member John Bradford is a veteran movie-trade reporter who now mail-syndicates his own Hollywood column. For his class on horary astrology—the astrology of predicting the future—he draws a horoscope chart on the blackboard and challenges the dozen students to guess what situation it represents.

"Those are some bad conjunctions up there," says a man of about thirty with a trim beard. "This person has a real problem." Bradford assures the class, "The chart only looks foreboding because the situation means so much to the person involved . . . but it's not really that world-shattering. Look at what's going on here in the sixth house!" It's explained that the sixth house covers children, real or spiritual. Before the hour is over—and with a minimum of prompting—the students have actually established that the chart depicts a man upset because he has to give his dog away to some friends in the country who will have more time to look after it.

The student body at the First Temple is the usual cross section of Americana one expects to find sampling the occult explosion, lots of elderly ladies, but also students, secretaries, showfolk, and hippie intelligentsia. "We're getting more young people than we used to a few years ago, but the overall number of students hasn't gone up too much," says board member Lila Gregory while in the adjoining lecture hall a teacher is filling in blackboard charts for Johnny Carson and Howard Hughes. "There's so much more competition around now. You wouldn't believe how many people study here for a while, then go off and start their own little classes without really knowing what they're doing. It's also surprising how many young prospective students refuse to sign the loyalty oath we require here as patriotic citizens."

One of their earliest dropouts to start a competing movement, according to First Temple of Astrology, was C. C. Zain, who changed his name from Elbert Benjamine for numerological reasons and in 1918 founded the Church of Light. The church only gets together quorums for a service twice a month now, but it has free astrology classes three times a week in its trim little storefront on Sixth Street at Western, not far from the First Temple.

After only two years of occult studies, Zain managed to contact the Brotherhood of Light, a secret society that went underground from the Egyptian Establishment in 2,440 B.C. and founded science. In 1909 he was called on to replace a dead member of the council of three who run the Brotherhood on this plane. After a year on the inner plane he was given his orders to prepare a complete occult system for teaching the Religion of the Stars. He started work in LA in 1915, founded the church in 1918, and finished the twenty-one-volume set of lessons in 1934. The black-bound volumes sell for $121.30 per complete edition, and the bustling Church of Light mailroom with all its up-to-date equipment shipped out $77,260 worth in 1968.

In the English-speaking countries at least, the modern revival of astrology as a symbolic map of human destiny can largely be credited to a proper Bostonian lady of the 1890's named Evangeline Adams. Though she was of *the* Boston Adamses, as a young lady she took up the peculiar practice of horoscope-casting and actually told fortunes professionally. After shocking the local aristocrats for several years, Evangeline's own horoscope told her to move to New York on March 16, 1899. She had made reservations at a chic Fifth Avenue hotel owned by a family friend, but when she told him she was going to see astrology clients in her room he wouldn't let her register. With chin held high, Evangeline Adams lugged her portmanteau up Fifth Avenue until she found the Windsor Hotel, whose genial owner, Warren F. Leland, wasn't worried about the disgrace of astrology on his premises.

In gratitude, Evangeline drew up Leland's chart while they were getting her room ready and was horrified to find that the hotelman was "under one of the worst possible combinations of planets—conditions terrifying in their unfriendliness." The next day, as the St. Patrick's Day parade was winding up, the Windsor Hotel burned to the ground and much of Leland's family was incinerated. The newspaper stories all featured Leland's awestruck tale of the astrological warning.

Evangeline Adams was at once in business with a vengeance. The clients at the studio she established in Carnegie Hall included King Edward VII, Caruso, J. P. Morgan, and Mary Pickford. In 1914 somebody at police headquarters decided it would be a good idea to arrest her for fortune-telling, and as her defense she volunteered to demonstrate the validity of astrology by doing a blind horoscope on any birth data provided by the judge. His honor gave her the date, place, and hour for a "Mr. X," and when she finished describing the anonymous party, he found her not guilty and said she had "raised astrology to the dignity of an exact science." Evangeline had given a dead-on personality sketch of the judge's son. Today New York is one of the few states where it's perfectly legal to advertise and charge fees for astrological horoscoping . . . due to the Evangeline Adams Decision. Evangeline died in 1932, having predicted her own death, of course. She had the first astrology radio show, beginning three times a week in 1930, and used to get 4,000 orders a day for her sun sign forecast pamphlets.

Though astrology is clearly the most popular part of the occult explosion, many astrologers tend to hold themselves apart from the rest of occultism. They see astrology as an overlooked science, at least as precise as medicine—which like horoscope-making also requires intuitive personal skills. But the more metaphysically oriented astrologers and their students are less interested in the precise techniques of divining the future than they are in relating evidences of the stars' effects on human destiny to the overall workings of a universal plan.

History credits the start of astrology to the Chaldean era of Babylonia, the cradle of Western civilization where for the first time nomadic hunting tribes gave way to settled agricultural societies. For generation after generation, the Babylonian priests climbed up on stone towers called ziggurats and watched the stately movements of the planets among the fixed stars. They had nothing but the naked eye to observe with, and naturally they assumed there was an unmoving flat Earth at the center of the universe. The effects of the sun and moon on agriculture and tides were obvious enough, so it seemed logical to expect that the other heavenly bodies had similar godlike powers. . . .

But hopefully the Babylonians weren't merely making up myths. It would seem that because of the pragmatic usefulness of their concepts even today, they must have been carefully observing what human events took place under different star patterns.

They invented the zodiac as a system for the twelve moon cycles that mark the circle of the sun around the Earth during the seasons of a year. The zodiac really doesn't exist anywhere in the sky, it's simply a method of keeping track of where the stars are month-by-month. The zodiacal signs tended to get their mythology from very practical sources. Aquarius the water-bearer came at the time of Babylonia's rainy season.

Western astrology was further refined from the Babylonian model by the Egyptians, Greeks, and Romans. But they really didn't tamper much with the basic structure. There were other independent astrologies too, the great Central and South American empires—Incas, Mayas, Aztecs—having their fully developed systems.

The marauding tribes out of Asia carried astrology back to China and India from their raids on Babylonia. The Oriental astrologies that developed in these two regions became very different systems from the original. Asian astrology never fell into a popular decline as the European branch did because of church disapproval. It is a near-universal belief in the East today, as much as ever. In 1964 the premier of Ceylon moved election day from March 24 to March 22 because of astrologers' advice on the best day for winning.

It was only gradually over the centuries that the Babylonians started applying astrology to the destinies of ordinary men. At first horoscopes were reserved for national problems and for advising kings. What is basically today's astrology was codified two centuries after Christ by Ptolemy, the great Greek mathematician/astronomer who lived at the Egyptian center of learning, Alexandria.

An astrological chart consists of an outer ring showing the zodiac signs and an inner pie cut into twelve "houses" representing the different aspects of life. Symbols for the planets are inserted to complete a map of the sky at the moment of birth. The various angles between planets are also meaningful for either good or bad, an idea based on what used to be seen as a slowing down or reversal of direction by the planets around the central unmoving Earth. However, recent scientific evidence has shown that the planetary angles do have surprisingly far-ranging effects.

Pagan astrology was understandably suppressed as Christianity became the dominant religion of Europe. It made a flashy comeback with the Renaissance era, which specialized in reviving the glories of the classic past. Typical of the renewed status was French Queen Catherine de Medici's utter reliance on astrologers following the birth of her son in 1544, which ended a lifelong infertility through the aid of some helpful horoscopes. Told by a favorite astrologer to "beware of St. Germain," she moved out of her palace in the Paris borough of St. Germain—known today as the Louvre Museum. When she fell ill in 1589 at her new palace, a priest was called in to take her last confession just as a standard precaution. His name turned out to be Julien de St. Germain, and Catherine died that evening.

The Age of Reason set astrology back again, even though the pioneers of modern astronomy—Copernicus, Tycho Brahe, Kepler and Galileo—all did some degree of work in pure astrology. A real body blow was Jonathan Swift's satire *Predictions by Isaac Bickerstaff* which genially insisted that the most popular almanac publisher of the day, a Mr. Partridge, would die on a certain day that year because it was ordained in the stars. The more vehemently poor Partridge screamed that he was still alive, the louder he was laughed out of business.

Astrology went back underground as part of the esoteric lore of the Rosicrucians, the Freemasons, and, most importantly, Theosophy. With the revival of interest in occult metaphysics at the turn of this century the cadre of astrology scholars began growing again. And inevitably, mass-market commercialization followed.

In England the popular founding fathers were Sephiral (Walter Gorn Old) and Alan Leo (ex-traveling salesman William Frederick Allen). You can imagine what his sign was! Leo founded Britain's *Modern Astrology* magazine and pioneered mail-order individual horoscopes in a real Charles Dickens' sweatshop operation at Hampstead. On the European continent the return of astrology was slow, steady, scholarly, and semiprofessional. Nobody was really able to make a living at it until Frau Elsbeth Ebertin produced some spectacular predictions of early Hitlerian triumphs. Even in the English-speaking world the general public wasn't aware of astrology until 1930 when the *Sunday Express* found circulation was increasing because of the astrological features by R. H. Naylor. One of his earliest forecasts was that British aircraft pioneers were in terrible danger—which was followed shortly afterward by the R-101 dirigible crash.

Soon Britain's other big national newspapers started covering astrology. But it took a few years before they realized it really wasn't feature stories the public wanted but their own daily horoscopes. Credit for developing the format of vague short-term predictions allegedly valid for everybody born under the same sign of the zodiac seems to go to Paul G. Clancy, founder of

American Astrology magazine in 1933. This is the oldest U.S. astrology magazine by two years, and it's still one of the biggest, a sixty-cent pulp monthly in trademark silver-foil cover published at Tucson, Arizona, and distributed by Hearst.

With the wonderfully standardized reduction of the destinies of the world's several billion people to twelve possible patterns, it now became feasible to make astrology the biggest business in occultism. No other form of divination could possibly deliver everybody their own supposedly personal mass-produced forecasts. The New York *Daily News'* syndicated astrology columnist, Constella (New England septuagenarian Shirley Spencer), switched over from a handwriting analysis column in 1955 after she saw the writing on the wall . . . or maybe the message of the stars.

"Don't get into any disagreements today and group activity is preferable tonight" is an example of typical astrology-column banality. It happens to be the Gemini horoscope from Jeane Dixon's March 10, 1969, column and it got a big laugh from Apollo 9 astronauts (and Geminis) McDivitt and Scott when Mission Control Center read them the advice during a quiet moment on the flight.

About 1,200 of America's 1,750 daily newspapers—with a total readership of 40,000,000—carry astrology columns. There are eighteen syndicated columnists, all but one of them human. The latest entry is *Astrodata*, written by an IBM 360 with 27,000,000 items of information on file. Its seventeen flesh-and-blood competitors were delighted to hear that the Houston *Post* cancelled *Astrodata* owing to a pile of reader complaints that the IBM 360 just didn't have that human touch.

Nearly all the columnists' daily sun-sign forecasts come across as bland commonsense that would be good advice for anybody on any day. About the only exception is Sydney Omarr, generally considered the most rational and intelligent of the younger astrology columnists. It wouldn't be easy to survey how effective his predictions are every day for all twelve signs, but at least he'll say something specific and stick his neck out a bit. "SAGITTARIUS: Some proposals which seem to lack substance could be successfully developed. Be versatile. Recognize fact that required backing is available. Visit by relative is featured."

Omarr is in his early forties, wears horn-rimmed glasses and a somewhat old-fashioned pencil mustache. The day I came to see him in his pleasant stucco-modern house in the Hollywood Hills it was the height of LA's annual autumn heatwave and he was working in a bathing suit with the air-conditioner at full blast.

"I believe in the information in my column," he insists. "Fate is character. Astrology shows destiny not with facts but with imponderables." Omarr's background includes being a CBS radio news editor in Los Angeles and the only officially assigned astrologer in Army history with a horoscope broadcast over the military station in Okinawa. He feels it's important to know that astronomers are against astrology because of what he calls paranoia about being linked up with their mother science. "Astrology is the missing link to man's relation with the universe," he says. "Real research is desperately needed."

The Big Daddy of astrology columnists is Carroll Righter, seventy, who's carried in three hundred and six newspapers as opposed to Sydney Omarr's two hundred and fifty. He's headquartered in the Hollywood Hills too, in a splendid old Graustarkian film-fantasy mansion with a tennis-court-sized swimming pool, perhaps a mile west of fellow-bachelor Omarr. Incidentally, both men are syndicated by the Los Angeles Times Service but it's Righter who maintains the prestige spot in the flagship LA *Times* with its 1.2 million circulation. "It's open knowledge that Buffy Chandler [the owner's wife] is an old friend of Carroll's," Omarr explains resignedly.

Righter is an enormously charming, personable gentleman of old Philadelphia lineage. He was taught his zodiac by no less a person than the great Evangeline Adams herself, who first met Carroll when he was fourteen; she insisted his horoscope showed he would be an astrologer instead of a lawyer. By now he's given up the splashy parties with which he used to greet each new sign of the zodiac cycle—with a live crab on hand for Cancer and a live but strongly tethered bull for Taurus. However, he still keeps teaching his weekly astrology class at $3 a head, simply for the love of rapping with fellow astrology fans—certainly he doesn't need the class fees since his annual income is in six figures.

Though he rarely leaves his mansion these days, Carroll used to be *the* social astrologer during Hollywood's Golden Time.

His client list included Marlene Dietrich, Ronald Colman, Tyrone Power, Susan Hayward, Robert Cummings, Van Johnson, Peter Lawford, and . . . Ronald Reagan.

Linda Goodman swears Governor Reagan is a secret astrology freak. "If not, why did he get sworn in at some strange time like six minutes after midnight?" she asks. Linda believes that Reagan is truly a humane, Liberal Aquarius who will drop his faked conservatism after he becomes President. However, the governor has a standard response to the many queries he gets from newsmen about his astrology. He says, "I am no more interested in the subject than the average man."

What Carroll Righter loves most about his astrological practice are the calls to help guide his celebrity clients. He even keeps a rolodex file with the star data on famous customers by his bedside in case somebody phones from an overseas film location during the wee hours. "If I don't get called late at night I sometimes toss and turn and wonder what's happened to everybody," Righter says. "I begin to feel not needed." He calls everybody by their astrological sign, claiming he can't remember names. And he insists that he discourages astrological hypochondria among the clientele; he'll hang up the phone if all they want to know is what clothes to wear that day. Like all successful seers, he has skill in presenting rotten news in encouraging terms. "If I find a strong indication, say, that someone is going to lose his job, I say: 'You know, nothing in life is certain. This is a period of change. Your chart shows that you have some interesting new beginnings. . . .' "

The long-time king of U.S. mail-order astrology is Zolar, whose real name is, fittingly enough, Bruce King. Now in his seventies, ex-clothing-salesman King is looking for a buyer to take over the empire he founded during the Depression when he observed a Professor Seward on the Atlantic City boardwalk selling horoscopes like hotcakes. It's a matter of some doubt among astrologers as to whether Zolar can so much as chart a horoscope himself. But Zolar was Mr. Astrology to the American public for decades when occultism was the concern of a minuscule minority. He accomplished this feat by consistently hitting the lowest common denominator of the occult with high-pressure ad copy promising instant revelations.

There are about 10,000 full-time astrology pros in the United

States with perhaps 150,000 part-timers. The top organization in the field is the American Federation of Astrologers which was incorporated (born) at the auspicious horoscope hour of 11:38 on May 4, 1938, in Washington, D.C., where it has its offices and holds an annual convention. International membership is some 2,000. By mistake, the AFA was invited to send a delegation to the Apollo 12 moon launch instead of the American Astronomers Society. Even after the mistake was discovered the astrologers couldn't be cut from the VIP roster.

Retired Navy Lieutenant Commander David Williams published *Astro-Economics* in 1959. He says 68 percent of the major aspects between Jupiter, Saturn, and Uranus correlated with the U.S. business cycle between 1761 and 1968. "The basic premise of Financial Astrology is that booms and depressions begin and end in the minds of men," he writes. "But men's minds are influenced by their emotions and their emotions are subtly influenced by changes in the earth's electromagnetic field, which is in turn affected by the interplanetary electromagnetic fields set up by the movements of the planets around the sun." Certain planetary patterns form angles that have been found to correlate with optimistic influences and others seem to be depressive. Williams says a clay tablet found in the palace library at Nineveh is inscribed, "If Jupiter seems to enter into the Moon, prices will be low in the country." In 1875 English economist W. Stanley Jevons reported finding a correlation between the eleven-year sunspot cycle and commodity prices . . . "The sun governs the vintages and harvests, and thus the prices of food and raw materials, and the state of the money market. The sunspot period is connected with the configuration of the planets."

Williams claims to have predicted months in advance the rising stock market of 1967-68 and the 1969-70 decline—which he said would continue till the final quarter of 1971. "Astrologically, the rising trend of the U.S. economy is due to the inflationary influence of the Neptune-Pluto sextile (60°) which has been within 3° of exactitude since 1946 and will continue in that relationship until February 1992 . . . So don't sell America short," he counsels.

The occult explosion has produced a new breed of culturally with-it young astrologers like Barbara Birdfeather, a slim, darkly magnetic thirtyish daughter of Mount Kisco artists. She had the astrology column in the short-lived but genuinely hip Hearst magazine, *Eye*. Now she teaches how to make horoscopes with her quirky, diarylike *Birdfeather Astrological Space Book*, written entirely in Whitmanesque free verse.

Kiyo, half Japanese and half Boston WASP, has been astrologer to the Hollywood hip set for some ten years, with a clientele that includes most of the top rock musicians. Kiyo lives on some charming hillside acreage in the deepest backreaches of Laurel Canyon, the pop music bastion of the Hollywood Hills. Among the rock stars renting cottages on her property is John Densmore, drummer for the Doors. Her tenants' daily communing at full volume with their instruments doesn't shatter Kiyo's calm as she works on charts for clients, teaches a Monday evening class at home and a Wednesday seminar at her friend Jane Russell's place, tries to write a book, and comforts waifs sent to her by leading Laurel Canyon hippies because of her famed skill at talking down kids freaked out on speed.

"I don't condone continued use of drugs at all, but there's no doubt that turning on has wakened many young people to the emptiness of traditional viewpoints. They are able to learn occult techniques very fast because they understand it naturally," says Kiyo. "Today's kids are much more attuned to the search for mystical realities than their elders; they are really comfortable living among the fast technological and social changes going on."

Kiyo grew up, for the most part, in Japan, attending private schools for the international colony and becoming interested in comparative religion because of her mixed heritage. She's a Leo divorcée and says the new occult youth have made astrology for the first time in America not "mainly a homosexual trade." Justifying astrological theory, she says "the birth moment, when you breathe your first breath, is when the influences of the universe first affect you. That's why the entire astrological chart is based on the birth moment . . . birth of a person, a corporation, or a conscious question."

A rallying point for astrology's comeback has been the Age of Aquarius theme. What this means is that about every 2,170 years the sun's spring equinox (day and night of equal length) shifts by one zodiac sign. We are now somewhere in the process of leaving Christianity's Piscean Age for the Aquarian Age, when the occult worldview holds that art, science, and religion will become one and usher in a new Golden Era.

Incidentally, *Hair*, the most popular theatrical packaging of the counterculture, has always maintained a staff astrologer with full credits in the program, whose job was to rule on opening nights and casting.

Among the more occult-oriented astrologers, it is commonly assumed that February 4, 1962, was a turning point in the new Age of Aquarius. For the first time in centuries, on that day the sun, moon, Mars, Venus, Jupiter, Mercury, and Saturn were all in Aquarius. The messiah of the space era may well have been born that day because, according to astrology, there were similar heavenly portents announcing Christ's birth.

As a fad, astrology has probably already hit its peak, although it will level off at a much higher plateau than ever before in an industrialized Western society. At Manhattan's Weiser Books, they've found sales in the astrology section have dropped off noticeably—shifting to Tarot, I Ching, and witchcraft for a while, and eventually settling on the loftier metaphysics. What happened is that several million Americans suddenly found out, mostly by word-of-mouth, that there was a lot more to astrology than the insipid generalities of the astrology columns and pulp magazines. They learned the personality and physique patterns associated with the twelve zodiac signs and found that it gave some unexpectedly valid insights into the people they knew. Next they wanted to know how to do full-scale horoscopes, but only a few made it. You really have to be taught chart erection by somebody else—it's not at all easy to learn from a book—and there aren't very many effective self-instruction manuals available. (Of the three or four how-to books I'd recommend, the best seems to be Davidson's *Astrology*, in paperback.) Still, the point is that there are too many people around now with an interest in, and a reasonably sophisticated knowledge of, astrology for the subject to be cavalierly dismissed by know-nothings.

The Birth of a Scientific Astrology

It wasn't until the 1920's that the first serious attempts were made to test the validity of astrology under scientifically objective conditions. Frenchman Paul Choisnard and the Swiss Karl Ernst Krafft both tried to collect case statistics which would bear out the principles of traditional horoscopes. But their projects were attacked both for the small number of sample cases and for important errors of astronomy.

A much higher quality of statistical astrology research is now being carried out by Michel Gauquelin, who has spent twenty years correlating the horoscope trends of prominent Western Europeans. Gauquelin, author of *The Scientific Basis of Astrology*, is a Sorbonne-trained social science statistician and technical writer with a suave Gallic disdain for both the ancient astrological tradition and the earlier botched attempts at scientific verification. In 1950 he was twenty years old and decided he was going to prove once and for all that astrology was useless. He looked up birth certificates and made horoscopes for five hundred and seventy-six medical professors. The results did not show any of the zodiac signs appearing at more than chance level, but, as he put it, these eminent physicians "showed an odd preference for being born at a moment when Mars or Saturn had just risen or was at zenith." Like any trained statistician, Gauquelin knew that a remarkable result means one should get more case histories—but the next batch of five hundred and eight major doctors held to the trend. In 1955 Gauquelin published an astrological survey of the biggest group of French celebrities for whom he could dig up birth dates. He demonstrated that success in different professions is associated with the rise or zenith, at birth, of either Jupiter, Mars, Saturn, or the moon. Since 1956 he and his wife, Françoise, have spent a month each year looking up birth times of prominent men outside France. So far they've covered parts of Germany, Italy, Holland, and Belgium. Along the way, Gauquelin began to suspect that maybe something in the genes tells a fetus when it's time to be born. So he got 15,000 birth records of parents and their children from around Paris and laboriously drew up the charts. He found that each generation of a family tended to be born under the same planets—at odds of 500,000-to-1.

Studies keep popping up to support astrology folklore. The Philadelphia Police Department published a 1961 report with the American Institute of Medical Climatology saying they clock in more crimes when there's a full moon. A Tallahassee, Florida, eye-ear-nose-throat man, Dr. Edson J. Andrews, kept a three-year tally of over 1,000 tonsillectomies done at his clinic and said that 82 percent of the bleeding crises occurred under the fuller moon phases. A Virginia health department neurological psychiatrist, Dr. Leonard Ravitz, says he found differences in electrical potential between the heads and chests of mental patients which paralleled seasonal lunar changes.

Dr. Giorgio Piccardi of Italy's Florence University discovered that the planets affect ionized water and other chemicals. In Tokyo, Dr. Maki Takata showed that the sunspot cycle causes changes in human blood chemistry all over the world.

The unpleasant jet-age phenomenon of time lag was proved by Northwestern University biologist Frank A. Brown, who demonstrated the existence of biological clocks. Long Island oysters brought to the university in Evanston, Illinois, were kept at constant darkness and temperature . . . but gradually they changed the rhythms of opening and closing their shells from the tide cycle of Long Island Sound. If there had been an ocean at Evanston, those oysters would have been right in tune with its tides. Apparently they were going on lunar time. Dr. Brown has since shown comparable effects in rats, crabs, and crayfish. He has also measured that oxygen consumption in carrots, potatoes, and other underground plants varies with the phases of the moon—just as in the centuries-old farmers' "superstitions."

RCA scientist John Henry Nelson doesn't know anything about foretelling destinies by astrology, but he knows that magnetic storms can be forecast with 85 percent accuracy by keeping track of planetary positions and sunspots. He uses astrological tables to help keep track of the positions between planets. RCA wanted to know about magnetic storms because they interfere with shortwave transmission and messages must be routed around the storm areas. Nelson read a paper on his work to a 1961 NATO Ionospheric Research Conference in Naples, where he suggested that the solar system acts like a generator with the sun as armature core and the planets as magnets whose movements cause changes in the power output.

"It's the biggest story of the century," says Sydney Omarr about the astrological birth control method invented by Dr. Eugen Jonas of Czechoslovakia—who claims 99 percent effectiveness in over 20,000 cases since 1956.

Dr. Jonas is both a psychiatrist and a gynecologist, a small, quiet man who is always overworking himself. Practicing at his hometown of Nitra, near the Hungarian border, he noticed that high-strung women seemed to have an increase of sex desire every thirty days. Being an astronomy-astrology buff, he wondered if this had anything to do with the age-old folklore about fertility and the moon. And he began to search for connecting principles between medicine and astrology.

Starting in 1960, he worked out astrological sex schedules for 8,000 women at the Bratislava Gynecology Clinic who wanted boys. He claimed results 95 percent right in setting the correct intercourse dates, also 87 percent right in predicting a baby's sex from the date of impregnation. He found in checking 5,000 children with birth defects that they all were conceived under the old malefic angles of bad planetary conjunctions by women born under a full moon. One woman had previously given birth to three stillborn babies and a premature deformed child. Jonas charted that she had only four safe days of conception each year. Following his schedule she gave birth to a normal child.

Dr. Jonas' Astra Research Center for Planned Parenthood has been funded by the Czech government since 1968 and really large-scale computer tests are under way to prove conclusively if the theory works. The Leningrad Gynecology Institute, UNESCO, physicians in Germany and Hungary, and several international conferences are following up his work. His book has been published in six languages.

The Jonas principle of astrological birth control is: A mature woman is most likely to conceive during the same phase of the moon that existed the day she was born. The baby's sex depends on whether the moon is in a magnetically positive or negative zodiac sign during conception—Jonas calls the fire and air signs positive, the earth and water signs negative. Birth control, baby sex choice, and increased fertility are a lot easier to chart than prevention of birth defects because there are less planets involved.

If Jonas is right, then the rhythm method's assurance that the tenth to fourteenth day of the menstrual cycle are a woman's most likely conception time is wrong, which might explain a lot of unwanted pregnancies.

When Dr. Jonas was submitting his case histories and statistics to the Czechoslovakian Federal Health Ministry to obtain a grant, his medical critics spread the word he was crazy. Jonas went to Hungary and got neutral psychiatrists to certify his sanity. In less extreme forms, this is the reaction from the cultural establishment anyone will encounter if he seems to be taking astrology *too* seriously. But although the new scientific evidence so far has not proven the truth of traditional astrology, it clearly demonstrates that the stars and planets have a far wider and more powerful effect on the Earth's living creatures than was ever imagined possible.

Chapter 9

Keys to the Unknown

HANSON BALDWIN, the New York *Times* military editor, is not exactly a mystic. But in 1967 he filed an article that began, "Coat-hanger dowsers, or divining rods, are being used by Marine Corps engineers at Camp Pendleton, California, and in Vietnam to detect tunnels, mines and booby traps . . . The traditional willow-wand dowser, employed for many centuries in the search for water, has been replaced, in combat use, by ordinary wire coat hangers or welding rods of steel, brass, or other metal three-sixteenths of an inch in diameter. The two wires are bent into L-shapes and held loosely in both fists. As the operator walks over the ground, they spread apart or point to hidden tunnels, mines or other objects . . . *This correspondent found a tunnel, previously unknown to him, with the device.*" (Author's italics.)

Vietnam veterans at Pendleton told Baldwin that the First and Third Marine Division engineers had been using dowsing rods against the Viet Cong "with marked success in the last years" along with electric mine detectors and the bayonet hunt-and-probe method.

Baldwin saw a demonstration of the coat-hanger dowsing rod by Major Nelson Hardacker of the Thirteenth Marine Engineer Battalion to troops leaving for Vietnam. A lieutenant colonel who didn't know where the faked booby traps, tunnels, and arms caches were on the Camp Pendleton-simulated "Viet Cong Trail" was able to locate them with two thin wires bent into L's about twenty-six inches long with eight-inch handles. The rods are held loosely at chest height, pointing forward and parallel to the ground.

Marine dowsing status is not quite official. Its acceptance is credited to Louis Matacia, an operations analyst at the Marine School in Quantico, Virginia, who started dowsing in Vietnam as a combat Marine in 1966 and later demonstrated its effectiveness for the brass at Quantico and Camp Lejeune.

The Russians are entirely convinced of dowsing's validity, according to *Psychic Discoveries Behind the Iron Curtain* which quotes a number of tests and reports by both the military and scientists like the top USSR water geologist, Professor G. Bogomolov. The Red Army has had successful dowse-ins with up to two hundred soldiers at a time. They claim dowsing works even if the metal rods are connected to recording graphs and you're riding in a truck or airplane. Electrocardiograms were taken which indicate that practically everybody has physiological changes when walking over land with underground water or metal, but only 30 percent of us can amplify this reaction by unconscious movements of the dowsing rod.

The Soviets say that weather conditions make a lot of difference in the effectiveness of dowsing. Lightning storms, of course, make it impossible to dowse, and even the angle of the sun may affect the results. This may be why Henry Gross, the Maine dowser who starred in historical novelist Kenneth Roberts' 1951 best seller, *Henry Gross and His Dowsing Rod,* admittedly failed miserably under test conditions with Dr. Rhine and other ESP researchers although he could sometimes be staggeringly effective in fieldwork. Roberts reports that Gross dowsed the first working freshwater well in Bermuda by moving his rod over a map at home in Maine.

England has had a dowser on the government payroll since the 1930's. Her name is Evelyn Penrose and she's supposed to be 80 percent effective as she travels around the world finding water for developing cities and new industry in the Commonwealth. Another English dowser, Robert Leftwich, found three out of five cans of water buried secretly by Manchester University President John Cohen who was, until the 1968 test, a firm skeptic.

Burly John Shelley with his white crew cut is the very model of a cautious, collected New Englander. By trade, the Maine grandfather has been art director of the *Farmers' Almanac* for over sixteen years. He graduated from Massachusetts School of Art and Pratt Institute. During World War II he was a Navy pilot and still participates in a reservist program that brings selected ex-fliers back to Pensacola Naval Air Headquarters every two years for a complete physical in order to find out as much as possible about the lifetime physiology of airmen.

Shelley was also the 1970 president of the American Dowsing Society. On his last flight to Pensacola, the Navy doctors challenged him, "If you're such a great dowser, John, let's see you dowse for your paycheck!" Shelley says, "I found it without too much trouble in a six-story building. Followed the rod up to the right floor and the right room. The only problem was when it pointed to a microscope and the check wasn't there, but then when I picked the stand up I found it underneath."

Shelley's dowsing began one Sunday afternoon when he was out painting at a field near Falmouth, Maine, and saw a couple of men waving a forked stick over the ground. "What are you doing?" he inquired.

"Dowsing," was the answer. "Want to try?"

They explained briefly what the dowsing rod was supposed to do. John took the willow branch and walked a couple of steps. The stick went down. He shrugged and went back to his painting. But now he couldn't concentrate on the brushstrokes. He cut himself another willow wand, dowsed the water line again and followed it up a hill where he found a little spring bubbling up out of the ground.

On his next trip to the local library he took out every book it had containing something on dowsing. Shortly afterward, he saw a newspaper story about Gordon McLain, a Vermonter who was then president of the American Dowsing Society. The society has 1,500 members, including a retired U.S. Forestry Service head and engineers, chemists, and physicians. Their publications have quite a few subscribers in Russia. The society was founded in 1961 in Danville, Vermont, which now has a big yearly dowsing convention. "There wasn't much to do in Danville during the winter, and they wanted something that would put the town on the map," Shelley explains.

When Shelley dowses with a willow wand, his preferred instrument, he notches a mark in one handle. "I don't like to change the flow of body current in a rod," he says. "I've found that my

right hand has positive electricity and my left hand negative."
When he uses a small chain pendulum to get answers from his
subconscious he finds that for him, clockwise means "yes" and
counterclockwise is "no." However, all of these factors should be
worked out by the individual dowser. "You should ask yourself
the question you want answered by dowsing," says Shelley. "You
can either concentrate on it mentally or say it aloud at the risk of
being thought a nut. The divining rod amplifies human senses."

A new addition to his dowsers' bag is the aurometer, an invention by Reverend Vern Cameron of Elsinore, California. The aurometer is a thin wire rod of metals very sensitive to electricity.
Set in a nonconducting handle, the rod rises up when brought to
the edge of a human being's aura field, usually about 6 to 12
inches around the head.

Dowsing circles feel that their skill (the scholarly term is radi-
esthesia) dates back to the dawn of mankind. They claim
30,000-year-old Trucilli cave paintings in Africa show a figure
with a stick that must be a divining rod. The Bible can be
interpreted to say the Queen of Sheba always had four dowsers
on her caravans to search for gold and jewels en route. Roman
chronicles tell of scouts, presumably dowsers, sent out to find
water in the desert for invading legions. There's wide circulation
of the belief that seventeenth-century England imported six
highly reputed German dowsers to find tin mines in Cornwall.

Dowsing came to America with the Pilgrim settlers, and since
everybody had to dig their own wells by hand in the centuries
before central water systems were established, it was taken seriously. Today's dowsers believe there were up to 800,000 hand-
dug wells on the northeastern seaboard and many of them—
perhaps even the majority—were found by what used to be
called water witches.

John Shelley, who sells a bit of real estate on the side, didn't
have that much confidence when a customer asked him to find
some underground water on the lot he'd just bought. Shelley
said the water would be found 120 feet down at the spot he chose
—it came in at 124 feet. "A dowser's mistake is a big pipe sticking
out of the ground and costing about $4,000," says Shelley. "You
have to be very careful." He now claims 93 percent accuracy in
finding wells around southeast Maine.

A salesman at *Farmers' Almanac* showed Shelley a map of his property showing where he intended to put in the house and garage. Shelley dowsed the map, pointed out where the well could be dug and told him the garage better be put someplace else or a "water vein" would undermine the floor. The salesman then confessed he'd been kidding John. Not only was the well already where Shelley said water could be found, but the garage was in and getting lots of floor cracks.

One way or another, all forms of divination rest on an unspoken assumption that the Grand Design of the Cosmos is reflected in various processes of this world and someone wise enough to understand the clues can read the unknown through all barriers of time and space. The very grammar of "divining the future" or dowsing with a "divining rod" comes from the old occult goal of tuning in on the voices of the divine gods.

In ancient times there were many different kinds of divination practiced. These are mostly forgotten today and a good thing too, because they often turned out to be grotesque. There was belomancy—throwing arrows into the air to see how they fall; capnomancy—observing the smoke from burning sacrifices; axinomancy—the movements of stones on red-hot axes; armomancy—the shape of shoulders; dactylomancy—fortune-telling by rings; gyromancy—spinning around inside a circle with letters marked along the rim until you fall down; phyllorhodomancy—the sound of crushed rose leafs; ornithomancy—the style of birds' flight; onychomancy—dirt patterns on the fingernails of virgin boys. In addition, there used to be numerous ways of divining the future from the entrails and other organs of sacrificed animals or humans.

But we shouldn't scoff *too* quickly at all these odd-seeming practices of our forefathers. For one thing, it now seems obvious that much of occult ritual was primarily a dramatic exercise for the purpose of psyching up the magician into the necessary state of mystical illumination. The entrails and smoke patterns were no more than props—rather tasteless by contemporary standards, but theatrical props nevertheless. And in view of all the other particles of truth which science has of late been finding in occult beliefs, perhaps it's worth another look to see if there's anything of value beneath the layers of superstition.

Certainly the uniqueness of every human fingerprint is an argument for being open-minded about palm-reading. As a matter of fact, not only fingerprints but handprints, footprints, and tooth X rays can all be used to identify an individual beyond doubt. Then there were the French criminologist Bertillon's millimeter-accurate head measurement records used by Europe's police for many years. And in 1964, two Tokyo dental instructors systematized the basic forms of lip-prints and showed that no two of these are alike either. So far, lip-prints have caught two Japanese threatening-letter writers and a murderer who left a lip-sticked tissue paper at the scene of the crime.

Tradition has it that Aristotle took palmistry seriously enough to write a book about it in letters of gold and present it to Alexander the Great. Sir Francis Galton, the father of fingerprinting, did not go in for occult speculations, but he spent most of the nineteenth century verifying that basic handprint patterns don't change during a lifetime. Since the 1940's, Dr. Hugo Debrunner, a Swiss psychologist, has been correlating handprints, handwriting, doodles, gestures, and physical build, and apparently is constructing an overall theory of projective personality testing.

Maxine Fiel, a Long Island housewife who has been studying palmistry since she was fifteen and first saw a hand-reader at a party, invented a palmistry game called *Touch* which is distributed by Parker Brothers, the *Monopoly* and *Scrabble* company. Mrs. Fiel says, "The more lines a person has on their hands, the more they suffer, the more they feel. If there are a lot of lines but each is apart from the others, separate and clear, you have felt deeply but managed to cope. It's when the lines are tortured and frayed, running into each other and scrambled, that you're apt to be uptight, mixed-up, and complicated. Lines on the hand do change as life changes."

This matter of palm-lines changing or not changing in reaction to your emotional state seems to be the source of the biggest dispute among palmists. "If you are right-handed, the left palm will keep the lines from birth and the right palm will change with your life," says Charles James, a teen-age palmistry prodigy who has done reading at the Factory Club during high school vacations. Charles believes palmistry foretells the future more accurately than astrology. He has now founded the Hollywood Occult Center, a brand-new mystery school where the hip young instructors teach subjects ranging from Advanced Magic to Astral Projection.

Small groups like the British Society for the Study of Physiological Patterns study the old palmist lore with open minds, not accepting the traditional interpretations until such time as they are empirically proven correct. The society was founded in 1945 by Noel Jaquin, the first palmist to work on large-sample studies of the psychological types associated with different kinds of fingerprint patterns. Jaquin also collected impressive evidence that interruptions in the orderly fingerprint lines was a warning of major illness.

On the non-occult level, more and more significance has been found in hand-patterns. Since 1945, Tulane University researchers have isolated a specific kind of palm-print that shows if an infant is a Mongoloid idiot. The latest discovery came in in 1970 from two Minnesota MD's, Milton Alter and Robert Schulenberg, who found that children born with certain heart defects have identifiably abnormal palm-prints. Apparently anything strong enough to damage the organs of a developing fetus would also affect the palm lines. The doctors recommend that palm-prints be taken of all newborn babies because the congenital heart defects often don't become noticeable until it's too late to operate.

By now handwriting analysis—graphology—is just about on the borderline of graduation from occultism to acceptance as a combination of psychology test and foolproof legal identification. Certainly there is no longer anything controversial about the kind of handwriting expert who works for the police, identifying forgeries and testifying in court about who wrote what.

The more ambitious branch of graphology, which claims to be able to analyze the entire personality in depth by studying the handwriting, doesn't seem to be nearly as ancient as most of the other divinations. This is understandable enough; it is, after all, only comparatively recently in history that most people have been able to read or write. Graphology is supposed to have begun in Renaissance Italy but didn't become popular till the mid-1800's in Paris when Abbé Jean Hippolyte Michon established a whole detailed system about how the loops in round letters, the crossing of a *t* or the dotting of an *i* revealed specific personal characteristics.

Psychotherapists *are* very interested in handwriting as an expression of personality, but they feel that real understanding of the way this works is in its infancy. Certainly no psychologist is going to claim that someone writes *k* with an odd slant because he is a secret foot fetishist. At this stage, it is the overall style of handwriting that can be useful to a therapist with a new patient. Obviously, garbled unreadable penmanship would lead to suspicions that the writer is seriously disturbed. Teeny, squinched-up little letters are probably written by somebody who's inhibited. The big, florid lettering comes from a flamboyant, expansive type. This is something, surely. But could it have helped Oedipus get over his problems?

There is one man who actually believes it could. He's Paul de Sainte-Colombe, ex-French Resistance fighter, who wrote *Graphotherapeutics*. He's been a popular figure on the U.S. occult circuit for the past few years, lecturing about how he successfully treated hundreds of disturbed children at his Paris center. If you clean up bad writing habits your psychological state will improve, Colombe claims. That's because if the subconscious influences the writing hand, then it must work in reverse too! He has been invited to demonstrate graphotherapy at various universities and medical meetings and was a consultant to the Youth Drug Study Unit at the Langley Porter Neuropsychiatric Institute of the University of California School of Medicine in San Francisco.

Today we don't hear too much about gypsy tea leaf readers—perhaps they have been made technologically obsolescent by the invention of tea bags. One of the last famous keepers of the tea leaf fortune-telling tradition is Arlene Dahl, the beautiful red-headed movie star turned wealthy cosmetics consultant. "I came across a book that explained all the symbols to look for in the bottom of the cup," explains Miss Dahl. "At first I took the book along to parties, but every time I had to check out something, I could feel I was losing my audience—so I started to improvise. But I was right too often and I got scared. When I went to London to make a movie, my English hairdresser insisted I read hers. Although I didn't know it, she and her husband had wanted a child for five years and when I read a new arrival she was overjoyed. A few weeks later she ran in and called me a witch—she was pregnant."

The way one reads tea leaves is to first drip a few of them into the cup, which is then placed upside down on the saucer and turned around three times. The leaves in the saucer show the past and those in the cup tell the future. The handle of the cup is December and the months are read off clockwise. Small specks near the rim of the cup are the symbol for money. A pair of shoes means taking a trip; romance is indicated by a Cupid's derrière.

Another discarded divination today is phrenology, the study of head bumps. The assumption behind this method is that thoughts shape the brain—which in turn shapes the skull from the inside because different faculties are located in different areas of the brain. Dr. Franz Joseph Gall, the founder of phrenology, came to Paris from his provincial Austrian hometown in 1806 and eventually claimed discovery of no less than forty-two "seats of thought" that could be felt by the bumps on the head. He placed intelligence at the front of the brain, emotion in the middle, and willpower at the rear.

The tenets of phrenology go completely against everything that medical research has discovered about the structure of the brain. However, the "science" was a great international rage during the earlier part of the nineteenth century. The main head-bump experts in the United States were the Fowler Brothers, Orson and Lorenzo. Dapper, with handle-bar mustaches and high-domed foreheads that were the mark of intelligence, the Fowlers were dynamite on the lecture circuit. They founded the American Institute of Phrenology and published authoritative works on the subject.

The sudden rise of U.S. spiritualism in the 1850's made phrenology passé as a major phenomenon almost overnight. It entered into the phase we remember today—carnival quacks with those huge charts of the human head marked off with numbers and dotted lines. Orson Fowler took his huge earnings and built himself a phrenologically significant eight-sided mansion which began the New England Gilded Era craze for octagonal houses.

Gematria, the mystical interpretation of numbers, is supposed to be a product of that great founder of mathematics, the Greek of 600 B.C., Pythagoras. It is also tied in with the *Kabbala,* the ultramystical Jewish decoding of the Old Testament, and even with arcane equations for astrological symbolism. As the numerology writers say, everything in the universe can be expressed in numbers and their relationships. But the problem is, of course, in interpreting these numbers as occult symbols of human destiny. It is doubtful whether a numerologist could offer anything like proof that just because the letters in the name your family chose for you add up to seven, you are "a mystic . . . thoughtful . . . contemplative and analytical by nature . . . a healer . . ." as one widely sold numerology paperback claims.

One of America's more unlikely occult scholars is Khigh Dhiegh (pronounced Ky Dee), the burly, shaven-headed, droopy-mustached actor who specializes in portraying Oriental film villains. Khigh was chief of the brainwashing team in *The Manchurian Candidate* and appears several times each season on TV's *Hawaii Five-O* as the wily Red Chinese spy, Wo Fat—a strange thing about this being that he has no Oriental blood at all; Khigh was born in New Jersey of mixed Anglo-Egyptian-Sudanese parentage.

But Khigh Dhiegh was a regular on the occult roundtable of the Long John Nebel late-night radio show for years. And he has established branches of his International I Ching Studies Institute in New York and Los Angeles.

The I Ching is a very old Chinese book of divinations from which one can obtain the correct course of action by tossing sticks or coins. Khigh thinks of I Ching as a catalyst which focuses conscious attention on information that is *already known* by the subconscious mind. "If you have thought of the question, you contain the answer," says the actor-metaphysician. "The best solution to every personal problem lies dormant within the inner self awaiting discovery."

The translation of I Ching is Book of Changes, and Khigh Dhiegh's nine-week courses do not stress divination techniques so much as the I Ching's inspired metaphysical diagram of the changes possible to man's state—and how these changes flow into one another, making an eternal circle of inseparable opposites. The ancient Chinese Taoist concept of yin and yang—which Khigh equates with flesh and spirit—exists in the real universe like the alternation between atoms and the submicroscopic spaces separating them . . . both atoms and spaces being necessary to create the myriad forms of matter.

I asked the I Ching, "Will the occult make important progress during the 1970's?"

Of the sixty-four hexagrams in the book, my coin toss chose number sixty. It is titled "Chieh," which translates to English as restraint and symbolizes water held by a dyke above a marshy lake. According to the new translation by John Blofield (supposedly not as weighty as the original Richard Wilhelm treatment, but more modern in its outlook), the text is: "Restraint—success! It is wrong to persist in harsh restraint." The commentary on this ambiguous little statement says, "The superior man employs a system of regulations in his plans for the widespread practice of virtue . . . Harsh restraint must not be persistently applied because it leads to exhaustion . . . When restraint is exercised in the work of governing, property suffers no damage and the people are not harmed. Joy is experienced in undertaking what is dangerous."

Because of the order of the coins, I got this more detailed advice: "He acts thus from his knowledge of when things can be carried through and when they will be blocked . . . Advancing now wins praise . . . Persistence in a righteous course brings to those in authority good fortune and freedom from error . . . The superior man nourishes the people and treats them with leniency . . . Making progress with a highly dangerous task is a way of obtaining control of the realm and of winning the people's allegiance."

Despite the generality of the book's terminology, there is an overall trend to this answer which seems clearly appropriate: It had been a poor time to bring the deeper ideas of occultism before the public until now, but conditions have changed and the people are ready if occultism is presented to them in the proper manner.

The occidental counterpart to the I Ching is the Tarot card deck. The most widespread occult tradition about the origin of Tarot is that it was invented by a great international assemblage of esoteric scholars in Egypt who fled to Fez, Morocco, around 1200 A.D. after war destroyed the library of Alexandria, repository of all ancient wisdom. These occultists decided to create a device for preserving their philosophic conception of how the mechanism of the universe works, flowing endlessly from one phase into the next, eternal opposites always blending into renewal. This teaching device was to express its ideas in the international language of picture symbols.

Historically, the oldest known reference to a Tarot deck dates from 1392. It was a pack owned by King Charles VI of France and is still on display in a Paris museum. The Tarot is apparently the ancestor of the standard playing card deck we use today. In southern Italy the game of tarocchi is still played with Tarot cards.

Today's Tarot deck has seventy-eight cards (properly called "keys"). There are the twenty-two picture cards of the Major Arcana with titles like the "Fool," the "Lovers," the "Devil." The other fifty-six cards are the Minor Arcana in four suits like contemporary playing cards, except that Tarot suits are wands, cups, swords, and pentacles.

There is no such thing as a universally agreed interpretation of the cards, just as there's no real proof of their origin. In addition, there are disagreements over how to lay out the cards for a reading. Some card-readers who use a standard deck claim they are working from a less-distorted tradition than the Tarot readers. Also, the Tarot answers questions only in terms of its very specialized frame of reference. Suppose you are mentally asking something as prosaic as: Will my boss give me a raise? The final card in the answer might be the "Star"—a naked girl pouring the waters of life from two jugs, one into a pool of universal consciousness and the other onto earthy matter, as the stars of cosmic energy shine down upon her. This shows the cycle of creation, but does it mean you're getting a raise or being laid off?

But in spite of any quibbles, divination with the Tarot is a far more evocative experience than using ordinary cards. The Tarot pictures have an eerie fascination. They are like windows onto another world, some place strange and different, but still hauntingly familiar—like snapshots from your dreams. All those vivid figures, living in silence among their bright-colored realms, yet absolutely bursting with life.

And as with the I Ching, Tarot's fortune-telling capacity is considered by aficionados the most plebeian thing about it. The deck may be used for meditation on the universal philosophic processes symbolized in the shifting patterns of the cards. Tarot and I Ching really have a lot in common; they're both what Khigh Dhiegh calls "acts of intentional chance" which use a Jungian "synchronicity" to connect the mental posture of the questioner with what is happening overall through the cosmos.

There is in Los Angeles even a Temple of Tarot and Holy Qabalah. It was founded by the late Paul Foster Case, whose book, *The Tarot*, is considered one of the best esoteric interpretations of the cards written in this century. Located in a small brick office building alongside the Pasadena Freeway at Figueroa Street and Fifty-first Avenue, the Temple of Tarot has a bustling mailroom which sends out dollar-a-week occult lessons and Tarot decks which the student colors himself, thus memorizing each picture as he puts his own personal touches on them. The chapel is a smaller room around to the back. It is decorated with brightly back-lit glass paintings of the Major Arcana.

An amazing demonstration of the creative beginnings of an occult insight is Morgan's Tarot, copyrighted in 1970. Whoever it was that invented the original Tarot must have perceived the flow of reality with the same touch of mystical genius as Morgan Robbins. Morgan is tall, spectrally thin and full-bearded. He makes his home in Boulder Creek, California, a village on the isolated coast south of San Francisco separated by mountains from Interstate Highway 101. When the Los Angeles distributor of his cards went up to Boulder Creek to find him, he had no clues as to where Morgan's house was. But as he was driving aimlessly about, he spotted a tall, skinny hitchhiker standing by the road like a Biblical Prophet. Morgan doesn't drive; he prefers to go where people take him! Each of his Tarot cards is a remarkable cartoon, freaky, post-psychedelic, and perfectly in tune with our time. Yet they have a timelessly universal quality that will affect people long after the immediate references are forgotten . . . just like the original Tarot, they illuminate this world by putting you into another one. Suiting the free-form spirit of this era, the seventy-eight cards aren't numbered or in suits and at this point we certainly don't need any commentaries to interpret them . . . although the commentaries will almost certainly come.

Again I asked: Will the occult make important progress during the 1970's? And I laid out Morgan's Tarot in a ten-card Celtic Spread, the most popular Tarot divination pattern.

Card one, representing the situation, was a nearly completed pyramid on a boundless desert with a single star overhead. Caption: "Keep up the good work."

Card two shows opposing forces—A flower coming out of a lightning bolt. Caption: "Power." Thus the power structure holding back the completion of the pyramid.

Card three stands for conscious factors—Two people under a lamppost on a tenement street. "Your mission is not yet complete" is the caption.

Card four, subconscious factors—The thinker is sitting on a rock with a thought bubble coming out of his head showing the bottom portion of the same thinker sitting on the same rock. "Think about it for a while."

Card five, immediate past—A diagonal strip with breaks on each side and a swirling butterfly pattern slipping through. "Somewhere, there is an energy leak."

Card six, immediate future—A bunch of people reclining against a backdrop of foothills. "Nobody here but us folk." The occult subculture becoming more influential?

Card seven, fears—A starburst. "Far out." Occultism too far out for the consumer-conditioned public?

Card eight, others' opinions—Earth, Saturn, and other planets orbiting. "There are NO MISTEAKS." A reason for occultism's rising and falling fortunes?

Card nine, expectations—An IBM computer spewing out tape. "I still don't understand."

Card ten, the outcome—No picture at all, just the words, "Your doubt is your faith if necessary in your particular case perhaps."

Morgan's Tarot couldn't be more correct. For the occult explosion to make any truly significant gains, those of us involved with the esoteric tradition must continue our doubts about the officially accepted version of physical reality and be satisfied with nothing less than rational, complete answers to these doubts.

Chapter 10

Magic—White, Black, and Satanic

IN A totally commonplace LA stucco blockhouse at a corner of Coldwater Canyon Boulevard in the family-residential heart of San Fernando Valley lives Israel Regardie, who was secretary to the last of the black magicians, Aleister Crowley, during Crowley's final burst of creativity in the early 1930's. Regardie must be in his late sixties, but he has a dapper ageless look. He is a shortish, broad-chested man with his all-black hair slicked back, and he wears a Hong Kong brocade vest over his sedate tie and white shirt. His shave is perfect and his breath mint-fresh for the close-up work he does. Today Regardie earns a living as a Reichian chiropractor—in effect, a lay analyst with a license to treat patients. His theory is that muscular tensions may cause mental stress and this is why he calls himself a Reichian—after Wilhelm Reich, the inventor of the theory of Orgone Energy, who believed he had mapped the real relationship between physiological and mental disturbances.

I have heard from several independent sources that Regardie is an extremely effective, if unorthodox, psychotherapist. But it is in his spare time that he has earned the reputation of being probably the most industrious, scholarly author on occult magic living today. Israel Regardie's first major work on magic, *The Tree of Life*, was published shortly after he broke with Crowley. (All of Crowley's intimates eventually reached a point where they had to struggle away from him—or else they literally had their lives destroyed.) It describes magic as a particularly demanding form of consciousness expansion directed at attaining mystical unity with a symbolic "Guardian Angel" which clearly represents still another view of the occult illumination/altered state of consciousness.

Regardie says his books are a clarification of Crowley's teachings and that the "Great Beast 666" himself understood magic primarily as a means of achieving control of the altered state of consciousness, with all its psychic gifts, by exercises of strengthening the will and direction of the powers of emotional passion—as opposed to the relaxed openness taught by Yoga and other forms of mysticism. "Yes, magic takes place in the consciousness," Regardie believes. "It affects the external world the same way a drunk does—through his state of mind—though of course on a much higher level."

This idea is expanded on in Richard Cavendish's *The Black Arts* (1967), the best book about the operative attitudes behind magical theory. Cavendish says that for magicians, good and evil are just two of the neutral forces within the universal design. Given that man has a spark of God within him, then the sorcerer believes it must be possible to reach Godhood by experiencing and mastering all the great spiritual forces of the universe.

The whole approach seems to have a lot more in common with Jung's contemporary speculation that alchemy and other branches of occult technique are really early maps of man's deeper psychological traits than it does with the popular assumption that classical magic consists of secret equations and formulas for manipulating human events and the forces of nature. But both interpretations—the popular and the psychological—can be found as far back as the earliest known document of magic ritual, *The Emerald Table of Hermes Trismegistus.* Legend says this is a slab of emerald engraved in Phoenician and hidden in a cave by Thrice-Greatest Hermes, the Greek god of invention who was based on the Egyptian god Thoth and later became the Roman messenger-god Mercury. In Hermes' function as "scribe of the gods" he is credited with authorship of some forty-two lost books which summed up the philosophic knowledge of the ancients. A Latin translation of the *Emerald Table* existed by 1200 and there were probably Arabic translations earlier. The opening sentence translated to, "As above, so below; and as below, so above . . . to achieve the miracle of the unity." The credo of the magician is to change the outside world by changing his mental world, hopefully to become eventually one with the powers of the universe.

What we generally think of as magic today is the medieval European tradition whose most important records we still have in more or less the original form. *The Grand Grimoire, The Grimoire of Honorius, The Arbatel of Magic, The Lemegeton, The Great Albert, The Key of Solomon, The Lesser Key of Solomon, The Testament of Solomon* . . . what majestically rolling titles. Unhappily, the contents of these magical textbooks are mainly recipes for summoning up the Devil or one of his demonic assistants for the majestic purpose of guiding the magician to a buried treasure. The books with Solomon in the title represent another powerful stream of medieval magic—the Kabbala.

The Kabbala is the Jewish occult tradition, more of a philosophic approach than a technique of magic-making. Exiled from their homeland for nearly 2,000 years, the Jews had only their holy book, *The Old Testament*, to cling to. Commentary after commentary sprang up, like the *Talmud* and the *Mishnah*. Little wonder that with all the creative force of a people funneled into exposition of a book, they would soon begin to see hidden symbolic meanings behind the words. To a large extent, the history of the grimoires is a history of faked "ancient Hebrew magic." Especially popular were nonsectarian adaptations of the ten sephiroth, or facets, of God. The twenty-two paths between the sephiroth are thought to correspond to the Major Arcana of the Tarot cards. The greatest nineteenth-century magician, Frenchman Alphonse Louis Constant, felt it was appropriate to take the Hebraic pen name, Eliphas Levi, for his work *Transcendental Magic*, which for the first time unified the concepts of the old grimoires in modern terms. Most important of these fake Jewish textbooks of magic is the *Sacred Magic of Abramelin the Mage*, written anonymously by some eighteenth-century Frenchman but purporting to be a translation of a Hebrew original of 1458.

In the book, Abramelin explains to his son Lamech how to adopt a six-month program of prayer, self-denial, and concentration in order to invoke a Holy Guardian Angel who will take him on a tour of the higher spheres—where elemental spirits can be tamed to do the magician's will.

An almost forgotten manuscript in the main Paris Library, *Sacred Magic of Abramelin the Mage* was rediscovered and translated by S. L. MacGregor Mathers in the 1880's. In 1887 Mathers founded the first modern English magical society, the Order of the Golden Dawn. A decade later, the twenty-three-year-old Aleister Crowley was initiated into the order—his first exposure to committed, well-informed occultists. Among the many illustrious members of this small but highly influential group were the poet William Butler Yeats and writers Arthur Machen and Algernon Blackwood. All of these men were highly influenced by the *Abramelin* system. Within a few years, Crowley was trying to take over the Golden Dawn leadership from Mathers and the two magi sent armies of evil spirits against each other. The bitter squabble and Mathers' death in 1918 virtually put an end to the Golden Dawn although there are still a few small branches here and there today—a secret chapter in the United States and an open group in, of all places, New Zealand. Aleister Crowley went on to found his own tiny society, Argentinum Astrum, and to take over a short-lived German sex-magic organization, Ordo Templi Orientis.

Israel Regardie began corresponding with Crowley about his philosophy during the late 1920's. Born in England, Regardie grew up in Washington, D.C., and joined Crowley in Europe from about 1928 to 1934. After the final break, he continued to study occultism on his own. "I'm basically a loner," he explains. "I avoid other occultists like the plague." But despite this careful disclaimer, Regardie seems to turn up in some of the most elusive occult activities going on today. A photo in the brochure of the Paracelsus Research Society showed him in their Salt Lake City alchemy laboratory, holding a test tube of what was supposed to be artificial liquid gold. And he is in touch with a mysterious couple, the McMurtrys, who preside over the official U.S. branch of the Ordo Templi Orientis from a post office box in Dublin, California, a small town north of San Francisco.

Regardie became a chiropractor shortly before World War II and then served in the U.S. Army. Afterward, he settled in Southern California for the climate, married briefly, and concentrated on developing his Neo-Reichian psychotherapy. "Today I wish I'd gotten an MD," he says, "then you're really free to try different therapies."

It wasn't until the 1950's that Regardie returned to public occult activities. The cause was his anger over the way Aleister
Crowley was being treated in print by the literary executor he
chose just before his death in 1947 at the age of seventy-two—
injecting up to eleven daily grams of heroin into himself until
the end. "It was like beating a sick dog; none of Crowley's real
genius and grandeur came through," Regardie says about the
John Symonds biography *The Great Beast* and Symonds' intro-
ductions to the new editions of Crowley's books. "Symonds made
out Crowley to be no more than a silly egomaniac."

Regardie shortly thereafter began putting out his own anno-
tated Crowley reissues for the energetic St. Paul, Minnesota, occult publisher, Llewellyn. "I think there's no doubt that Crowley had considerable greatness as a teacher and writer," says
Regardie of his old mentor. "Most authorities worthy of the
name would agree that Crowley's *Magick in Theory and Practice*
is the finest single work ever written on the subject. True, he was
certainly a very difficult man, but nothing like the monster of
depravity and evil that the gutter press of his day made him out
to be. If I had to describe him in only one phrase, I'd say he was
a Victorian hippie—And I'm sure that's why he's become so popular again with the kids who can see him in that way. His major
fault was a lack of good judgment—typical in the way he chose
for his literary executor a man who held his work in contempt.
He associated with absolutely the wrong people. If he sometimes
acted with an appalling lack of consideration, that's because he
had no diplomacy. Fifty years before Tim Leary, he was absolutely open in his advocacy of drugs and promiscuous sexuality
—both heterosexual and homosexual. In short, he had a helluva
good time and most people hated him for that, right off."

The main episode of Aleister Crowley's long, full life which
caused the English popular press to make him a regular Sunday
supplement bogey labeled "The Wickedest Man in the World"
was his proprietorship, from 1920 to 1923, of the "Sacred Abbey
of Thelema" at an isolated villa near the Sicilian village of Ce-
falù. Orgia were practiced most evenings, to use his own term for
the method by which he raised the olden gods. Disciples went
mad or died, drugs were consumed voraciously, animals were sacrificed, sometimes after participating in the orgia. Crowley maintained a small but shifting harem at the abbey, ladies he

named Alostrael, Cypris, Metonith, Scarlet Woman. It ended only because the energetic new regime of Mussolini grew embarrassed by all this and threw them out. "Sex magic is the most difficult of all roads to power because it is a great effort for the mind to remain concentrated on the ceremony," he confided to his *Magical Record* shortly before the expulsion.

Crowley was a brewery heir (he may have set records for his squandering of a substantial inheritance), raised in a family of Plymouth Brethren, a sect better known in the United States as the Pilgrims. It was his mother who first took to calling teen-age Aleister the Great Beast 666, after the blaspheming monster mentioned in the Biblical book of Revelation (13:1-6). Her displeasure was due to Aleister's early religious irreverence and also his propensity for bedding the servant girls.

One of the more frightening chronicles of what it meant to be under the sway of Aleister Crowley during his heyday is Crowley's diary of *The Paris Working*, which was obtained by Jean Overton Fuller for her biography, *The Magical Dilemma of Victor Neuberg*.

Neuberg was a starry-eyed young Cambridge student who accompanied Crowley on a trek across the Algerian desert in 1909 where they conjured up the "mighty devil Choronzon," with the aid of quantities of hashish and performance of a homosexual rite on an improvised sand altar "in the sight of the sun." With Neuberg protected inside a magic circle, Crowley crouched in a Triangle of Solomon and allowed the demon to take possession of him; appearing in turn as a hairy, horned beast, a beautiful whore, a wriggling snake, and a naked pseudo-Crowley who broke into the protective circle and tried to bite Neuberg's throat.

The Paris Working was a series of twenty-four sex magic sessions in January and February of 1914, with Crowley taking the feminine role and Neuberg reporting visions of the higher dimensions. A sample of the dialogue they recorded: "CROWLEY: How can one invoke Mercury better? NEUBERG: Use a gold pentagram, placing the same in a prominent position; drink yellow wine and eat fish before the ceremony. Let the clock be removed." By the time this adventure ended, Neuberg had enough of Aleister Crowley. But at parting, the magician put such a powerful curse on him that poor Victor had a two-year nervous breakdown. In time, Neuberg recovered and fought for his country in World War I, married, and became a father. He was an important poetry editor during the 1930's and responsible for publishing the first printed verse of Dylan Thomas.

The classic of all Southern California occult rumors is that Aleister Crowley lived in Pasadena for long enough to found a Black Magic Coven whose membership remained active until well into the 1950's. If so, there must have been some pretty doddering old occultists involved by the end. The only time Crowley spent in the United States was World War I—his period between Neuberg and the Abbey of Thelema. According to his own *Confessions,* Crowley spent most of this American period playing at bohemianism in quaint Greenwich Village. For a while he had a job editing a pro-German propaganda magazine; after the Allies won he explained his treason by claiming all those calls to destroy Britain were really meant as satire against his employers. He did make one swing around the country in 1915. There was a brief stopover in Los Angeles, and he told his diary he couldn't wait to get out of this boring orange-grove country village.

The high point of the Pasadena coven myth came in June, 1952, when CalTech rocket propulsion expert Jack Parsons blew himself up under extremely mysterious circumstances. (A coven is really a congregation of witches, not a circle of magicians, but public terminology was somewhat confused before the occult explosion came in and that's the way they were known.) Parsons, at thirty-seven, had invented many of the basic processes in JATO (jet-assisted takeoff) and was married to a lady who later became famous as Cameroun the Witch. Parsons got blown apart in his garage laboratory on the grounds of the luxurious Busch estate while packing for a hush-hush trip to Mexico where he was reportedly going to experiment with his new formula for an explosive "more powerful than anything yet invented."

Another chemical ordnance expert named George Santmeyers, who had worked with Parsons for five years on various industrial projects, insisted it was absurd to think that a scientist as knowledgeable about explosives as Jack Parsons would have thrown cordite and fulminate of mercury wrappers into a trash can and then let a coffee can full of mixed fulminate of mercury slip from his fingers to explode on hitting the floor. For an extra bizarre touch, when Parsons' fifty-eight-year-old mother got the news of the blast an hour later, she committed suicide by swallowing forty-five sleeping pills while an elderly wheelchair-ridden friend looked on, unable to stop her. The final sentence in the Los Angeles *Times'* story was "Rumors that Parsons had been involved in mystic cults some years ago were discounted by Santmeyers."

But that was only the public version! "Cameroun stayed with me at my Malibu Beach house for six months, pulling herself together after Jack died," says Renate Druks, a bronze-tanned lady with long black hair who looks the image of a proper sorceress even though her work is making children's art education films and for the past decade she's been a member of the Huxley-Isherwood-Heard set's Vedanta Hinduism. "I have every reason to believe that Jack Parsons was working on some very strange experiments, trying to create what the old alchemists called a homunculus, a tiny artificial man with magic powers. I think that's what he was working on when the accident happened."

Renate lives in a small apartment in one of those wonderfully rococo old Hollywood hillside buildings. The walls are hidden behind ranks of large, unearthly oil paintings, including the eerie wedding portrait of Katharine (*The Graduate*) Ross and James (*Rain People*) Caan commissioned for the stars' earlier film, *Games.*

"I was never really a witch, but I did study magic for a while with the last mistress of Aleister Crowley, a wonderful old lady in her eighties named Jane Wolf," she says. "I took it up mostly in self-defense; there were some scarey things going on at Malibu Beach in the late fifties. A man named Smith had a very active black magic circle, and I wanted to protect myself against the evil atmosphere. I only cast a curse once. There was a very unpleasant building inspector who was giving all my friends at the beach a tough time. Everybody begged me to put a small curse on him so I gave it a try. The next time he was due back to check my wiring another inspector came. I asked him what had happened to the regular man. He just shook his head and said, "Everything."

The climax of the Malibu black magic days came when Renate threw a "Come as Your Madness" costume ball at her little beach house. The guest list included the important avant-garde authoress Anais Nin and Kenneth Anger, one of the very first of the U.S. underground film-makers. The party's weirdness inspired Anger to make the first contemporary occult-psychedelia film, *Lord Shiva's Dream* (the initials spell LSD). All the foremost California occultists of the early 1960's were featured. Renate Druks did the truly awesome makeup, putting highpriestess Cameroun in silver talons and creating an unforgettable spiderweb face for Samson De Brier as the Great Beast 666. Samson also played Lord Shiva in a different getup. The film was shot in De Brier's weird old cluttered museum of a house in the hills above Hollywood and Vine, a fascinating junkpile of occult, literary, and showbiz lore whose style would be possible only in Hollywood. Samson, another of those elderly but ageless occult loners, is extremely leery of talking these days about his magic background, much preferring to concentrate on his memorabilia of Valentino, André Gide, and James Dean. He pops up at all the Motion Picture Academy screenings, researching the Oscar vote choices for a busy scriptwriter friend! "I'm mainly interested in my film work," he says. "I don't want my name still associated with the black arts. I have to be very careful about my powers; I was very angry at a friend's husband and found myself wishing he was dead. The very next week he was killed in a plane crash."

The Fellowship of Ancient Mind made a dramatic entry into the occult spotlight on March 11, 1969. The Great Earthquake Prediction Rumor was getting under way to panic thousands of Californians with the message that the entire state would crumble into the Pacific Ocean sometime in April. Arch-Druid Tyrhon, bearded, bespectacled, and wearing a clerical collar, led a line of psychedelic-robed young people into Los Angeles City Hall to take out a license for restoring the city after the disaster. As can be imagined, they were an instant hit with the press, popping up on all the TV news shows. They then disappeared briefly and suddenly resurfaced again in a cubicle of a rent-an-office suite in the utterly plastic California Federal Savings high-rise on Wilshire Boulevard's "Miracle Mile."

"When we saw that the suite number was 1313 we knew this was for us," said the then twenty-seven-year-old Arch-Druid Tyrhon. "We needed a straight office like this so people will realize we mean business. *Time* and *U.S. News & World Report* were here this morning, and ABC News is on the way. That first wire-service story on us was pretty garbled; it wasn't that we didn't have among ourselves the sixty-six dollars for a salvage permit, we just decided we didn't need that kind of license. Our purpose was to teleport the great artworks in town to safety before the earthquake hits. For that we only have to get permission from the owners to make it legal. And we're not predicting any definite date for the quake; it's just due within a couple of years. This is why our superiors in the fellowship ordered us to reveal ourselves now; people can always take care of themselves in a disaster, but artworks are the first to be destroyed."

According to Arch-Druid Tyrhon, the Fellowship of Ancient Mind is some six thousand years ancient, its goal to produce an ever more powerful circle of psychic adepts for "a long-range goal that would be incomprehensible to outsiders." He said, "I have been a member since 1966; a Lebanese adept initiated me in Madrid where I was editing a travel magazine. The fellowship seeks out new telepaths when they're ready to join. There are two hundred and fifty members in Los Angeles and six hundred in the United States. I was teaching our membership in Palm Springs and writing some science fiction until I came here to help Arch-Druid Morlock." He said the LA chapter had recently run off a practice project for the big art-lift. "We flew a fully loaded Mercedes-Benz the ninety miles from Hollywood to Palm Springs in twenty-three minutes, jumping it through the outer dimensions miles at a time along the freeway . . . No, I can't explain why the other cars on the road didn't notice anything unusual happened; that's just the way teleportation works."

Within a year, the Fellowship of Ancient Mind had been through lots of changes. Tyrhon was spending most of his time in Europe making underground films. Arch-Druid Morlock hinted this was all part of some mysterious plan. Morlock is about the same age as Tyrhon and has currently adopted the hairless look. His skull is completely shaven and he wears all-white clothing—loose Mexican peasant shirt with an amulet dangling around the neck, white jeans. Like Tyrhon, he was something of a prodigy as a science-fiction writer. The Arch-Druids drop in and out of the occult shop business. At one time or another, they separately ran Hollywood shops called the Compleat Enchanter and the Magical Mystery Museum. For the moment, Morlock maintains no more than an occult concession counter at the Psychedelic Supermarket near Hollywood Boulevard.

But his main project is now a mystery school with a name that is secret, although it is advertised in the Los Angeles *Times* classified pages as Honorius. (The title choice is strange; the *Grimoire of Honorius* was one of the bloodiest of the medieval magic texts, prescribing the slaughter of a lamb and the tearing out of a black rooster's eyes to summon up the Devil, all the while praying sweetly to God.) The school is a two-room affair, almost bare except for a few occult props, located in a quaint old office building on a street fittingly titled Cosmo Alley, 100 yards west of Hollywood and Vine. Each six-week class is $20, or $800 for the year's twenty-eight courses in subjects like Introduction to Demonology, Beginning Lesser Elemental Spirits, and Astral Projection Lab.

"All occultism is advertising for an esoteric school," says Morlock. "The secret of the occult is that there are no occult secrets. Every teaching is notes to ourselves, and the incantations are formulas to remind us we must verify our own information and time, the only things there are in a personal universe." He tells of being a staff writer at Universal Films during the past year. "It all went to this; I'm proud to say I personally lost $8,000 on the school last year."

The Man Who Brought Back Satan

If there is anybody who could have eliminated the fear of making Devil-worship respectable for the first time in Western history, it is Anton Szandor La Vey—a unique combination of occult scholar and outrageous prankster—who shaved his skull on Walpurgisnacht, 1966, and proclaimed himself high priest of the First Church of Satan.

Soon he was appearing on the Johnny Carson show, wearing a horned hood and brandishing a ceremonial-magic sword as he explained that his church altar is a live and naked woman to symbolize the pleasures of the flesh. "Evil spelled backwards is live," he gave as the Satanic credo.

Already there are over 9,000 members of the Church of Satan, with active "grottoes" in France, Italy, Germany, England, Switzerland, Ireland, Mexico, Brazil, Argentina, Japan, South Africa, Ceylon, and India. U.S. grottoes pay homage to Satan in New York, Chicago, Los Angeles, Denver, Detroit, Tulsa, Shreveport, and Albuquerque. At a rate of $18 per person to join and with various other smaller dues, La Vey has estimated his annual income at about $25,000—tax exempt, of course, as with any legally certified religion.

Anton spreads the faith from his black San Francisco-Victorian house on quiet California Street, just south of the Golden Gate Bridge. The interior is a masterpiece of pop occult decor, a Disneyfied Charles Addams setting that's exactly what you would imagine as a sorcerer's lair. The walls are black and the lightbulbs red; each room has some of La Vey's cheerfully ghoulish paintings; there's a deformed skeleton and stuffed animals peering out of unlikely corners; even the bathroom has black towels and black toilet paper. Drinks are served with Marquis De Sade napkins on a marble gravestone coffee-table made by Anton's wife and high priestess, Diane, a cuddly-cute blonde who bustles about the premises as if she had just stepped out of a sexy-housewife TV commercial.

Everybody who's ever written about the Church of Satan has been struck by how well-adjusted the La Vey family life is. Anton and Diane's six-year-old daughter Zeena had the world's first Satanic baptism. And Karla, Anton's darkly lovely eighteen-year-old daughter by a pre-Satanic first marriage, is starting college as an art-drama major. The only member of the household who came to a comparatively unhappy end was Togar, the La Vey pet lion who spent his days chained in the front hallway and bedded down nightly in a large cage overlooking the kitchen table.

San Francisco had never gotten around to passing a no-dangerous-pets law until Togar, and they couldn't make it retroactive. The item used to make the network TV news every once in a while. Angry neighbors would assemble on the sidewalk in front of Anton's house and the reporters would ask what it was about the lion that bothered them. Strangely enough, nobody ever mentioned being afraid that the full-grown lion would break loose and eat them up. The main complaint was that his roaring kept the neighborhood awake nights. Eventually Anton did have to voluntarily commit Togar to the San Francisco Zoo.

He made the mistake of offering to board an acquaintance's female jaguar while the owner was away. Unfortunately the jaguar went into heat and lust-maddened Togar almost tore down the building trying to get at her. "Togar has already sired the zoo's four lion cubs," says Anton proudly. "But we don't go and see him very often though; it's too sad."

La Vey had just made a dramatic entrance through a bookcase which swung open—the house always has a couple of secret panels he keeps changing around. He's put on a bit of bulk since founding the Satanic Church but is still quite an imposing figure. A shaven-headed six-footer with deep-set eyes and a black goatee, and a baritone voice that drones hypnotically, he's an extremely plausible, charming conversationalist.

Anton La Vey says that's his real name and that he was born in Chicago some forty years ago of mixed Rumanian-German-gypsy parentage. He was something of a minor youthful prodigy, and at sixteen he was playing second oboe in the San Francisco Ballet Orchestra. He ran away with the Clyde Beatty Circus his last year in high school, rising from cage boy to assistant lion trainer and also taking over as the circus calliope player. At eighteen he switched to a carnival as a mind-reader's assistant and there learned hypnotism and various occult fundamentals. Then he returned to San Francisco, married, graduated from the City College, and became a police photographer, snapping shots of the gorier events around town. After three years of this, he went back to the keyboard as Tony La Vey, local nightclub organist. Meanwhile, however, he kept studying his steadily growing collection of occult books.

By the early sixties he was having friends over every week for a Magic Circle discussion group. Some of the more recognizable names involved were Crowleyite film-maker Kenneth Anger, author Steven Schneck (*The Night Clerk*) and Monique Van Cleef, the whips-and-leather queen who came West after Newark police raided her seventeen-room sadism brothel.

A high point of the Magic Circle period was rumored to be Anton's hush-hush dinner of long pig—which is the polite cannibal term for human flesh. Only about five of the circle were brave enough to show up. It was not quite clear exactly what the dish was and under what circumstances it was obtained. The facts seem to be that a University of California medical student contact provided Anton with a genuine female thigh from an anatomy lab. There was a show of much reluctance before anybody present tried a serving. Those few who ultimately partook reported that the meat was delectably soft and sweet, just as tradition would have it.

La Vey's magical prowess was steadily increasing at this time, it seemed. The office building of a corporation which had been annoying him one night mysteriously fell down. But the trick Anton repeats most often is finding a parking space for his black Cadillac in the narrow old traffic-choked streets of San Francisco's North Beach theater-restaurant district. This *is* truly a feat of magic, as anyone would know who has ever tried it on a busy weekend, and Anton never fails. "I create the parking spaces in visual thought forms as I'm driving over," he explains.

It was also during the years of the Magic Circle meetings that La Vey finished working out his concepts of occultry and Satanism. "The black magic left-hand path is used for honest gratification of the ego—greed, pride, lust, anger, any of the seven deadly sins," he says. "The fact is we all have the will to power in some form, if we only had the guts to admit it. We would all like the opportunity to practice black magic.

"And the only way a hex, curse, or blast will work properly is if it's perpetrated against someone who truly deserves it, a person who has interfered with one's progress or wantonly destroyed the tranquillity of another's existence. Many people are deserving victims, and there's no need to sacrifice babies or animals or the town drunk or anybody who isn't causing others trouble. Satanism is the worship of life, not a hypocritical, whitewashed version of life, but life as it really is, concerned with the fullest gratification of the ego on this plane of existence."

To some extent, Anton's Satanism retains the stern morality of the former police department employee. He believes in an ordered society that can protect its inhabitants against crime, is totally against drugs as a magic tool, and remains unsympathetic to the hippie ethos because of its denial of the ego. One of his most popular recent interview topics is how Charlie Manson is just another mad-dog killer as far as he's concerned and should be drawn and quartered. He was thoroughly offended by the sudden plague of supposedly Devil-inspired murders in California, calling the bootleg Satanists "kooks and creeps out of their mind on drugs."

Acting as a sort of sorcery therapist, Anton had begun to see patients even before the Church of Satan got under way. He still devotes each Wednesday to his practice when he is not on the road. He gets many cases of demonic possession for which he can usually prescribe the curing spell—often it involves changing the shape of the room where the ceremonies go on. Anton anticipated the Czechoslovakian experiments in arriving at the conclusion that shape is a key factor in amplifying psychic forces. When he is dealing with a patient whose problem is sexual perversion, he recommends acting out the erotic fantasies instead of self-destructively sublimating. He believes that many of the more obnoxious people in the world are really secret masochists who constantly try to provoke bystanders to punish them.

Since the respectable sales of his paperback *Satanic Bible,* Anton has had three other book assignments, which he works on when he finds the time, as well as a column in the *Inquirer*-type tabloid, *National Insider.* Still another sideline is technical advising on films that deal with black magic. He says he was on the payroll for both *The Mephisto Waltz* and *Rosemary's Baby,* in which he even appeared on screen in the bit part of the Devil who impregnates Mia Farrow. This was by no means his only return to show business since those nightclub organist days. In the early period of the church, when he was trying out all sorts of different stratagems for celebrity, Anton La Vey and His Topless Witches Sabbath appeared at a North Beach nightspot. He said at the time, "Of course there's no conflict in reenacting black magic rituals at a nightclub. Satanism belongs where people are having pleasure, not where they are being made to learn false guilts." A little later he even posed amid arrangements of nude altars for a nudist magazine.

At the San Francisco opening night of *Satanas,* a quickie exploitation film of his black sabbath rites, Anton made a personal appearance and distributed free Satanic Bibles to the audience. The starring nude altar was one of La Vey's prize converts, a pretty, honey-blond PTA chapter president from Oakland. She is also one of the volunteer helpers who comes in one evening a week to help Diane at the files, just as at any church social. Some

Satanic products on the market are $20 pentagram wall plaques, a $5 Satanic Mass recording, and a $2 poster of "the High Priest in ceremonial garb with the traditional nude altar" captioned "Satan Wants You, Join Now."

Since the Church of Satan is registered in California as a fully legal religion, Anton has been able to perform Satanic marriages as the press cameras click away at a buxom nude altar atop his fireplace. There was also a Satanic military funeral, with the required Navy honor guard in attendance, for a young sailor who had joined the Church of Satan a few months before dying in a car crash. Quite a few of his members are young servicemen.

Naturally, the most colorful Satanic ceremonies are open only to church members in good standing. Anton's black masses are quite esthetic affairs, with candles, incense, and chanting. Every once in a while he does something more spectacular like an Exorcism of Shibboleths, a ball to which everyone comes costumed as the thing they fear most. Aside from the nude altar, a staple of La Vey ritualism is the human sacrifice—who submits to a ritual spanking. If this role is not being played by a genuine masochist who really wants to get spanked, he is allowed to pad the seat of his pants—participants often use a copy of *Playboy*.

The Church of Satan's mimeographed monthly newsletter, *Cloven Hoof,* isn't supposed to go out to nonmembers, but I managed to get most of the 1970 issues.

One issue had a sermon about the proper attitude a woman should have when obtaining the "great honor of being a nude altar, which is not to be taken lightly." Anton decreed, "Each grotto should have at least one woman who can be depended on. The purpose is NOT to add variety by changing altars from week to week. Physical beauty is of secondary importance. Dedication, awareness, an unshakable belief in the power of magic, and an unyielding faith in Satanism are the most important requisites. Under NO circumstances must an altar girl feel as if she is being put to task or 'helping out' by serving. The topless dancer or stripper is too accustomed to using her body as a livelihood to become enthused about displaying it for overt magical purposes."

Another *Cloven Hoof* carried an announcement of his birthday, with a reminder of how grateful all Satanists should feel toward the high priest. The next month on page one, Anton was able to report his "profound appreciation for the devotion of the entire membership. I was pleasantly overwhelmed by the mountainous assembly of cards, telegrams, greetings in letter form, and gifts (I admittedly favor Mammon!) which awaited me."

Chapter 11

The Real Witches

ONLY a few years ago, witches were believed to be as mythical as vampires and werewolves. But with the coming of the occult explosion, suddenly thousands of Americans and Europeans were announcing themselves as witches—and redefining witchcraft as a religion for the practice of magical techniques which produce paranormal but natural psychic powers.

The start of the modern witchcraft revival can be traced quite directly to British anthropologist Margaret Murray's 1921 book, *The Witch Cult in Western Europe*. It was Dr. Murray's theory that witchcraft was really the nature-worship pagan religion of pre-Christian Europe, gone underground to escape from Church persecution. Most other archaeology and history experts didn't feel there was enough remaining evidence from early medieval Europe ever to prove Murray's vision. But this idea of a lost pagan cult had a certain romantic resonance which kept it from dying out—it seemed to fill a growing modern need to explore again some of those mysterious areas of man's psyche.

It was the Murray theory that inspired the first modern occult scholar who actually decided to come right out and proclaim himself a witch. Gerald Gardner had spent most of his adult life as a colonial customs official in British Malaya, but apparently his heart was really back home with the mysteries of the Druids, elves, and faerie-folk. When he was evacuated back to England during World War II he took his pension and became the first twentieth-century witch activist, even appearing as witch spokesman on British TV and radio. He wrote an influential book called *Witchcraft Today* and founded a witch museum and the fund-raising Witches' Mill Restaurant on the Isle of Man in the Irish Sea, recruiting publicly for a coven—the first such in centuries. (England did not repeal the law that made witchcraft liable to a one-year sentence for fortune-telling until 1951.) It was Gardner who made the claim that all the underground witches in England convened for a Grand Coven to "whistle up a wind" for a mysterious storm which disabled most of the Spanish Armada so Sir Francis Drake could beat them. England's other Grand Coven, according to Gardner, was called in 1940 when seven hundred witches gathered on Salisbury Plain to raise up a "cone of power" which produced an unprecedented calm of the English Channel so all the small boats could cross to evacuate the Army from Dunkirk. Both of these exploits are articles of faith among modern witches.

By the time Gardner died in 1964, he had organized the nucleus of an ongoing witch society. He bequeathed everything, including the four-hundred-and-sixty-nine-year-old building with the museum and restaurant, to Monique "Niki" Wilson, a pretty witch of French parentage who is married to Scotch ex-RAF pilot Colin Wilson. (About forty years old, she was actually born in Hanoi. She met Colin in Hong Kong after World War II, and together they converted to Gardnerian witchcraft.) It seems certain there had been some few scattered underground witch circles in England all along. Gardner claimed he obtained the accounts of the ceremonies in his books direct from this source. As more and more English witches began to reveal themselves, the ones who didn't choose to ally themselves with Gardner tended to claim they were from "hereditary covens" and had been passed the true secrets of the craft by their ancestors.

In the early 1960's, Sybil Leek, a personable antique dealer and part-time TV correspondent from the south of England, revealed that her magical heritage went back to 1134 when her father's ancestors were sorcerers to the czar. Her initiation into a coven took place in France, however—in the secluded "hills above the Gorge du Loup (Wolf Canyon)"—and so there were no English witnesses. But she was caught up in the earliest groundswell of the occult explosion, becoming the first American witch celebrity when she came here to make publicity appearances for her book about selling antiques in the Gypsy forest. She migrated to the United States in 1964 and, after various changes of residence, now lives in Melbourne Beach, Florida, near Cape Kennedy. Her output of books on every facet of the occult has been staggering—Sybil Leek is apparently an accomplished witch, psychic, medium, ghost-hunter, astrologer, numerologist, palmist, graphologist, and even phrenologist. In her *Playboy* interview of January, 1969, Sybil made the unfortunate prediction that Russians would be the first to land men on the moon, and they'd do it in 1970.

King of the Witches is a recent biography of Alex Sanders, who on examination turns out to be the king only of the 1,623 witches he recruited through public appearances and organized into one hundred and seven covens. Sanders is an interestingly beat-up-looking man of about fifty, frail, five feet seven, and balding. His biography recounts the story of a dissolute youth with all the temptations of black magic—down on his luck, he had cast a money spell and a wealthy couple stopped him on the street to say he was the image of their dead son and they wished to adopt him. He had discovered his witch heritage as a slum child when he stumbled upon his grandmother performing a ceremony. Grandmother was seventy-four when she initiated the teen-age Alex into her version of third-grade witchdom by the ancient ceremony of removing his virginity.

If there are any who deserve the title of Premier American witches, it's the Bucklands, an English couple now living deep in Long Island suburbia at Brentwood village. Raymond and Rowen Buckland are the only personal associates of Gerald Gardner residing in America.

"In 1964 we felt it was time to call public attention to our religion as a means of reaching people who'd be potentially interested in joining," says Ray Buckland, a trim, debonair man with a neatly Satanic Vandyke beard. So they invited out reporters from the two local dailies, the *Long Island Press* and *Newsday* to watch them celebrate a genuine Halloween Witches Sabbath. The Bucklands shooed their two young sons off to bed like any ordinary parents, except they were wearing black robes embroidered with gold. They led the blasé newspapermen down into their cellar—which instead of being decorated as the ordinary playroom had been furnished with black velvet drapings, incense burners, candles, with the pentagram star diagramed on the floor. . . .

Then the Bucklands coolly slipped out of their robes and performed a nude invocation to the spirit of the autumnal equinox, Ray chanting and the lithe, long-haired Rowen moving in a rhythmic dance. As traditional witches, they are required to perform their rituals minus clothing so their bodies will be fully opened to the powers of nature. The newsmen's eyes popped, and the photographers were snapping pictures as fast as their flashguns would recycle. Though most of the photos never got past the city desks of family newspapers, a couple of prints retouched with eerie shadow made page one the next day.

"Our neighbors in Suffolk County recognized us from those newspaper stories even though we didn't have our names or faces printed," says Ray. "The thing that gave us away was one photo of Rowen in the kitchen, which had the same very distinctive design in all the houses of our subdivision. Also, Rowen's hair was very long for those days, so it seemed like after a week of buzzing to each other on the phone everybody in the neighborhood put two and two together. They call us 'our witches' and fortunately seem to think it's classy to have witches living on the block. We'd already lived there two years, and Rowen had done a lot of baby-sitting for the neighbors so they all knew we weren't up to any of that *Rosemary's Baby* nonsense. They also knew Rowen was interested in herbs. A clerk at the hardware store where we shop asked her if she knew something he could take to make him less tired while he was working at three jobs."

Ray commutes to Manhattan for a job as travel brochure editor with an international airline. "My co-workers seem to get a kick out of me, but my bosses are a bit shaken if I'm in the news too much," he says. "They throw Harper Lee up to me; she was a reservations phone girl for the line while she was writing *To Kill a Mockingbird*." In London he had been a store manager, a commercial artist, and the manager of a Dixieland band. They decided to emigrate when a relative of Rowen's came back to England on a visit and explained what the American standard of living really meant. But before this, Ray and Rowen had been interested in the occult for years, and they gradually focused on witchcraft as the religion they were looking for. They corresponded with Gerald Gardner and then joined one of his covens.

According to Ray, there are now eighteen American covens under Buckland leadership. This would have to be the biggest witchcraft organization in the country, spanning from Boston to San Francisco to Kentucky and across the border into Toronto. Ray has written several occult books and is now on the big-league lecture circuit, while Rowen sharpens her herb magic and is high priestess of the home coven. Their Brentwood cellar is a witchcraft museum; too small to be open to the public, it offers guided tours for the area schoolchildren. The Bucklands hope to build a full-scale museum in Cooperstown, New York, and move the whole family to a more relaxed smalltown atmosphere. "Cooperstown is a kind of summer tourist museum center," explains Ray. "They come up to see the Baseball Hall of Fame, and there are all these other little museums close by."

As it is, the Bucklands' Brentwood coven holds regular esbats (not quite as large-scale as the sabbat festivals) once a month. They used to have weekly meetings while they still lived in the New York City borough of Queens, but their present Suffolk County home is rather far out on Long Island. However, if any affiliated witch has a problem, a special service can be put together anytime.

"I believe in magic," Ray says. "I've seen it work, and I don't worry about people thinking me naïve. What happens in a spell could be a coincidence every time, but it's a coincidence you have made, and witchcraft can affect both physical nature and the actions of people. . . . One thing our coven did in Brentwood was to solve a neighborhood problem of two teen-age boys who were running riot. This family had moved from Brooklyn to Suffolk and was living next door to a man who had a wonderful garden. He was dreadfully worried these hooligans would wreck his garden as they'd broken up so many other places in the area. So when he went away on vacation he got us word he'd like his garden protected somehow. Since the whole coven has to agree before any spell can be cast, I called the coven; everybody agreed the best thing to do under the circumstances was to move the family back to Brooklyn. So for whatever reason, the kids messed up other places while the man next door was away, but they didn't touch his garden. And before the end of the month they suddenly picked up and moved back to Brooklyn for no obvious reason that anybody could see.

"When the high priestess of our New Jersey coven had a hysterectomy and it seemed as if complications would make a second operation necessary, Rowen sewed a cloth doll to represent her disorder and made a cut into it. Then she sewed it up with a healing ritual. Again, for whatever reason, Deirdre didn't need the second operation after all." — *False Healing*

Ray won't even try to guess how many witches there are in the world today, and he's in a position to know, if anybody is. He says Sybil Leek has been quoted at various times as saying she is the only witch in England and that there are 20,000 witches in the world. Niki Wilson, the Gardnerian heiress, says there are 3,000 witches in England—which is a more reasonable estimate.

From the visible manifestations of the witchcraft scene, it's doubtful if there are more than 6,000 or 7,000 really active practicing witches around today—those 3,000 in England, including Alex Sanders' organization, perhaps 2,000 in North America, and another 1,000 or 2,000 scattered around the globe. Contemporary witchcraft is more conspicuous than numerous and in the popular mind it still suffers from the wrong image—mythical black magic Satanists instead of the real world's nature-worshiping neo-pagans who follow the right-hand path of white magic.

A theory of the witch religion can be assembled from various occult writings, and it offers a surprisingly consistent view of world history. The earliest patron of witches is the Greco-Roman goddess of the moon and night. There were various names for this figure, but the one that lasted longest was Diana. Somewhere along the line, witch worship came to embrace the mysterious *Horned God*, who isn't really Satan but a personification of the active principle of nature.

Today's witches claim that their religion is the only survival of a powerful body of occult knowledge. The source of this knowledge is suggested to have been the rebellious angels called Sons of Heaven in the Bible's Apocryphal Book of Enoch. The Enochian saga is that these Sons of Heaven saw the daughters of men and lusted after them, taking them as wives and passing along their superior knowledge to the giant children of these mixed marriages. The hybrid race ran amok within a generation or two, and God was forced to send his loyal angel armies to wipe them out. Only scattered shreds of their great magic secrets remain.

The few survivors of this super race intermarried themselves back down to human size and drifted west to Europe in nomadic tribes. Some may still be nomads as the gypsies. Others evolved into the Huns. Hence Germany's Brocken, in the Hartz Mountains of Bavaria's Black Forest—the best-known Witches Sabbath setting in Continental Europe. Even after World War II there were occasional reports of Black Forest witch hysteria involving use of the drugs henbane and belladonna. The most effective weapon for ending this witchcraft of the left-hand path was not the sporadic church or government educational campaigns, but the coming of television to fill the nights in these isolated villages.

The most powerful contingent of all is believed to have settled in Britain long before the Celts with their new iron weapons arrived from northern Europe around 500 B.C. They called themselves the Pyrtani; various later invasions would call them Picts, Elves, or Heathens. The only people to whom they told anything about themselves were the Celtic shamans we remember as the Druids. The Pyrtani were great archers, buried their dead in mass mounds, and had a kind of astrological religion that they practiced in open-air stone circles. There may be some ancestral link with Merlin, Morgana Le Fay, and the Lady of the Lake. Halloween was their major festival, along with Beltane (April 30), Lammas (August 1), and Candlemas (February 2). By 100 A.D. the Romans had pushed them to the northern tip of Scotland, and there were a few rumors that they had impregnable fortresses made of stones fused by fire.

From the Vikings to the Spaniards, every European race had its strikingly similar witch legends. But none of these pockets of magic culture survived, whether because their level of technology was backward or perhaps because they were simply overwhelmed by sheer weight of numbers in a growing medieval Europe.

In the June, 1970, *American Journal of Psychiatry*, Dr. Robert Anderson calls the great witch hunts of approximately 1450-1750 an "epidemic of mass psychopathology" which grew out of social breakdowns in the last period of European feudalism. Government and Catholic authorities officially defined witchcraft as an anti-Christian movement that gave evil supernatural powers to those who made a deal with the Devil. *Malleus Maleficarum* (*Hammer Against Witches*), the standard textbook of inquisitors for two hundred years, was written by two fanatical German priests, Kramer and Sprenger, who became the first traveling witch-hunters. They proclaimed, "All witchcraft comes from carnal lust which is in women insatiable . . . wherefore for the sake of fulfilling their lusts they consort even with Devils." The book stands as a classic of distorted sexual fantasies; apparently there was nothing a lustful nymphomaniac witch liked better than to castrate a man so he couldn't have sex with her.

The Inquisition's version of Witches' Sabbaths sounds like great fun. Satan would appear as a goat or a big dark hairy man, and all the witches would kiss his butt. Frenzied dancing followed and culminated in an incestuous mass orgy with demons and each other. Next came an ornate banquet of rotten flesh, presumably human. Each witch would boast of her sins to the Devil, who rewarded evildoers with gold that turned to feces. The grand finale was a black mass, using urine, instead of holy water, and fecal wafers, with guarantees of eternal damnation for one and all. The entire affair must have been a barrel of laughs. No wonder—according to the witch-hunters—hundreds of thousands of pleasure-seekers were involved. Especially when one could fly to these happy events with an ointment that included bat's blood and baby fat, as well as mind-benders like deadly nightshade or hemlock which could certainly cause anybody to *think* they were flying.

By the early 1600's the more advanced nations of Europe were beginning to abolish their witch trials. The last official witch hanging on record was in Poland in 1793, and burning at the stake had been considered bad taste much earlier.

Considering the awful reputation that had been given to witches, it is not surprising that the whole movement went into eclipse for nearly one hundred and fifty years. Out in the countryside here and there, some old lady might have a reputation for herb spells, but that was about it. And actually, it was mostly this brand of harmless eccentric the witch-hunters were sending to the torturers during their three-hundred-year reign of terror.

A full moon floats above the dismal warehouse streets of Southwest Los Angeles and a handsome twenty-year-old who looks like a poetic surfer parks his beat-up MG in front of a small duplex. A heavy-set, bespectacled, middle-aged man opens the door, and the kid says, "I want to find out about joining your coven."

In the disarray of the living room, books on sorcery jostle the Dr. Spock baby manuals for shelf space. "The craft has come down from neo-paleolithic times; it is the old religion," says Fred Adler in an accent that still carries traces of his native Hungary even though he has been in America for twenty-seven years. "There were at least nine million witches in Europe when the Inquisition struck—most of the real ones were able to go into hiding. That's why only common implements are needed to cast a spell; a kitchen knife, a kettle, lard and soot. When the soldiers came in, everything went back on the shelves."

Fred Adler was a lawyer in Cincinnati. Since he and his family moved to California in 1964, he's been a purchasing agent for a local Defense Department buying office. "The craft is a great help in negotiating contracts," he says. "I don't try to cover up my interest in witchcraft around the office; the boss is very interested in these things."

Mrs. Martha Adler, benign and motherly, comes out wearing a housedress. She's just getting over an ear infection. Martha is an ex-nurse; she and Fred have been married for twenty years and have two boys just starting grade school. "Fred and I didn't find out we were both interested in witchcraft until after we were married," she says. Apparently they both had ancestors who were versed in occultism. "Excuse the condition of the place," she apologizes. "We just rent here and we're shopping around for a bigger house to buy. Would you like a drink of mead? That's the Druid's honey wine."

Fred passes around some of the rather beautiful amulets he makes and sells through occult shops. He gives a token with a seashell imbedded in rock to the young would-be male witch. (Fred doesn't believe in the authenticity of the term "warlock." There's room for debate on many of the finer points of the craft, such as: Does the size of a coven *have* to be thirteen witches? and How do men and women rank in witch hierarchy?)

"Hold this amulet for a minute and notice if you feel anything," Fred Adler says. After a moment the kid answers, "I feel cold chills going from my hand all the way up to my shoulders and neck." Fred tells him, "I have found this charm very helpful in discovering people with the basics of psychic sensitivity. We got it one afternoon when Martha and I took the kids down to the marina to make a gift to the ocean. We did a little chant and poured some crumbs and wine into the Pacific. The inlet had been absolutely calm, but suddenly there was one small, gentle wave and this stone and seashell were lying at our feet."

The Adlers usually try to have a training coven and a real coven going. But they've been a bit disorganized lately; Fred was supposed to be transferred to a job in Australia by the Pentagon, but during his physical they found he had mild diabetes. The family was living at a motel for a while as they went house-hunting again. They hope to have their covens fully operative soon once more.

"We're traditional witches here," says Fred, which means they use nude ceremonies. "One coven can't generate enough power to stop a war, but we've had a very high batting average with healing spells. We are, of course, practicing only white magic—the left-hand path destroys all those who try to use it."

"When we were getting started fifteen years ago," says Martha, "we joined a very powerful coven in Cincinnati. The Midwest is very interested in witchcraft. You know the witches' newsletter, *Waxing Moon* published by Jo B. Wilson in Topeka, Kansas."

One thing that seemed obvious about the witches I met was that they tend to be artistic persons who enjoy the aesthetics of organized group ritual for its own sake. This is why they're attracted to witchcraft rather than to other approaches to occultism.

Sara Cunningham is a tall, slender, dark-haired lady in her early thirties who put in almost fifteen years as a commercial artist, saving her money so she could quit and devote her full time to the craft. Now instead of drawing posters, she makes love amulets and goes into trances to paint portraits that really appear to change expression as you look at them.

"I always wanted to be a witch when I was a kid," she says. "I *knew* the grown-ups' scare stories were only propaganda. A witch was really a nice, pretty lady who lived in the deep forest and talked to animals." She has four cats, including her familiar, Pepperpot. A familiar, in witch terminology, is a pet that has a magical bond with its owner and assists in carrying out enchantments.

A few Halloweens ago, Sara had the unlucky distinction of becoming the first witch ever arrested in California. The police sent up a stooge to ask for a Tarot card reading, and she was busted under the anti-fortune-telling laws of Los Angeles. She has since sent off for one of those mail-order ordained minister certificates which makes her, as a religious practitioner, immune from arrest.

Like most other serious witches, Sara says it's not correct to charge money for craft ritual or counseling. Occasionally she used to accept fees for trance Tarot readings. Those first years as a full-time witch under these ground rules were not easy. She had a charming but small house in the Hollywood Hills with an extra apartment—she thinks it was a disgruntled ex-tenant she evicted who turned her in to the cops. She had a weekly class in witchcraft at her home for several years. Then Sara inherited a small amount of money and was able to move to a roomier place in Pasadena. She doesn't teach anymore but has a filled-up coven whose rituals tend to be a highlight of most TV documentaries on California occultism.

She says she's the seventh daughter of a Black Irish seventh daughter and was a tomboy adopted by a physicist in Yuma, Arizona. "The witch name for the craft is wicca, which means wisdom in the old language," says Sara. "Wicca is really a method of enlarging your mind to develop ESP awareness. It doesn't deny God and is meant to be used for helping others. Now that I'm a high priestess I am not allowed to defile myself by having sex with a man."

It's a sunny LA afternoon and a suave, graying Frenchman is leaving Sara's pleasantly cluttered home with a folded paper instructing him how to cast the spell that will end his particular problem. "Some girls come to you for a love charm," she says, "and you find they expect it to get them a man who's perfectly happy with his wife and has hardly noticed this girl's attentions. No way. There has to be a foundation to work from. You've got to be very careful with spells. All negative vibrations you send out really do come back at you with redoubled power."

It seems Sara was having trouble with a thoughtless neighbor parking in front of her door all the time, back when she lived in Hollywood Hills on one of those quaint, rustic paths so narrow a car can barely get by. "Finally it got to be too much and one night I slipped out with my candles and oil to make an incantation that would exorcise the cars from my door. I should have spelled out what I wanted in more detail . . . Within forty-eight hours the engine simply dropped out of their car. Then a few days later the transmission went on their second car while they were driving down the hill and one of the passengers got hurt slightly. I should have put into the incantation that nobody was supposed to get hurt . . . And then by the end of the month the negative vibrations came back and made my Mustang go ker-blooey. I blew three tires in a week and had to trade in the car."

The contemporary writers of how-to witchcraft books generally do not try to convince their readers that there's a magic force within the ritual itself. Paul Huson, the handsome young warlock who wrote *Mastering Witchcraft*, says, "The success of a spell depends on the emotion you put into it. You can use anything you like to turn you on and get the current flowing. This is the rationale behind the traditional trappings of witchcraft. Tie the emotion to a single, sizzling bolt with the help of a pattern of spoken words, the charm or incantation. It is the awe, the shiver of emotional excitement aroused by the name of God that is its chief magical value—you can use your spouse, lover, favorite star, or dictator . . . It's all a way of getting at your deep mind . . . contacting entities that are really forces dependent on your attentions."

The most visible witch around today, Mrs. Louise Huebner, agrees with this in her book *Power Through Witchcraft*.

"Witches use props to get in the mood. I use candles, bells and other things because I was raised to believe they were necessary and I am comfortable with the old methods. What you are doing is psyching yourself into believing that because you do one action another will result. If you do it often enough, like using candles, you become very confident in that action and it works for you. My grandmother, a good, old-fashioned fortune-telling witch, feels that the flame of a candle can change the atmosphere and create vibrations. That may be true although I'm not sure. I believe it is my own energies and the action only helps me. A very strong person can do without the candles and other objects.

I know I'm becoming more and more able to cast spells without props."

Louise Huebner is a mother of three whose husband, Mentor, is a top Hollywood set designer. She looks the part of the seductive witch with her curvy figure, long black hair, dark eyes, and creamy complexion. As a matter of fact, she won a scroll naming her Official Witch of Los Angeles County for a public spell aimed to "increase the sexual vitality" of LA. This was probably the largest-scale spell of modern times; Louise did it at a 1968 free summer entertainment fest at the Hollywood Bowl. Adorned in one of her sexy silver maxi-robes, she passed out red candles, garlic, and chalk and instructed one and all to draw magic circles around themselves and chant three times, "Light the flame, bright the fire, red the color of desire." As the occult explosion kept growing, Supervisor Eugene Debs became aware that his tongue-in-cheek proclamation of Louise as official county witch was being used for a lot of solid commercial mileage and he disavowed the whole thing. Louise's return bombardment was unilaterally to rescind her LA sexual vitality spell. But effects of the spell and its revocation on Los Angeles sexuality both remain debatable.

The Huebner haunt is a pleasant, rambling house near the peak of Mount Washington, overlooking the downtown smog through a lattice of trees. The place is filled with Mentor's paintings, the activities of the three kids, and a Mexican housekeeper, plus a motley assortment of animals . . . cats (including Louise's eighteen-year-old familiar, Othello), dogs, rats, snakes, turtles, and giant beetles. When not in her designer robes, Louise is chic and miniskirted. "I have to cast a spell at least every two weeks or I feel frustrated," she says. "I go into a dark room and concentrate on a candle flame; I might burn incense or play music . . . anything I think would turn me on so I feel, 'Okay, now my subconscious has taken over.' I'm psychic—it's a chemical thing, most of my family is too."

Louise gives her pedigree as a sixth-generation witch, going back to Yugoslavia. She grew up in Great Neck, Long Island, the liberal Jewish New York suburban mecca, spending most of her childhood years with her grandmother, who she says could break a glass by mental energy, call praying mantises to come in and sit on her hand, read tea leaves, cards, palms, and horoscopes. Grandma also was a sculptor and musician and had eight kids.

"Until five years ago almost all my work was in astrology, but all of a sudden the interest in witchcraft was there," says Louise. She began building up her showbiz credits making supermarket appearances in the small towns east of LA where she would do fast horoscopes and psychic readings. By 1965 she was doing the same thing on KLAC, the radio station that invented the audience phone-in format. Other local stations call her in for things like Halloween midnight specials and Valentine's Day funky forecasts ("Cancer and Pisces are fated; One hour after meeting they're mated"). She also writes a weekly column for some twenty community newspapers in the *Santa Monica Outlook* chain. Her book, *Power Through Witchcraft,* was excerpted for a Warner's record album under the title *Seduction Through Witchcraft,* which says something about the different marketing approaches in the two media. Louise read her own words, like the recommendation that orgies are good for releasing magical energy, with bleeping electronic effects in the background. Coming up is a witches' cookbook and hopefully a TV series. She has been welcomed to Salem, Massachusetts, as a dear departed daughter and was mobbed on Wall Street when *Life* photographed her organizing another sexual vitality spell during lunch hour.

On a Saturday afternoon I am doing some research shopping in Gilbert's Book Shop at Hollywood and Vine. Along with Larsen's, the Cherokee, and Pickwick's—also on Hollywood Boulevard—this store has one of the best occult book selections in Southern California.

A pair of very All-American, cute, straight, high-school girls come in and one of them asks, "Which is the best book on how to be a witch?"

A logical response seems to be the question, "Why do you want to be a witch?"

"I already am a witch," she says with assurance. "My family belongs to a fundamentalist church in Burbank, and the minister is always warning us to keep away from magical spirits. But I made a love spell that got me the boyfriend I wanted—and I'm going to *keep on* doing witchcraft!"

Chapter 12

The Magical Monsters

WE must also face the dark side of the occult explosion. As so often, the first Distant Early Warning signs of a new social trend came from the avant-garde. During the winter of 1969, Israel Regardie's North Hollywood home was broken into, and his irreplaceable first-edition collection of Aleister Crowley's works disappeared. Within a few months, the same thing had happened to most of California's outstanding Crowley collections.

Regardie's wide occult contacts pretty soon gave him a good idea of who was responsible for the burglaries. Then in August, 1969—shortly before the Sharon Tate household was mass-murdered—every serious occultist in America knew there was a new group of berserk Crowleyites on the loose. The general public didn't know this because journalism in the United States is not widely staffed with reporters who have studied the occult tradition.

The story was a small one but bizarre enough to make all the wire services. Indio, California, out in the date-growing desert east of Palm Springs: Inhabitants on a strange farm commune became annoyed with six-year-old Anthony Gibbons on June 20 for starting a fire that burned down one of their houses and injured a flock of goats.

So little Anthony's parents burned his fingers with matches; then he was chained in a packing crate for fifty-six days as the summer desert heat kept up its usual 100°-plus. Somehow the police eventually got wind of this and arrested the communards. Eleven members, including Anthony's mother, were brought to trial and apparently received light sentences, after which they disappeared—reportedly to Mexico but not for long.

The significant factor in all this came in the bottom paragraph of most of the dispatches. The cult responsible for this child torture was known as the OTO—which UPI spelled out as Ordi Templar Orientalis. Well, that's reasonably close. But we can see that the OTO is really Ordo Templi Orientis, the long-forgotten German sex-magic fraternity which offered Aleister Crowley leadership of its chapter in the British Isles, only to have him absorb the short-lived group into his own would-be magic organization, Argentinum Astrum.

This particular OTO tribe is said to be led by a woman named Jean Brayton (the spelling is problematical). The membership is certainly an object of interest to the FBI. Federal investigators have questioned occult storekeepers in both San Francisco and Los Angeles about the whereabouts of Jean Brayton's OTO. The rumor is there are two interstate murder warrants out on them.

After Anton La Vey made Satanism feasible again, it was only natural to find more free-form underground Devil-worship cliques turning up. Anton himself knows of two or three San Francisco groups put together by his Church of Satan discards who were more interested in kinky orgies than in ceremonial magic. At least they've been nonviolent so far.

Ben Harris of the Timeless Occult Shop on Sunset Strip, the most reliable pipeline to the new occultism in Southern California, says he knows of three Satanist groups in the process of forming, as well as two existing ones in the LA area. In nearby Manhattan Beach, there's a quite respectable bunch of Devil's disciples grouped around a gentleman named Polk. The other extant Angeleno Satanists are reputedly a much more militant crowd, all for smiting the enemies of Satan. They carry guns but so far have only used them to hit people over the head with. The front for this group was a walk-up saloon with Satan in the title, on the raffish eastern end of Sunset Boulevard. It had closed down by the time I began these investigations; all that could be seen out front was the padlocked entry and corny window paintings of the Evil One. The inside decor was supposed to be equally heavy on the cutesy Devil motifs. The leader, Don B., has a funky carnival background that he draws on in creating his rituals.

Only a couple of years ago in Houston, Texas, the police raided a Satanist club and found hidden graves full of animal bones. . . .

As an occultist, Sirhan Sirhan can be dismissed as a dim-witted sorcerer's apprentice. In an earlier time, his symptoms would have probably been classified as demonic possession. As it was, his modern demonology was more indirect . . . Robert F. Kennedy as anti-Arab Zionist fink.

According to the Rosicrucians AMORC, their records show that Sirhan answered an ad in June, 1966, and was dropped from membership after only one month because he didn't pay the $2-per-lesson fee. In jail, he set aside $20 to activate his membership and at one point in court testified that he joined the Rosicrucians because he hoped to develop the mental powers to produce psychic phenomena, visual hallucinations, and thought transfer. During the preliminary hearings, the defense made an attempt to show that Sirhan might have read the May, 1968, *Rosicrucian Digest* which contained an article saying, "Dare to plan something different, just write it down and see how it gains momentum." Sirhan's May 18 diary entry is the famous "RFK must die before June 5." Sirhan's other occult stir was when he requested two Theosophy books for his jailtime reading, Madame Blavatsky's *The Secret Doctrine* and her follower C. W. Leadbeater's *At the Feet of the Master*. This of course prompted the various Theosophical societies to join the Rosicrucians in taking newspaper ads to deny that the assassin ever was active in their movements and that anyway they teach nonviolence. Robert Kaiser's semiofficial Sirhan biography, *RFK Must Die,* raises some tentative evidence which might mean Sirhan Sirhan was hypnotized into murder by parties unknown—Sirhan's raving automatic writings that he claimed he couldn't remember, his ease at going into deep hypnosis during psychiatric interviews, his unusual pauses before answering key questions under hypnosis. But for the immediate future, these speculations are certain to hit the same blank wall as the suspicions of facts yet hidden about the assassinations of President John Kennedy and Reverend Martin Luther King.

Charles Manson is a different story. The five-foot-six, one-hundred-and-thirty-five-pound illiterate ex-con wasn't merely a marginal loner acting on his delusions like Sirhan (wherever Sirhan's delusions came from). Manson was able to control a self-contained tribal family—consisting at any one time of up to twenty women and six males all bigger than Manson—simply through the force of his personality. His ability to lead groups of young people into the most grotesquely self-destructive acts imaginable can only be described as a magical power. Rasputin and Hitler are two historical figures who clearly put the same hypnotic spells over their associates. It's what all the great magicians, Aleister Crowley included, were able to do.

Drugs, of course, helped a lot in Manson's mind-manipulations. But it is the basic talent of a sorcerer to invest his most commonplace actions with an aura of magical significance and get all those around him to share his peculiar vision. Charlie was just so ingratiatingly plausible it hurt. I wrote one of the few critiques of Manson's music. It covered not only an obscure album put out by one of Charlie's jailmates who went on to become LA majordomo for the Rolling Stones, but also the entire four hours of existing Manson tapes from his many recording auditions. Charlie had lots of chances to get a record contract; he was just too undisciplined to follow through. His light voice and pretentious antisocial songs were nothing special, but good enough for airplay, and there have been far worse hits. The time I had to put in listening to those tapes made me feel as if I knew him on a certain level. Particularly revealing was a very strange, muddy tape made after an LSD orgy at the home of Harold True who was the next-door neighbor of Leno and Rosemary La Bianca who got carved up the night after Sharon Tate's massacre with "Death to Pigs" smeared on the refrigerator in their own blood.

Manson, for obvious reasons, was limpidly relaxed the night of the taping and couldn't sing more than a couple of bars of anything before his attention span broke and he started spouting off the little acid guru epigrams he always punctuated by a high, self-conscious laugh—which in retrospect can easily be recognized as the sound of impending madness. Charlie loved cute wordplay that didn't say anything. "Everything is the way it is because that's the way love says so. When you tune in with love, you tune in with yourself. That's not really a philosophy, that's a fact and everybody who's got love in their hearts knows it." Heavy thinking! But all the girls on the tape said "Yeah" with great enthusiasm and after a while it began to sound rather profound. There was *something* about the way Charlie said things.

It was Manson and the Tate/La Bianca slaughter that really made the general public aware there was something extremely dangerous about this new mixture of drugs and occultism. In Hollywood itself, the murders produced an unprecedented malaise that lasted for several months, almost until the Family got arrested. This was really cutting it close to home. Though Robert Kennedy's murder was local too, it had been too major a catastrophe for anybody to feel *personally* threatened. But if you weren't safe in a $200,000 house in a chic canyon, where were you safe?

This genuine feeling among Hollywood image-makers that the fabric of life was falling apart was brilliantly captured by the classic *Esquire* issue, March, 1970—"Evil lurks in California." It was great on the climate of desperation, even if sometimes absurd on facts—with the magazine's long-established horrified-fascination reflex to all things Californian. For example, the story called two of the most namby-pamby teenybopper rock clubs in town, the Climax and Thee Experience (both now defunct), hotbeds of ravening Satan freaks. Naturally their New York research team turned up all the easy people—Morlock, Samson De Brier, Ben Harris. Their real coup was discovering beautiful Princess Leda Amun Ra who, they said, attempts to have sex with swans which she steals from public parks under the very noses of the guards. Even for *Esquire* on California, this was a bit much. I immediately assumed Leda was just another Sunset Strip doper who had picked up a dab of occult jargon to hallucinate on.

Hollywood's movie-recording-TV community is surprisingly small and open. At an old friend's party I met someone who lived a few houses down the street from Leda's consort, dubbed by *Esquire* "The King." So I dropped by one afternoon.

The King goes by the name of Garrison in real life; he's twenty-eight and as an actor has appeared in about sixty movies and TV shows. He is physically a remarkably beautiful male, relaxed and likeable, with a refreshing air of sanity no matter how bizarre the experiences he's describing. *Esquire* said he drives a gold Jaguar with a TV set on the dashboard and is an astrologer who gets $1,000 a horoscope. The actual Garrison has a three-year-old Thunderbird convertible and lives in a teeny but charming basement apartment with one of those superb Hollywood Hills views. He's got a cat, a horse at the beach in Malibu, and a young son from a marriage before he got turned on by LSD.

"Sure, Leda's for real," he surprised me by saying. "She's in touch with an invisible world that has both good and evil angels. She does have zombies around her, mostly homosexuals fucked up on acid and magnetized by Leda's strength and power. She did steal the swan from the park like *Esquire* said. Leda is always getting away with things that are so outrageous nobody believes she's actually doing it, and so they don't try to stop her till it's too late. She lives in the hills just across the freeway, and if you drop in on her any afternoon, she'll talk to you . . . but she won't really *tell* you anything unless you share the holy sacrament with her and go to one of her all-night sessions."

Leda's holy sacrament is, of course, LSD, and the problem with dropping one of her caps is that she makes up her own formula, spiking the dealers' acid with ingredients like speed or strychnine. According to *Esquire,* their photographer on the Leda story "innocently bit into an LSD-spiked apple at the castle and came closer to evil than any of us had planned." According to Garrison, the photographer knew perfectly well what he was sampling and wound up with a three-day stay in the psycho ward of Sawtelle Veterans Hospital after he was found wandering down Sunset Boulevard pulling fire alarms.

"Leda got into the magic thing around 1967 when she divorced her husband and split the suburban scene," says Garrison. "Her four-year-old son lives with her at the temple but I doubt he's aware of what's going on yet." Leda doesn't go club-hopping as much as she used to. When she does pop into her 1937 MG and head down the hills, often as not it's to the cavernous Citadel of Haiti, an obscure discothèque in the unfashionable Vine Street area of Sunset.

"My experiences with Leda have shown me that black magic, physical and mental vampirism and cannibalism really exist. If I had wanted to stay with her any longer I would have had to make a pact to sell my soul for the left-hand path. I always had my own place and my outside life, but we were together a lot for two years until I took off about five months ago. I loved a lot of the things I had there and it was very tempting. But I was not ready to turn in my soul for material life down here. Like it says in the Dylan song 'Frankie and Judas Priest' . . . 'don't mistake the house across the road for heaven' because it's a whorehouse and Frankie screwed himself to death in sixteen days and sixteen nights. I feel that I know a lot about the occult by now; I read some of the books at Leda's but most of my knowledge came from talking with people who are into it. Acid was my open door to a new kind of thinking, and I've had enough of the left-hand path. I didn't know what I was getting into when I started; now I want to be in a more positive metaphysics."

Leda's live-in crowd currently includes a permanent guard named Michael, who never sleeps. When there's enough LSD on hand, the temple hosts an all-night bash every Saturday and Leda can be observed, according to Garrison, "appearing in all her reigning glory with thunder and lightning and fire."

He had one final contact with the dark world of Princess Leda. "I ran into some of Leda's people a couple of Saturdays ago and decided to drop in on her ceremony for old times sake. Leda never threatened me or anything like that when I took off. She seemed to feel that if I was enough of a fool to give it up she wouldn't lower herself by trying to stop me. I say if you're a strong person, you have nothing to fear from Leda; she won't *force* you to do anything against your will. But when I came over that night she started improvising a ritual that became a Satanic wedding of the two of us. It was the hairiest experience I've ever had, the longest night of my life, and it took all my strength to get through it. I wasn't sure I was *permitted* to leave; I was never so happy as when dawn came."

We now descend from psychedelic sorcery to absolute bottom. . . . The sudden spate of brainless Devil-worship murders in California. Meet Steven Craig Hurd, twenty, leader of a Devil-pack consisting of three teen-age boys and a thirty-one-year-old woman. On two consecutive nights in June, 1970, police claim that they killed an Orange County gas station attendant and a schoolteacher, a mother of five, not far from President Nixon's San Clemente summer residence. They apparently forced their way into Mrs. Florence Brown's station wagon when she stopped at the intersection of Interstate 5 and Sand Canyon Boulevard. She was killed in an orange grove near the University of California's Irvine campus and buried in a shallow grave after they cut out her heart, lungs, and an arm to sacrifice to the Devil. The idea was to steal her car for a jaunt up the coast to San Francisco to see the "Head Devil"—definitely not Anton La Vey according to Hurd's lawyer, who also said his client's biggest worry in jail is that there's a Bible in his cell.

The next month another pair of Satan cultists and self-admitted cannibals were nabbed in Salinas for the murder of a Montana social worker near Yellowstone Park. Two young Wyoming hitchhikers, Stanley Baker, twenty-two, and Harry Stroup, twenty, were given a lift by the social worker. They shot him with a .22, hacked his body into six pieces, and ate the heart. Baker told police his craving for human flesh began after he got an electric shock at the age of seventeen. At the time of their arrest they had finger bones in their pockets.

San Francisco's Zodiac Killer isn't exactly a berserk astrologer. He seems to be the usual insane mass murderer after the fashion of the Boston Strangler. Metaphysics, however, enters into his ideology to the extent that in one of his letters to the San Francisco *Chronicle* he wrote that everybody he killed would have to be his eternal slaves in Paradise, signed "Zodiac." The record shows that he has murdered five people since December 20, 1968, though he is currently claiming thirteen. He prefers to sneak up with a gun on couples parked at lovers' lanes in the northeastern Bay Area countryside. The few survivors said he was wearing a hood.

At this writing, the very latest occult-tinged mass murder was the Santa Cruz Tarot killing. This had more to it than just demented occultism. Radicalism, ecology, drugs, and an instant hippie drop-out entered into it—the whole gamut of counter-cultural factors carried to maniacal limits. A wealthy Japanese-American eye surgeon named Victor Ohta was shot along with his wife, secretary, and two of his four children in their ultra-modern home at the wooded community north of Big Sur. The house was set on fire and a note left on the doctor's Rolls-Royce. "Today World War 3 will begin . . . anyone and/or company of persons who misuses the natural environment or destroys same will suffer the penalty of death by the People of the Free Universe." It was signed with the four knights of the Tarot Minor Arcana—wands, cups, pentacles, and swords.

Fortunately, there was a partial fingerprint on the note and within a few days—acting on a tip from outraged local hippies— police arrested runty John Linley Frazier, twenty-four, an ex-auto mechanic who freaked out on the pollution problem after getting heavily into mescaline. Frazier was picked up in his mother's cabin a few miles away from the scene of the crime he had boasted about to neighboring hippies two weeks before he committed it.

How much is the occult explosion responsible for this sort of thing?

It is certainly a contributing factor. But I suggest there are good reasons to believe occultism isn't directly to blame for tripping off violent acts . . . although the whole subject is extremely involved.

For one thing, the new style of occult crime is only a tiny part of the seemingly tremendous increase of violence on all levels of American life today—a violence apparently caused by nationwide tensions over the many rapid social and technological changes going on throughout the United States. However, violence levels are hard to judge. America has had no shortage of violent civil disturbances in its past, but these episodes are nearly all forgotten except by the historians. There was New York's Civil War Draft Riot, which left more dead than practically all other U.S. riots combined—mostly Negroes hung from lampposts by the Irish. And who remembers the Haymarket Square Bombing of 1886, the Whiskey Rebellion during the Presidency of George Washington, the bloody Chicago Police Strike, the 1894 Pullman Strike put down by the Army?

Even in the most peaceful of societies, there are always a few poor wretches who never had a chance in life from the day they were born. Charles Manson and James Earl Ray, the assassin of Martin Luther King, are almost ludicrously perfect examples, born of unintelligent, promiscuous, teen-age mothers and raised in chaotic fatherless homes. It would have taken a miracle to keep them out of trouble. People like this are a time-bomb in our computerized society, liable to go off and murder at any time for the most obscure of motives.

And anybody who needs a motive for the murder he's going to commit anyway tends to fall back on the more obvious social trends available. If, for some reason, goldfish became a hot social topic, a popular fad, there would be at least a few Goldfish Murderers—stuffing the fish down the throats of their victims or signing death notes "The Phantom Guppy."

But the occult explosion is just the newest expression of a force as old as the oldest of human societies. It represents a deep need in mankind's psyche, a vehicle for the hallucinatory approach to the discovery of an ideal universal plan. The line between the idealistic and the delusional is very thin. What is called psychosis today used to be called demonic possession and for good reason. Even before there were popular modern occult symbols around, insane murderers must have felt they were operating according to the rules of some higher existence to which they had risen above the grubby mass of men.

Magic and the occult *are* dangerous. Nobody who has studied the esoteric tradition would recommend fooling with magic in ignorance. But there are many other dangerous things around —the hydrogen bomb, sexual repression, political turmoil. None of these is going to disappear either, because they are currently part of the human situation. The best we can do is learn how to harness their power constructively. In fact, it is all we can do.

One thing is sure, until man's psychic energies—including the spectrum of occult powers—are fully mapped out and brought under conscious control there will be no end to murderers who are madmen posing as magicians.

Chapter 13

What You Can and (Probably) Can't
Fake in Occult Phenomena

WOULD you believe I could see through a blind-fold over cotton wads bandaged on my eyes? That I can see any-thing written in a completely dark room without using mechanical gimmicks? That I can make a table wobble around though I'm standing several feet away and don't have any stooges sitting tableside? Would you believe I can produce spirit raps better than the Fox sisters without using my hands or feet? That I can be tied to a chair in a dark seance room and make luminous spirit ectoplasm appear, moving and growing?

Well, I *can* perform these miracles. And so could you if you sent $12.00 to Robert Nelson Enterprises at 336 South High Street, Columbus, Ohio 43215. It's $3.50 for the X-Ray Eye Act, $1.50 for Super-Normal Vision, $2 for the Mystery of the Gyrating Tables, $4 for the Joe Spook Spirit Rapper, and only $3.50 for the Ectoplasm Kit.

Robert Nelson is a portly, dignified-looking man with a neat pencil mustache. He's been in the Mentalism supply business for more than fifty years, but he started young as a kid magician. Mentalism is the correct term for the stage magicians' specialty of mental magic—mind-reading acts as opposed to sawing a woman in half. Nelson has written some forty how-to books on the subject and has produced a delightful one-hundred-and-thirty-page catalog listing all the gimmicks available for fake telepathy, clairvoyance, precognition, and hypnotism.

Some of the more important tools of the trade are miniature microphone-receivers ($249), a mini code-transmitting unit that sends pulses instead of sound for undetectable close-up work (price on request), impression clipboards that secretly copy what's written on the inserted paper ($6 to $32, depending on how close-up they can be used), pads with built-in carbon paper ($1.50).

Mentalism is a relatively recent category of magicianship, inspired by the nineteenth-century spiritualism craze which first popularized ideas of psychic phenomena. Some categories of magic tricks were actually invented for fake seances, the most obvious being spirit writing on slates. This soon became so familiar that even magic shows avoided the trick as too corny. (Nelson's Deluxe Spirit Slates are $7.50.)

Before World War I the first code mind-reading acts appeared. Generally they consisted of a man and a woman. The one working the audience would pass information to the oracle onstage by translating it to an oral code. The code was basically a memory feat and required hours of daily practice. But it wasn't quite as complicated as it seemed. Take four words—please, what, yes, now. These could be made to mean one set of things the first time the assistant says something to the oracle and an entirely different set when used in a second, third, or fourth sentence. That way a few common word combinations code dozens of different items. Even more baffling seem the silent codes. Somebody in the audience picks a card, any card. Without a word, the assistant lays it on a table, facedown. The mind-reader immediately names the card . . . The performers had a mental image of something like a checkerboard on the table. The message lies in what part of the tabletop the card is placed and at what angle it's laid. There's another branch of mentalism called muscle reading. It's a very spectacular skill you can learn with a lot of practice . . . Something is hidden in a room without the muscle reader's knowledge. He takes one of the witnesses by the arm and "leads" him to the hiding place, cued by nearly imperceptible unconscious movements of the person trying to keep the secret. A really outstanding muscle reader doesn't even need to feel the body; he can stand on a stage and see the audience swaying away from the seat where the selected target has been hidden. Bob Nelson used to include muscle reading in his shows, and he says that with enough experience you just *know* on the subconscious level where things are hidden.

But a whole underworld breed of phony psychics and spiritualists use these same effects not for entertainment but for purported ESP advice. These con artists generally don't appear in theaters or nightclubs, they give "consultations" at their homes or offices, often they travel and appear at meetings in hotel rooms. Or with so legal loopholes available today if they aren't on the road traveling the hotel metaphysical circuit, they might pick up a mail-order ordination and found their own arrest-proof church.

There is a lot less of this hard-core occult fakery than there used to be thirty years ago. The public is better-informed, for one thing. But the main reason is that it simply doesn't pay enough these days to go through the effort of bugging a prospective client's house or hiring investigators to compile a dossier on him. The average neighborhood psychic adviser usually can't command more than $3 to $10 per hour. And a session with a comparatively big-name consultant won't cost more than $15-$25, except for the handful of psychic stars who make most of their income by lecturing anyhow.

The only tool a fake ESP consultant really needs, however, is ever-present human gullibility. And there is a little-known art called "cold reading" which takes fullest advantage of this. Cold reading is the sort of thing traditionally associated with gypsy ladies or carnival fortune-tellers. Shrewd practical psychologists, these people are able to size up clients by appearance and make clever guesses about them. They can tell by the customers' expressions if the guess is right or wrong and immediately change to another line of patter. The cold reader is able to make a question sound like a statement and he feeds back the customers' own information in dramatic, mysterious form. Once he has convinced the client that he sees into the past, all he has to do is predict the future the client wants to hear. "In six months you will meet a tall, dark man," etc. The Nelson catalog offers a special of nine books on all aspects of private-office cold reading for $41 . . . "Sold with the distinct understanding that any information derived from this exposé will be used for legitimate purposes only."

Nelson's Catalog also has a $3 book giving no less than thirty-four methods of reading sealed messages, and there are more listed in Ted Annemann's *154 Practical Mental Effects*, the standard textbook of mentalism. There aren't so many different principles for what the trade calls "sealed billet reading," but these principles can be applied in many different ways. For instance, you can "X-ray" the writing inside most envelopes by holding them up to a strong light. Nelson sells several innocuous-looking props with a built-in light that you can use in front of an audience without being spotted. Also, if you wet an envelope with alcohol it will become transparent until the stuff dries. It's easy to sneak an alcohol-soaked sponge into a pocket or out of sight on the table. You keep your fingers wet and rub the unopened envelope as you "tune in on its vibrations." If you want to open the envelopes to "verify" the contents after sensing them psychically you can use the one-ahead method which requires no props . . . The first question you answer is directed to a stooge planted in the audience and then you open the second envelope. But what you really answer is the question from the first envelope and you stay one-ahead all through the show.

The way you read folded questions is to rip off the corners and palm the middle piece where the writing is. In the old days, a lot of stage mentalists used to hold a little crystal ball in one hand to look into the unknown dimensions. What they were really looking at was the writing they had palmed by this center-tear method . . . or maybe a sheet of questions collected in advance by an assistant using the gimmick clipboard or copy pad.

Mae West, still going strong at seventy-seven, is the chief celebrity fan of dashing Dr. Richard Ireland of Tucson, Arizona, who reads written messages through bandages and a blindfold and says, "I'm not a mentalist; I'm psychic." According to America's senior sex symbol, "There are forces in the room that speak to him. The part of the mind they come in on is the part where you dream, but they do it while you're awake. I'm trying to get USC to set up a department of parapsychology."

Ireland doesn't try to X-ray the questions through their envelopes; he just rips them open onstage. It costs $3 to see him at a hotel meeting room and $15 for one of his private consultations. The admission is $5 to the celebrity nights Mae West hosts for him at her legendary beachfront Santa Monica mansion.

Here are some of the ways to work the blindfold vision trick: The first thing to keep in mind is that cloth is often not as difficult to see through as might be imagined. If you put most handkerchiefs or silk scarves over your eyes and looked into a strong light, you could probably see quite adequately. And even with the most formidable-looking blindfold you can often peek down along your nose and have a little strip of sight directly below. Vision through extra-thick blindfolds such as sleep goggles is accomplished by punching a lot of pinholes through the padding. If cotton pads are put over the eyes, you can squeeze the lids tight and then blink the pads up over your eyebrows under cover of the blindfold. Bandages may also be doctored so that it's possible to blink them out of the way—you scrape most of the adhesive off with a blade and fill the strip with pinholes, then rewind the bandage around the spool again.

Considering all of this, it was only to be expected that when reports started coming out of Russia during the early 1960's that a homely twenty-two-year-old girl named Rosa Kuleshova had taught herself to read with her fingers, magicians like the Amazing Randi—who replaced Long John Nebel when he left WOR—were quick to say, in effect, "Hah, we knew all about doing that stuff when Kuda Bux had his X-ray vision act in the thirties."

But the point is: Just because some psychic abilities can be faked under loose conditions, it does not prove that these same psychic abilities do not genuinely exist! And it is extremely doubtful whether any phonies could remain undetected by the test techniques which have been developed by contemporary parapsychology.

Life magazine sent reporter Bob Brigham to interview Rosa, and he found her to be genuine—after she read his business card with her elbow while he was pressing down his fingers on her eyelids and the position of Rosa's forearm completely blocked the card from view. If you have any doubts this is a foolproof test, please press your own fingers firmly on your closed eyelids and try to open them. Not only is it impossible to open your eyes against the pressure, it is also true that once you remove your hands and do open your eyes, you won't be able to see anything clearly for up to a minute.

Rosa Kuleshova had some blind relatives in her Ural Mountain hometown, Nizhniy Tagil, so she kept them company learning Braille. Then she got the idea that it might be possible to teach the blind how to read more than Braille bump codes with their fingers. She began practicing daily and kept it up for six years. In 1962 she showed her doctor what she could do, allowing him to select the blindfolds and apply them. He brought her before a regional science convention, and soon she was whisked off to the Moscow laboratories of the Soviet Academy of Science.

The most exotic test conditions were devised. Rosa passed with flying colors every time. They wrapped her head like a mummy, shielded her with screens and huge cardboard neck collars. She could distinguish colored papers under glass and sometimes even under metal. Rosa Kuleshova became an instant celebrity, a TV star and hot lecture attraction. As happens so often with new psychic fads, eyeless sight became a national craze. All over the USSR, people were trying to read with their fingers and many soon claimed they could. Practically all were exposed as phonies with no difficulty, but a few actually did test out.

The Soviet scientists investigating this phenomenon turned up long-forgotten reports that Europe's nineteenth-century mesmerists claimed to be able to hypnotize people into skin sight. As recently as 1920, French novelist Jules Romains published a paper on his successful private research with skin sight. By 1963 Russian experimenters were trying to teach children and adults, the blind and the sighted, how to see with their skin. Many of the results were spectacular. Dr. Abram Novomeisky took eighty art students and found that nearly one out of six could learn to recognize the difference between two colors with their fingertips after half an hour of practice. The volunteers reported that different colors feel smooth, sticky, or rough, and you can feel this for several inches above the tinted paper, even if it's covered with glass or metal. The first blind child to learn to see with her fingers was Nadia Lobanova in 1963. At a 1965 psychology conference, Dr. S. N. Dobronravov reported that he'd found skin sight potential in 72 percent of the seven-to-twelve-year-old children he tested.

As for poor Rosa Kuleshova, the pressures of fame hurt her badly for a while. She was caught cheating blatantly and had a nervous breakdown, losing her eyeless sight. The psychologists coaxed back her mental balance by getting her to play cards with them blindfolded and by the time *Life*'s man arrived, she was better than ever at skin reading. She had even learned to follow the shifting patterns across an oscilloscope screen with her fingers.

And of course in 1970, completely independent of all this, came the U.S. development of a machine that scans light waves, replays them as electrical impulses on the skin of a blind person's back, and so transmits visual images directly to the brain, bypassing the eye completely.

The most bizarre development in contemporary occultism has been those "psychic surgeons" who supposedly open up a patient's body by merely touching it or by no more than pointing at it as blood comes up and organs splurt out. However, by the end of 1968, the doyen of bare-handed miracle surgery, Dr. Tony Agpaoa of the Philippines, had been rather conclusively exposed as a sleight-of-hand artist who palms animal blood and tissue from the instant-healing incisions. There were a few cases of patients, just arrived home, who needed an operation to remove the very organs Dr. Tony had supposedly plucked out.

Having started off accepting only donations for his wonderful "God power," Dr. Tony is now said to be gambling, living high on the hog in a splashy resort mansion and paying kickbacks to the tour organizers who arrange healing pilgrimage flights from North America. In 1968 the Filipino police chased him all over the islands for practicing medicine without a license. And these damning disclosures come from Harold Sherman, a long-time psychic researcher who wrote the original *Wonder Healers of the Philippines* in 1967. (Sherman apparently achieved a remarkable well-authenticated success in picking up telepathic communications from the Arctic expedition of Sir Hubert Wilkins in a 1938 experiment.) Sherman still feels he has seen humbler miracle surgeons in the islands taking up the cause where Dr. Tony fumbled.

Another stamping ground for miracle surgeons is Brazil, which has a strong, rather Voodooistic tradition of spiritualism for which the mediums are not supposed to charge fees. Trance surgeon Lourival de Freitas operates drunk with unsterilized kitchen implements and no anesthetic. Unbelievable as it seems, an English writer named Anne Dooley claims she had her infected tonsils removed by Lourival during a painless thirty-five-minute operation, and now she can breathe smoothly again after many years of inoperable bronchitis. Still, she warns against seeking out trance surgeons unless you are considered incurable, and she also makes no claim that they are infallible.

Today no psychic research topic is more controversial than the case of Ted Serios, the heavy-drinking Chicago bellhop who was supposed to be able to think blurry photographs of all sorts of scenes onto the sixty-second-developing films in Polaroid cameras pointed at his head. He apparently lost this gift—at least temporarily—in 1967 with a final photo resembling curtains coming down. But witnesses say that at his peak, Serios could will photographs which looked like the preselected target pictures hidden from him in sealed envelopes.

"Ted worked with the Polaroid because if a regular camera is used, there's always the suspicion of faking pictures in the darkroom," Dr. Jule Eisenbud said at the 1970 ESP Seminar at the University of Maine. "You should have seen what he did one time to the patterns on an oscilloscope screen at my hospital. The electrical engineers were tearing their hair out."

Dr. Eisenbud is the Denver psychiatrist who tested Serios for two years and then wrote about it in *The World of Ted Serios*. He is a debonair, silver-haired man, suave and imposing. His first public involvement with parapsychology was as an expert witness to the Bridey Murphy hypnotic sessions, which took place not far from his home. Eisenbud began publishing occasional articles in the ESP research journals. As the result of a piece trying to demonstrate that it was inherently impossible to have a repeatable psychic experiment, he began to get insistent letters from Curtis Fuller, the publisher of *Fate* magazine, assuring him he'd change his mind about the repeatable ESP experiment if he would come to Chicago and investigate Ted Serios.

Fate published the first story on Ted Serios in 1962. Eight years before, when Serios started working at the Chicago Hilton, a fellow-employee named George Johannes, who was an amateur hypnotist, discovered that Serios was excellent at going into hypnotic trance. Eventually Johannes began experimenting with suggestions that Ted have out-of-body experiences. The results seemed encouraging enough so that he tried to get Ted to clairvoyantly locate hidden treasure around Chicago. When immediate riches were not forthcoming, the idea occurred to him to try making Serios' visions more accurate by recording them on film, first with regular cameras and then—when strange shapes began appearing on film—with instant-picture Polaroids.

This was a spontaneous rediscovery of thought photography, sometimes known as spirit photography or thoughtography. Louis Daguerre invented the first workable photographic process in France in 1839, and within a couple of years "spirit photographers" were claiming they could think the faces of the dead onto photographs. One after another, the stars of spirit photography were exposed at their double-exposures and the British Society for Psychical Research just tried to forget about the whole thing in order to avoid further embarrassment.

Shortly before World War I, Tokyo University professor Tomokichi Fukurai started receiving thought photographs from various professional and amateur psychics. The Japanese have always been enthusiastic about cameras, so that the emergence of pioneering thoughtography in Japan should not be a surprise. Over this span of years, it's impossible to fill in the facts about Fukurai's procedure that would allow us to be sure how cheatproof the work was. But so many phony thought photographers had already been uncovered that the entire subject was discredited as a subject of serious scientific investigation.

The year Dr. Eisenbud's book on Ted Serios appeared there was a critique of its experimental practices in *Popular Photography* by Charles Reynolds and David Eisendrath, Jr., who were each photography authorities as well as expert amateur magicians. They didn't actually catch Ted cheating while they watched him work—nobody ever has. What they did was to suggest Ted could be slipping a tube containing microfilm inside his gizmos. These gizmos were simply the cylinders rolled from the stiff, black paper that comes with each Polaroid film pack. Serios insisted he needed them to "focus his thought waves on the camera lens" and to block out excess light from the sides. Between tries he would keep the gizmo in his pocket. The two investigators noted that Ted's pockets were never searched and that once he refused to let them examine his gizmo after getting a picture. They also pointed out that Ted's drinking during experiments would fit in with the psychology of the card sharp, who may not cheat at more than a couple of hands to win the game but can't afford to be caught even once and has good reason to be nervous. Usually, Ted got only a couple of hits per session, and these tended to come toward the end when the attention of the people supposed to be watching him understandably wore down.

However, there were sessions where Serios got dozens of different pictures, and for a while Eisenbud had been stripping him and sewing him in a monkey suit to rule out any hidden film clips.

The microfilm-tube pictures the *Popular Photography* writers offered as their comparison samples were a lot more restricted than Ted's work and certainly weren't produced secretly under test conditions with hostile witnesses looking on. Dr. Eisenbud found other photography experts to testify that the nature of Polaroid cameras and film made it impossible for this kind of trickery to work. A mainstay of his argument was that Ted's pictures never came out the same way twice, so he must have been making and hiding an impossible amount of microfilm tubes in his pockets to get those results.

But a much more spectacular argument for the genuineness of Ted Serios' thought photographs is the kinescope film edited from a six-hour experiment with Ted at the studio of KOA-TV, the NBC station in Denver.

We see Serios lurching around in a black knit shirt with nothing up the short sleeves. If he isn't dead drunk, he is performing the greatest imitation of a lush since movie character-actor Jack Norton. Ted is a wiry little bantam of a man who looks as if he belongs in a gangster film playing the mob runt. Born in 1918 at Kansas City, Missouri, of a WASP mother and a Greek diner-operator father who used to wrestle professionally, Serios is one of life's natural losers. However, he's no menace to society and has never been jailed for anything more serious than being drunk and disorderly.

The secret target theme Ted is supposed to reproduce is "Wheels" from a *Life* pictorial history of transportation. He is surrounded by four TV newsmen, three cameramen, a squad of Eisenbud's friends with some special knowledge of photography —such as the audio-visual services director of the University of Colorado Medical Center, a Denver University technical photographer, a professor of engineering optics. These observers are all taking notes on each other with their stopwatches clicking as they break open the new boxes of Polaroid film to load cameras that Serios isn't allowed to touch. A reporter from the Denver *Post* is rolling up the gizmos.

The kinescope shows Ted producing a few vague circular images on the Polaroid film, then later some fuzzy pictures which could be the dim outlines of cars and buses. He grunts and belches, exhorting fate like a crapshooter while he shoves his hand at the camera lenses as if to force pictures onto the film.

By the time Ted has finished his sixth quart bottle of beer, he is cheerfully incoherent and increasingly megalomaniac. The crew and observers are disgusted because nothing has happened for hours. They begin to pack up, and Serios is crushed at no longer being the center of attention.

"Let me at the video camera," Ted suddenly yells. He burps and comes running at one of the RCA Orthicons, giving it his full whammy. The lens picks up a wild-eyed Serios coming at it, pushing his hand out, apparently holding a gizmo. Then an image comes in from the edge of the picture and all at once the entire screen is filled with a strange jumble of moving patterns.

The slow motion replay lasts almost three minutes, a sequence of pictures that looks a lot like wheels, autos and buses, fading in and out. One of the images holds distinct for at least a second. There is no way in the world this could have been done with microfilm tubes or sleight-of-hand or magnets or any other natural method yet known.

Chapter 14

The Psychic Gift

MOVIE star Glenn Ford bought the rights to *Psychic,* an autobiography of Peter Hurkos, during the mid-1960's and was planning to produce the film and star in it. "While I was working on this project, Peter and I became good friends," says Ford, "and I witnessed some incredible things."

When Hurkos visited the country house Glenn Ford was then building in Wisconsin, the famous Dutch-born psychic announced, "This cement foundation is no good in one place." Ford says, "I frankly didn't pay too much attention. But the next year a big rain undermined the wall at the exact spot Peter had pointed out and my whole cellar was flooded."

Shortly after the rainstorm made Hurkos' prediction come true, he was shown a car that Ford had just bought his son to drive at college. Peter Hurkos told Ford, "I see this car painted red and going over a cliff."

"By this time I had enough faith in Peter so that I got my son another car and had him sell the first one at school," says Glenn Ford. "A few months later, the car we'd sold went down a cliff along Angeles Crest Highway. Fortunately, nobody was injured seriously . . . But the wreck showed that underneath a coat of black paint the auto was really red!"

Most remarkable of all was the evening Hurkos and Ford were dinner guests of Dr. Alex Harley, Santa Monica Hospital chief of staff. At the party were eight professors from UCLA Medical School, including a dentist who used hypnosis in his practice.

"Peter agreed to let himself be hypnotized," Ford says. "And when he was under, he started telling the doctors what operations they had performed that day, what happened in the surgery room, what the patients looked like and how the next day's laboratory test results would come out. I don't even see how he could have known all these guests were doctors. But Peter's better if he comes in cold and doesn't know anything about you . . . He told one doctor that he'd operated in the afternoon on a Mexican woman for kidney stones and there had already been two prior operations, but this time there wouldn't be any malignancy showing in the tests. *Then, right in the middle of this, Peter stopped and told how there was a Cuban missile crisis coming up and President Kennedy would have to announce it in a few weeks.* The whole thing was taken down on a tape recorder!

"I've seen Peter Hurkos be wrong, but I've also seen him amazingly accurate many times," says Ford. "Before I met him, I hadn't really been that convinced of the existence of ESP. I have a great respect for Peter, and the only reason my movie of his life story never came off was that we couldn't arrange clearances to use the names of all the key people involved. If these permissions were wrapped up, I'd go ahead with the film in a minute."

The psychic gift is the raw material of occult powers, down-to-earth and with no coating of esoteric dogma. The most universal format for a spontaneous psychic experience is someone sleeping —or at least in a very relaxed, passive state of mind—who gets a brief, vivid picture of a person close to him who is in a desperate emergency, often in the process of being injured or of dying. Is there any family that *doesn't* have a story like this? My family has this one: Back in czarist Russia, my grandmother dreamed that her oldest son—gone off to America to prepare the way for the rest of the clan to immigrate—was lying hurt on a strangely patterned wood floor and dressed in some kind of a white suit. Of course a letter soon came with the news . . . My uncle had broken his leg when he slipped on the scaffolding in his white coveralls early in his new career of installing the fancy wooden floors that were all the rage prior to World War I.

This sort of in-the-family spontaneous psychic event has probably done more than anything else to open people's minds about the reality of ESP and occult divinations. The 600,000-circulation London *Evening Standard* started a Central Premonitions Registry in 1967 after psychiatrist J. C. Barker verified twenty-two cases of advance psychic warnings about the Aberfan,

Wales, disaster where a mountain of coal waste behind the mining village "crept" and buried alive one hundred and fourteen people. The American Central Premonitions Registry was recently started by ASPR member R. D. Nelson, thirty-four, manager of the New York *Times* college and school service department. Nelson and his wife, Nancy, currently have over 1,000 predictions filed at their apartment. Hunches and dreams can be mailed to Box 482, Times Square Station, New York, New York 10036.

These registries are exactly the tool we need to find out how historical precognition actually works. Three million copies have been sold to date of Ruth Montgomery's *A Gift of Prophecy: The Phenomenal Jeane Dixon*. Washington, D.C.'s socialite crystal ball seeress became internationally famous on the strength of her prediction in the *Parade* syndicated Sunday supplement of May 13, 1956: "A blue-eyed Democratic President elected in 1960 will be assassinated." However, by 1960 she was predicting that Richard Nixon would beat John F. Kennedy. And Ruth Montgomery's 1970 memoir of her journalistic career, *Hail to the Chiefs*, complains that her *Gift of Prophecy* publishers "insisted on deleting most of my references to Jeane Dixon's many wrong predictions, leaving in mainly those on which she had hit correctly." It's a good thing Jeane Dixon is wrong a lot, because she predicted World War III would come in 1958 over a Red Chinese invasion of Formosa.

The greatest psychic of the classic occult era was Nostradamus, the Latinized pen name for Michel de Notre Dame, a French medical professor credited with heroic service during the Marseilles plague of 1546. As a seer, he was the favorite of France's Queen Catherine de Medici. But he is remembered today for his book, *Centuries*, published in 1555, a prophetic history of the era to come expressed in more than nine hundred ambiguous poetic quatrains.

The first of his historic predictions came true four years after publication. Nostradamus had written, "The young lion shall overcome the old on the field of battle in single combat. He will pierce his eyes in a cage of gold. This is the first of two blows, then he dies a cruel death."

In 1559, Nostradamus' patron, King Henry II, was jousting in a tournament with one of his young noblemen. They were both wearing lion emblems as the Comte de Montgomery's lance accidentally slipped through the gold cage of the king's visor. Henry II died with a splinter deep in his eye which kept him in agonizing pain for ten days. The second blow Nostradamus predicted came when the heir to the throne, Henry III, was stabbed to death and the assassination ended France's rule by the House of Valois.

Merlin, King Arthur's wizard, has been credited with saying, "Henceforward I shall not speak before the people or at court save in obscure words, nor will they know what I mean until they see it come to pass." Even today, this is a standard technique of commercial oracles.

But there's a lot more than this to Nostradamus, according to Stewart Munro Robb, a musician, writer, translator, and psychic researcher who interpreted Nostradamus' correct prophecy of the entire course of World War II in British newspapers during England's most desperate hours. Robb says there is no problem in understanding what Nostradamus is saying before-the-fact if you teach yourself what he means by his precise choice of words and symbols. He believes Nostradamus predicted a big war for the end of the twentieth century when "The Oriental . . . shall pass through the sky . . . and shall strike everyone with his rod." But this would lead to an era of peace and prosperity lasting for some 2,000 years, after which the world would end in what reads like a nuclear holocaust at a date estimated as 3797 A.D.

To return to Peter Hurkos. He is rough-hewn, likeable as a teddy bear, and extremely earthy. His unpretentiousness has probably been a vital factor in helping him keep his sanity while past, present, and future jumble together within his mind. It's hard to believe that someone as robust as Peter is already in his sixties, but he was born in 1911 in the Dutch town of Dordrecht. His early life is a prototype of the European working-class situation between the two world wars. He sailed as a merchant seaman, got married and had children, came ashore to work with his father as a housepainter. In 1941, near the start of the German Occupation, he took his famous fall from a four-story building. He had major brain surgery and was in a coma for four days. Apparently the injuries to his midbrain caused some significant rearrangements in the circuitry of the neural switchboard. His psychic visions began almost immediately after he regained consciousness. The first was about a patient who was leaving the ward that day. Peter suddenly *knew* that the man was a British secret agent and would be shot down in the street by the Gestapo that very afternoon. His frantic warnings were dismissed as hallucination by the hospital staff and Peter was unable to prevent the tragedy.

Following his recovery, he served in the Dutch underground with bravery and was decorated after V.E Day by Queen Wilhelmina. But Peter found it impossible to go back to a normal life in peacetime. The psychic impressions that kept bombarding him made concentration on a regular job beyond his powers, his tormented confusions understandably made him difficult to get along with, and his first marriage broke up. To this day, Peter's memory and attention span are far below normal, and he's the first to admit he often can't find his own shoes.

He began hanging around a coffeehouse in The Hague, giving psychic readings for small change. But in a comparatively short time, he developed a solid reputation with feats such as telling a distraught wife where her missing husband would be found drowned and psychically detecting a rich young firebug who'd been considered above suspicion in the investigation of a rash of arsons. Peter received a written commendation from the Pope for helping solve the murder of a priest in Amsterdam—and indirectly for not revealing that the murderess was mother of the priest's illegitimate child. Peter based himself in Paris, was able to be of help to the French police, and earned his living giving psychic demonstrations across Europe. Dr. Andrija Puharich, a Yugoslavian-American neurologist turned ESP investigator, read a *Paris Match* story about Peter's successful work aiding a medical researcher on a polio vaccine project, and he invited Hurkos to his Maine laboratory for what was originally to be six months of testing, but which stretched to two and a half years. "Dr. Puharich showed me I could do a lot more than I thought I could," Peter says of this period. "In the beginning, I would say, 'No, I must be wrong, it doesn't seem possible.' I was confused and unsure. That's over. Now when I hit, I catch it and know it. I understand it more now and I'm more sure of myself." He now feels that his psychic "TV pictures" are now about 87 percent correct.

Peter Hurkos insists that the Charles Manson mass murder is

his last crime case. The strain of spiritually reliving these gory events makes him sick for days. He says he is under police orders not to reveal the results of his visit to the Sharon Tate murder house until all Manson's appeals are heard by higher courts. But a story was printed well before the arrest of Manson and his followers to the effect that Peter has said a group of LSD-fogged killers was involved and that the actual physical murderer was a bearded fellow named Charlie who also had the initials D. W. — Charles D. "Tex" Watson? Peter's last psychic detective job on public record was concerned with the 1969 Ann Arbor coed murders. Even when first contacted about the case by the Detroit *Free Press,* he visualized a description of a slight, intellectual, motorcycle-riding student that tallied almost exactly with John Norman Collins, an Eastern Michigan University senior arrested for the crimes some weeks later with the help of key clues found by Peter in the Michigan college town. Peter has never asked for or gotten more than expenses and small fees from the citizens' groups that usually recruit him for murder investigations. Sometimes the promised payment never comes through at all—as in the Boston Strangler case, according to Norma Lee Browning's authoritative new biography, *The Psychic World of Peter Hurkos.* Incidentally, Hurkos insists to this day that he found the real Boston Strangler and that Albert DeSalvo just confessed to the crimes to get some money for his family by selling the story . . . learning the details from the genuine Strangler whom he'd met in the insane asylum.

Peter will still accept assignments to find missing persons. One recent success was the locating of a private plane lost over the Arizona mountains for two weeks with five men aboard. He ran his finger over a map laid upside down so the place names wouldn't distract him. On March 28, 1970, a sheriff's posse found the Piper Cherokee on Taylor Peak near the town of Pima, almost exactly where Peter had pinpointed it, in a heavily wooded area that had hidden the crash site from air searchers.

He has lived in Hollywood since 1960 and now has a sprawling ranch house in the Studio City area of the Hollywood Hills. A neighbor and close friend is retired World War II General Omar Bradley. Peter does remarkable things with his luxuriant garden and began playing operatic arias by ear on his $6,000 electric organ as soon as the delivery man told him how to turn it on. He's never had any painting lessons either, but around 1967 he suddenly began sitting down at his kitchen table in the middle of the night and fingerpainting very good representational landscapes and still lifes in a couple of hours. He sells a lot of these pictures right off the walls and has given away even more. Over the years, Peter has become quite a dashing figure. He wears Filmland's colorful, expensively casual clothes; his first involvement in the Sharon Tate murders came about through his being a regular customer of victim Jay Sebring's ultra-expensive barber salon. He even has a *Peter Hurkos Predicts* column in *Rona Barrett's Hollywood* ("Raquel Welch: I see divorce in your future. You and your husband, Patrick Curtis, may be indignant at this prediction, but I tell what I see!") Peter rarely gives private consultations anymore, but he has a fairly active schedule of public appearances. He's played at nightclubs and at a Lake Tahoe casino, but now he mostly gives demonstration-lectures in theaters and colleges. When his gift is working at full wattage, the psychic hits make smashing entertainment in themselves. But when he's on a cold streak, Peter is just too honest to be able to cover it up with a showman's glibness. He himself admits he'd rather be taking part in some solid ESP research program, but so far a psychic talent as wildly spectacular as Peter's is scares off the major foundations that are currently the only source of funds for parapsychology in the United States.

Despite all the glamor and pizazz of his life today, Peter Hurkos makes no secret that he'd prefer to be back painting houses or gardening. "I don't concentrate at all and it comes . . . like a TV picture. If it was only eight hours a day I would be the happiest man in the world. But it's always there, day and night, day and night."

Hurkos is often compared to another Dutchman of about sixty, Gerard Croiset, who remained in Holland and has been associated for more than twenty years with the ESP research of Professor W. H. C. Tenhaeff at Utrecht University. Croiset is reported to have psychically traced four hundred of five hundred lost children successfully, usually just phoning in his visions of their whereabouts. But for some years Croiset has been devoting most of his career to treating up to one hundred patients a day at his spiritual healing clinic. Many of his clients keep coming back year after year, thoroughly convinced that Croiset has worked wonders for them.

There exists a fascinating ASPR confidential report from 1964 when Croiset was in New York in connection with his biography, *Croiset the Clairvoyant.* He made a psychometry reading of an object from a murder case and came up with clues that proved to be true when the police checked them out. The New York detective lieutenant taking part in this demonstration said he'd be happy to work with the Dutchman again any time. Croiset's healing produced measurable muscle movements in the leg of a paralyzed patient at Rockland State Hospital with the director of research looking on. At an ASPR meeting, Croiset worked his healing on a polio-crippled MD who reported noticeable sensations in his paralyzed leg.

There is also what appears to be an absolutely foolproof long-distance precognition experiment made with Gerard Croiset in January, 1968, by Dr. Jule Eisenbud, the psychiatrist who carried out the thought photography work with Ted Serios. Eisenbud flew to Holland and made a film of Croiset describing a man and a woman who would attend a public ESP meeting at Denver a couple of weeks later. Eisenbud also filmed the actual meeting at Denver International House. The audience filled out questionnaires as they entered and then watched the movie of Croiset. The woman described in advance by the Dutchman was supposed to have had a recent emotional upset dealing with page 64 of a book she was reading. A Mrs. Olinger said she'd been upset at a page in a cat book about putting felines to sleep. "I recently had to put my daughter's beloved old cat to sleep and felt very guilty over it," she said. Phoning home verified the book page as 64. Then a Mr. Tuck confirmed detailed statements Croiset had made about him, such as, "He has a coat with green spots, made by a chemical from his work in a scientific laboratory."

Why do so many top psychics seem to be Dutch? "All the peoples along the North Sea have inherited psychic gifts," says Lotte von Strahl, one of Europe's great ESP stars during the 1930's. About five-feet-nine, and bursting with white-haired regal presence, Lotte is the daughter of a Dutch diplomat and the widow of a German baron, an opponent of Hitler. She became a psychic to Hollywood celebrities after arriving in the United States following World War II and finding that without a college degree her fluency in nine languages and high-level international contacts qualified her only for a job mopping office floors.

"No, no, my dears, you know what you can do with that," she said and hung out her shingle as a psychic reader. When she moved in the cream of Continental society during the thirties she donated her talents free to the European police and to pioneer ESP researchers. She still prefers the challenge of performing clairvoyant diagnoses for doctors and psychometry for criminal lawyers. But the Louis XIV living room of her antique-filled little apartment across from UCLA is crowded with photos gratefully autographed by the likes of Goldie Hawn and Laurence Harvey.

The New York chapter of the Association for Research and Enlightenment is on two floors above a Chinese restaurant around the corner from Macy's. The reception room is a warm little library full of books on metaphysics and psychic phenomena. Gathered around the coffee table is a constantly shifting group of younger people—bright-eyed theatrical and Greenwich Village intelligentsia types by appearance—cheerfully pasting the addressograph labels on about 2,000 ARE monthly newsletters. "Young folks and even hippies are checking out Edgar Cayce," says Shane Miller, sixty-three, a biographer and author of children's books who's been in the ARE for more than twenty-five years. "We have a group of about forty young people who take over our meditation hall Wednesdays to do their own thing and it's really been exciting what they come up with. Cayce left a laymen's movement; he believed his gift was latent in everybody and should be developed."

Edgar Cayce is generally accepted as the most powerful psychic of modern times. He died in 1945 at the age of sixty-eight leaving behind 14,249 psychic reading transcripts dating from 1923. A $100,000 Remington Rand information retrieval system has just been installed at ARE headquarters in Virginia Beach, Virginia, to open up the mass of material with the use of some 200,000 indexed topic cards. Cayce, born to a fervently religious farm family outside Hopkinsville, Kentucky, in 1877, was apparently able to put himself into a hypnotic sleep in which he could answer questions about the illnesses of persons perhaps thousands of miles away—and eventually his answers to questions about the meaning of life grew into a complete, complex theory of reincarnation, destiny, and lost chapters from history.

The Association for Research and Enlightenment is led by Cayce's two sons, Hugh Lynn and Edgar, Jr., together with Gladys Turner, who was the stenographer who transcribed Edgar Cayce's sleep prophecies for twenty-two years. In 1956 there were only 2,000 ARE members worldwide, but with the occult explosion came a Cayce revival and membership is now at 13,000, growing faster than ever. Nobody is sure exactly why, but America's most active ARE cities are Cleveland and Pittsburgh. There's also a sharp new focus of interest around Phoenix, where a clinic specializing in Cayce's system of medical treatment has been opened by a husband-and-wife team of MD's who belong to ARE. The organization itself began in 1931 in response to a trance answer by Cayce about what would be the best way to carry on his psychic teachings.

The basic ARE activity is called the Search for God group. Ideally consisting of twelve members, it conducts discussions around a textbook of meditations taken from the Cayce readings by the first such experimental group in Norfolk, Virginia. Cayce's meditation technique is known as affirmation, a way of holding but not seizing metaphysical ideas that is said to heighten perceptions and quiet the restless state of normal waking consciousness the sleeping psychic described as a "monkey mind." ARE functions also include healing prayer meetings and even economic healing groups. "Cayce taught that healing power can be raised within a group and can be broadcast mentally," says Shane Miller.

Photographs of Edgar Cayce show a gentle, bespectacled man looking a bit like a smaller Dwight Eisenhower. He didn't get beyond grade school and apprenticed himself to a photographer. In 1901, when he was twenty-four, he mysteriously lost his voice, and a year of traveling from doctor to doctor brought no help. Then a touring theatrical hypnotist was able to make Cayce speak naturally again while under trance, but posthypnotic suggestion didn't take. Finally a local osteopath and amateur hypnotist got the idea that a hypnotized Cayce might be able to diagnose himself. Put to sleep, Cayce announced that nerve strain was paralyzing the muscles of his vocal cords and "It may be removed by increasing the circulation to the affected parts by suggestion while in the unconscious condition." Shortly after this treatment restored Cayce's voice, the osteopath-hypnotist developed severe stomach problems and tried Cayce on a sleep diagnosis. The prescription of drugs, diet, and exercise cleared up the symptoms in short order.

Hypnotic experiments like this were not at all uncommon around the turn of the century, and the osteopath kept bringing around more and more local patients who found that Cayce's ideas for treatment cured them. Often included in the readings were bits of clairvoyant information about the patient's past and distant surroundings that checked out with a phenomenal degree of accuracy.

Soon Cayce learned to put himself into trance sleep without any hypnotist's aid, and he found he could diagnose patients many miles away, as long as they were in a preappointed place at the time of the reading. Once, when challenged, Cayce psychically traced the morning route of a skeptical executive to his Manhattan office from down in Virginia Beach. The report, phoned to the executive as he arrived at his desk, included such details as the buying of one more cigar than usual at a tobacco store and walking up the stairs to the office instead of waiting for the elevator. Asked to read on a murder in remote Canada, Cayce said that one of two spinster sisters shot the other because they were both in love with the same man and the pistol was stuffed down a drain in the house—he even gave the serial number. When the gun was found, the sister confessed. As always, Cayce refused a reward. He never charged a set fee for his trance readings, merely accepted donations based on the client's ability to pay. He also consistently refused to make public appearances or advertise, continuing to support his family as a photographer until the demands for his readings made this impossible. The drain on his health of going into psychic trance more than twice a day—which he was continually doing in response to emergency pleas by the desperately ill—may have shortened his own life.

The ARE claims that when Cayce's prescriptions were followed, cure was almost inevitable. The organization was in no position to be able to keep complete follow-up records over the decades, but certainly the hundreds of letters on file at ARE headquarters testify that Cayce diagnoses led to spectacular cures in cases judged hopeless. One grateful patient was wealthy enough to build a block-long oceanfront mansion at Virginia Beach for a Cayce Hospital where physicians, osteopaths, and chiropractors treated the ill using the sleeping psychic's recommendations. Unfortunately, the hospital was founded in 1929, and its benefactor promptly lost everything in the Stock Market crash. It was only with the new Cayce resurgence that the ARE was able to buy the building back to use as its international center.

Cayce's second phase began as accidentally as his sleep healership. A wealthy printer from Dayton, Ohio, convinced him that his psychic gifts were being wasted unless Cayce also used them to explore philosophic issues. In 1923 Cayce began giving the first of his 2,500 life readings. The devout Christian, a lifelong Sunday school teacher, was at first horrified to find that his psychic voice insisted on the reality of reincarnation. But as the system expanded, it focused on Christ as the ultimate perfected soul who had worked out all his karma.

Shane Miller says, "Cayce was something like an Old Testament prophet. What I like about his system is that it teaches that you are responsible for your own karma."

But others, although genuinely awed by Cayce's psychic record, may find it impossible to accept the metaphysics that came through in his trances. A not untypical Cayce past-life reading informed a wheelchair-bound mother of three that she had suddenly been stricken down by polio as punishment for having persecuted the Christians in Nero's Rome. By now, many ESP experiments such as the telepathic dream study at Maimonides Hospital have indicated that all psychic phenomena are filtered through the confused misinformation of the subconscious mind —which subjects every ESP insight to rather classic Freudian patterns of symbolic distortion. It's reasonable to expect this process to operate more strongly on abstract philosophical speculations which don't have the anchor of a human target situation to focus on.

A remarkable thing about Cayce readings on any subject was that they apparently never contradicted themselves, even though delivered during trances as far apart as thirty years. Cayce's lavishly detailed history of the lost continent of Atlantis has the sweeping grandeur of an epic poem. But by far the most exciting thing that has happened to the ARE movement since Cayce's death was the 1968 discovery of undersea ruins off the coast of Bimini Island in the Caribbean Sea—ruins that appeared to be the pillars of some great temple. "There will be new lands seen off the Caribbean Sea," Cayce had said in 1934. And it was in 1940 that he predicted, "Poseidia will be among the first portions of Atlantis to rise again—expect it 1968 and 1969—not so far away . . . The temple will rise again."

One of the greatest and most unique modern psychics, Eileen Garrett, passed away in September, 1970, at the age of seventy-seven. She was quite a formidable Irish lady who never lost her zest for life despite much illness and travail . . . the deaths of several children and husbands. Spurts of psychic intuition she'd had from childhood were channeled during the twenties at the British College of Psychic Science, directed by the remarkable Hewat McKenzie, one of the toughest-minded and least doctrinaire of spiritualist researchers. Mrs. Garrett became a trance medium, complete with control spirit voices, and her prowess at announcing obscure personal details from her sitters' lives made her one of the two or three most respected British mediums of her day.

Then in 1929, McKenzie died and Eileen was invited to visit the United States by the ASPR. She took a trip down to Duke University and was tested out with the then-new ESP cards of Dr. Rhine. Her results were not spectacular, and she said she could never work up sufficient interest in card guessing to feel attuned to the test situation. Rhine's younger associate, Dr. J. Gaither Pratt, now of the University of Virginia, put Eileen into more mediumistic experiments, having her perform seance readings of strangers hidden from her by a screen. Pratt says she came up with some astonishing hits, but the Duke Parapsychology Center never followed it up or published a report because of Rhine's insistence on concentrating on the accumulation of mass statistics of ESP in average persons.

But Eileen Garrett was gradually coming to believe that her spirit controls were part of her subconscious and that the real road to understanding paranormal phenomena was through psychic research. She threw herself into this work with her usual gusto.

She had always been a businesswoman and a writer, and before World War I she ran a literary coffeehouse that was a rendezvous for authors such as D. H. Lawrence. In 1941, after a hairbreadth escape to America from occupied France, she founded a magazine and publishing company that were from the first more metaphysical and less literary than she intended. In 1951 she rearranged her activities around her new Parapsychology Foundation. The foundation is now one of the most important organizations in ESP research. It has given grants for many of the most ambitious psychic research projects of the past twenty years, with the help of patrons like former Cleveland Congresswoman Mrs. Frances Bolton. It has one of the best libraries of paranormal literature in the world at its offices on East Fifty-ninth Street in the heart of Manhattan's art-gallery row. (In a typically canny investment, Eileen bought the entire building for the foundation and supported the salaries of the twelve staff members by rentals.)

Eileen Garrett also held private group seminars each summer with top ESP scientists on various topics at her villa on the French Riviera and published a scholarly journal which she dropped after ten years only because there weren't enough quality research papers around to fill all the parapsychology magazines now in existence. Her unexpired subscription list was a great boost in helping James Bolen start his *Psychic* magazine in 1969.

For four decades Eileen Garrett's most famous exploit as a medium was her contact with the captain of Britain's R-101 dirigible two days after it blew up on its maiden flight in October, 1930. She was in seance trying to contact Sir Arthur Conan Coyle when her guide Uvani broke through with Flight Lieutenant H. Carmichael Irwin, who started reeling off his near-hysterical orders as the R-101 went down, complete with detailed mechanical terms and obscure naval slang that Mrs. Garrett, who didn't even drive a car, would have no reason to know.

And in the ASPR Journal of January, 1968, is a thoroughly authenticated report of a more current Eileen Garrett performance *which must be taken to prove clairvoyance*. Lawrence Le Shan, a well-respected parapsychologist based at Mills College in New York, wrote that he phoned Eileen at the foundation and said nothing but, "I have a problem requiring your assistance.

Do you have a few minutes you could spare me today?" He showed up with a two-inch square from a shirt worn by a Midwestern doctor the day before he disappeared from his home. Le Shan had never met the doctor or any of his family; it was Mrs. Le Shan who looked up the doctor's wife—an old schoolmate she hadn't seen for years before their marriage—while visiting the Midwest.

In two sessions ten days apart, Eileen came up with the following correct information as tape-recorded and transcribed by Le Shan: A man disappeared . . . His wife is upset and seeking his whereabouts . . . I see him at La Jolla . . . I am sure he thought of going to California and then on to Mexico." She accurately described the doctor as in his middle forties and about five-feet-ten, who has recently lost weight, a former child prodigy who lost his father as an adolescent. At the final session she predicted that the doctor would contact his wife very soon now if he hadn't done so already. Two hours after this a letter from the doctor in La Jolla arrived at his home. He had decided to return and face his problems.

With Cayce and Eileen Garrett dead, the most powerful psychic living today may well be Bulgaria's Vanga Dimitrova, a blind woman in her fifties who looks as if she had just stepped out of a Brueghel painting of peasant life. In the old days people would crowd into her yard at the Bulgarian border village of Petrich and demand readings. Sometimes she gave as many as fifty a day, and her health was breaking down. But by the middle of the 1960's she had become a governmental research project. A committee now screens the applications for sessions so that Vanga won't be overworked. Fees are $5 for Bulgarians and $30 for foreigners. Vanga gets a salary of $200 a month. She is given a thorough physical daily to be correlated with her long-term results. Every year, 3,000 questionnaires are sent out to people read by Vanga, asking them to rate the accuracy with which her predictions came true. The total statistics so far show that Vanga Dimitrova is seeing into both the past and the future 80 percent correctly.

For all practical purposes, Shirley Harrison is almost unknown south of Boston. But in northern New England she got wide attention when she successfully predicted where two downed private planes would be found in 1964 and 1965. At a 1966 demonstration for the psychology department of Maine University's Gorham branch she scored 80 percent right in tests such as holding a sealed box and accurately describing both the ring inside and its owner.

Shirley is a petite, quietly attractive mother of six who has never taken a cent for what she calls her God-given gift. She says she had her first vision at the age of five, when she described to her mother that man she'd seen puttering in the garden next door and was told it was a neighbor who'd died long before her birth. In 1963, at the age of forty, she wrote to Mrs. Louisa Rhine at Duke University, went down and was tested by William Roll of the Rhine's parapsychology center. Shirley successfully did things like holding a tightly wrapped package and identifying the contents as a book of obscure Civil War poetry.

In 1966, after a local charity benefit lecture, she told a reporter she'd just met, "We have a lot in common, we both have daughters named Margaret and know somebody named Hale who lives in West Greenwich Village, we were both married in 1945 and are Congregationalists." This turned out to be absolutely correct, and was reported in the *Biddeford-Sacco Journal*.

Before another meeting at a Holiday Inn in Aroostook County she described where the body of a murdered newsboy would be found two months later in a bog outside a town Shirley had never been to. She has few precognitive intuitions about her own family, feeling that it's because she's too emotionally involved. But occasionally things do happen, like the night in 1954 when she routed the family out of bed at their Lake Sebago summer cabin; by daybreak two sturdy-looking pine trees had toppled over and smashed the cabin to the ground. While she was engaged to her husband Michael during his World War II military service, she insisted on one of his furloughs that they leave their train at Boston and continue on to Maine via bus. The train they got off was derailed en route.

Shirley Harrison was the founding force behind the very serious-minded Maine Research Association for Parapsychological Study, and she organized an ESP seminar in the summer of 1970 at the state university's Gorham campus—attracting packed houses and the top names in international parapsychology—on an organizational budget of $150. But the association is in no way an ego showcase for Shirley. They practically had to drag her onstage at the seminar sessions because she wanted to be in the audience learning more about her talents.

Present techniques for training the psychic gift rely on learning by actual practice. This sink-or-swim approach does, in fact, seem to produce valuable results, according to the testimony of many students. England's best-known ESP school using this approach today is the College of Psychic Studies, the former London Spiritualist Alliance. Their star teacher is a courtly bachelor medium named Douglas Johnson who has performed televised seances in both England and the United States with his spirit guide, Chaing. His psychic classes meet for an hour weekly in groups of six to eight. They start by meditating in darkness for thirty minutes, focusing on an image suggested by Johnson. A discussion follows to see if other images came into the meditation and were perhaps shared telepathically by more than one student. Next a mystery visitor comes in with some item to be passed around for an exercise in psychometry.

"The first thing one must realize is that one can't be right all the time," says Douglas Johnson of his classes. "But also the thing which may seem to be absolute nonsense might prove to be a very good hit . . . . Some people develop more quickly than others. But I have found that those who are slowest—if they have a gift—in the end their gift is the most stable one. One must possess the latent ability though, much the same as a gift for music or painting." He also stresses that every person's ESP produces different psychic symbols whose codes he must decipher. Johnson sees an open book with the right-hand page in either light or shadow, depending on whether the client's life is entering a positive or negative change.

A lady technical personnel administrator from Hughes Aircraft has opened her castle-like Hollywood Hills living room for a five-week psychic development course by Fred Kimball, whose two specialties are teaching groups and reading the thoughts of animals. Kimball says he gets TV type images from animals in response to his mental questions, but the creatures have a very small vocabulary and have trouble expressing complex thoughts. He's good enough at this to have convinced a number of Los Angeles talk show hosts he is no faker, and the author of a 1967 story in *West,* the LA *Times* Sunday supplement, swears Kimball's conversation with his Siamese cat checked out on the details of the trailer camp where the writer lived with his pet.

Kimball tries to teach his students to assume a state of ESP concentration. "It takes about fifteen hours practice at concentrating and then they'll never lose it," drawls the retired merchant seaman who had a youthful fling at pro wrestling. "Some students follow me to a couple of these five-week classes, but I won't let them come back more than twelve hours because they just sit back and read everybody off." The mystery guest is a key part of his method, as with Douglas Johnson's. He has his classes concentrate deeply for six minutes on some stranger he's brought in, trying particularly to see if they can spot a colored aura. He also believes that during the true state of ESP concentration, an itch at any part of the body carries a specific psychic message. He has made detailed diagrams of this ESP itch circuitry. A lot of it must have been suggestion, because if you think about being itchy you will probably soon begin feeling that way. But as Fred Kimball explains this theory, a crowded roomful of people who look well-bathed are scratching themselves as if caught in a flea circus.

The lady who's tonight's mystery guest listens to what the students guessed about her and now it's her turn to match it with a names-left-out life story. She starts by stammering, "But . . . almost three-quarters of what you said about me was right!" Kimball chuckles with satisfaction, "Not bad for the third lesson."

Chapter 15

Spiritualism Makes a Comeback

IN the harsh, glaring lights of the television studio, what started out as a panel discussion about life after death became a videotaped seance. Arthur Ford, the septuagenarian dean of American mediums, had put himself into trance. His spirit guide since 1924—Fletcher, a French-Canadian killed in World War I—was passing along to former Episcopal bishop of California James A. Pike words supposed to be from Pike's son Jim, who'd committed suicide during a bad LSD trip at the age of twenty.

"I will tell you this much, Dad—he called you Dad—the beginning was someone he calls Halverston," Fletcher reported via Ford's vocal cords, in answer to Bishop Pike's query about the events leading up to his son's suicide. "I don't know, is the name like Halverston or Halbertson . . . He's here now, this Halverston. I've seen him here; he seems to have come over about the same time the boy did. Do you remember such a person?"

"I think I do . . . I didn't connect him," Bishop Pike hesitantly replied.

Arthur Ford went on, "Wait a minute, wait, check it out. He had . . . his name was Marvin . . . and, uh . . . something about some modern music or modern dancing, or art or something in the church, and, uh. . . ."

"There's such a person," Pike broke in. He now remembered Marvin Halverson as a young man working for the National Council of Churches, director of an office studying the church's relationship to contemporary arts. The two were even on a TV panel together once, but Pike hadn't heard anything about Halverson for at least two years and had no idea his son Jim even knew Halverson.

Checking around afterward, Pike was able to find someone who knew that Halverson had dropped out, gotten heavily involved with drugs in Berkeley, and died a year after Jim. Bishop Pike then had a private sitting with Arthur Ford, asking Jim's spirit for a further explanation of the events that led to his suicide. Ford reported that the breakdown began when Jim ran into "some—not old friends—but some people I had known—from the West Coast." He then launched into a detailed, lengthy narrative, naming names of living people who had been with Jim just before he killed himself. Pike was actually able to trace these witnesses and for the first time he put together the full story of his son's death.

It was this experience that made Bishop Pike finally decide to write his best seller, *The Other Side,* which put him on public record as a believer in psychic phenomena and the possibility that communication with the dead can exist. More than anything else, the notoriety over the book and Pike's 1967 TV seance is what has brought spiritualism back into the limelight for the first time in almost fifty years. Most Americans probably assumed that spiritualism had died out by now, the victim of exposé after exposé of seance fakery.

"Yes, I have come across frauds," no other than Arthur Ford admitted in *Psychic* magazine of October, 1970. "When people started telling them they're wonderful, they believed it. They got greedy, egotistical, and unbearable. Then they try to force it—but you can't turn it on like that . . . But if some woman has a husband and kids to support, and she sees five or ten bucks coming through the door, she's going to try to get it. And so she gets a bad reputation. I don't think anyone ever starts out as a fraud. There isn't enough money in it."

Ford called himself a lower-case spiritualist "in the real sense of spiritualism as a philosophy . . . not as a cultist or a sectarian . . . But I do give the Spiritualist Church credit for keeping the subject alive until the scientists were compelled to look at it."

Arthur Ford died on January 4, 1971, a few days before his seventy-fifth birthday. He had been a member of the American Society for Psychical Research since 1921 and an ordained Disciples of Christ minister since 1923. He said his first spontaneous psychic experiences happened when he was a World War I second lieutenant and saw in his dreams next day's casualty lists. In 1927 he sailed to England for a look at what their Society for Psychical Research was up to. The night he arrived he went to an SPR lecture and the speaker—Sir Arthur Conan Doyle—suddenly invited Ford to step up and demonstrate his budding mediumship. Next day's London *Express* quoted Doyle, "One of the most amazing things I have ever seen in forty-one years of psychic experience was the demonstration of Arthur Ford." Sir Arthur then gave a long list of Ford's psychic hits that audience members had verified as correct.

But until the TV seance with Bishop Pike, Arthur Ford was remembered mainly as the medium involved in the 1929 controversy over Houdini's code message from beyond the grave. When Houdini, America's greatest magician, died in 1926 he made a pact to come back in spirit and communicate with his wife Bess if such a thing were possible. A reward of $10,000 was offered to any medium who could come up with the two-word code message. On January 8, 1929, the New York *Graphic* bannered a front-page scoop that Arthur Ford gave Bess Houdini the message, "Rosabelle, believe," spelled out in the "talking code" the Houdinis used during an early career mind-reading act. Rosabelle was Houdini's private pet name for Bess because of a song she sang in their first vaudeville days. Mrs. Houdini then signed a statement that Ford had delivered the correct code message, witnessed with the signatures of a United Press reporter and the associate editor of the *Scientific American*. But two days later, the *Graphic* branded its own scoop as a hoax, claiming that their reporter had tricked them by somehow finding out the message and code in advance. The paper hinted just short of libel that Ford, Mrs. Houdini, and the reporter were all in it together. Brought up on charges before the New York United Spiritualists League, Arthur Ford easily cleared himself. He always maintained that Fletcher brought him the code message exactly as stated and the accusations against him were a typical smear by one of the most notorious scandal sheets from the heyday of American yellow journalism. By this time, there have been too many charges, countercharges, and denials for anybody to reconstruct exactly what happened. But certainly no one has ever come near proving that Arthur Ford took part in fraud. And although

Houdini's widow never again publicly admitted the authenticity of Ford's message, she never specifically denied it either.

Prolonged ill-health and cardiac trouble put Arthur Ford into semiretirement in Miami during his last years. He gave only four trance sittings in 1970. Two were for doctors, one for a U.S. Senator, and the fourth "was for an astronaut who came anonymously. I didn't know who he was at the time of the sitting. Afterward, he wrote me a very beautiful letter in which he said everything checked out."

According to National Council of Churches figures, there are at least four hundred spiritualist churches and some 150,000 Americans who name spiritualism as their Christian denomination. Certainly every respectable-sized city in the United States has at least a couple of listings in the phone book under *Churches, Spiritualist.*

The oldest nationwide spiritualist denomination still functioning in this country is the National Spiritualist Association of Churches, founded in Milwaukee in 1893 and now headquartered at Cassadaga, Florida. The first major schism came in 1913 when the National Spiritualist Alliance and the New York General Assembly of Spiritualists split from the parent body. The split-offs and new denominations still continue through today, fueled by the many shades of opinion within spiritualism over whether life after death is a series of reincarnations, or progression through ever-higher states of being, or simply an ESP telephone line to the Judeo-Christian heaven. The fastest-growing spiritualist denomination currently is the Universal Church of the Master in San Jose, California. UCM leadership was taken over in 1966 by Robert A. Ferguson, a dynamic minister still in his thirties, and the membership has shot up to one hundred and twenty-five active churches throughout the country with some congregations as large as one hundred and fifty.

Spiritualist magazines like *Chimes* of Encinitas, California; *Cosmic Light* in Jamul, California, and the *Psychic Observer* of Box 8606, Washington, D.C., 20011 feature page after page listing more spiritualist churches, associations, publications, and mail-order ministries than even the most devoted seance believer could sample in one lifetime.

Today's mediums come in all forms, but the prototype of a contemporary spiritualist psychic would be a sweet, elderly lady drawn to exploring the afterlife by a desire to contact her own loved ones and a history of spontaneous ESP experiences as a youth. Spiritualist theory has it that in general, women are more open and sensitive on the subconscious levels than men.

"I'm not usually taken over by the spirit guide anymore," says Brenda Rowland Crenshaw in her sunny east Hollywood Hills living room. "Trance work usually develops first, but the best way for a medium to reach the other side changes as she progresses." Mrs. Crenshaw, an attractive, well-bred English lady has been one of the best-known spiritualist mediums on both sides of the Atlantic for more than thirty years. Her guide is a nameless Oriental gentleman, and there's also a spirit nun who helps her out before large audiences, such as the crowd of seven hundred that saw her passing along messages from departed loved-ones at a church in LA's Southgate district in 1969.

Her best-known spiritualistic feat took place before a packed church auditorium in England. Suddenly a German officer who had died in battle during World War I began speaking through Brenda. He gave his name and announced that he had come to thank an English nurse who tried to help him as he lay dying. The nurse than stood up in her seat and identified herself. The officer said he had given her his crucifix just before passing away. And the nurse then took it out of her handbag for all to see.

Brenda Crenshaw never advertises and won't accept a client who isn't recommended by someone she's already sat for. She does two sittings a day and is currently booked three months in advance. To get herself in the proper mood for a sitting, she likes to play hymns on her stereo and join in an opening prayer with the client. "During the Blitz when bombs were coming my way, I would hear a voice singing 'Nearer My God to Thee,' and I knew it was time to go down to the shelter," she says.

At the age of twelve, she began to see beautiful diagrams in the rain and dust on her windowpanes. With the moral support of a psychic aunt, she joined the Spiritualist Association of Great Britain and started taking their mediumship development classes. Before she left for California in 1955, she was booked two years in advance for platform demonstrations and private sittings. James Crenshaw had been reading about Brenda in the spiritualist press, and when they met while he was visiting England, it was love at first sight. They describe their life together as blissfully happy, until Crenshaw got hit by a runaway auto in front of their house. "By all rights, I should be dead," says James, who is still in fragile health. "It was only Brenda's psychic force that pulled me through."

James Crenshaw is a Hollywood freelance writer who specializes in showbiz and occult reportage. In 1950 he published *Telephone Between Worlds,* a biography of Richard Zenor, founder of the Agasha Temple of Wisdom at 460 North Western Avenue, which teaches a faith based on Zenor's trance recountings of the philosophy of Agasha, an Egyptian thinker who lived 7,000 years ago. Zenor began as a prodigious teen-age medium in Terre Haute, Indiana, reported to be capable of materializing ghosts and levitating objects. He met his wife Thelma when she started coming to his seances to contact the spirit of her dead first husband, who gave his consent to the widow's remarriage by telling her through Zenor, "I'm satisfied. Now that you're taken care of, I can go on." Once when a fire was threatening their home in Woodland Hills, Mr. and Mrs. Zenor carried on an excited metaphysical discussion about why their spirit guardians hadn't warned them of this, or was it their karma to have the house burn down, all the while hosing down their yard.

San Francisco has at least a dozen active spiritualist churches and the longest-established medium is Reverend Florence "Mom" Becker, a Buddha-like woman in her eighties who does blindfold billet readings Wednesdays and Sundays at her Golden Gate Church and is said to have performed seances for Franklin Delano Roosevelt.

New York City's most important occultism center during the twenties and thirties used to be the Carnegie Hall studios, but all that's left of this now are a couple of mediums and the Yoga Guild of America. The focus for New York City's traditional spiritualist activity has shifted to the Hotel Ansonia, a massive old pile that used to be one of the gems of the West Side during its opulent gaslight era. The Ansonia is at Seventy-third Street and Broadway, just across from Needle Park, the famous meeting place for junkies. Hundreds of little spiritualist sects have come and gone through the hotel's double-doored sitting room suites through the years. At a certain section of the gray marble lobby, the Ansonia's seance-going tenants sit around and chat about their latest paranormal phenomena. When the desk clerk was asked where to find one night's seance, his bored reply was, "Which seance do you want—the third floor, fifth floor, or fourteenth floor?"

Caroline Chapman's Manhattan apartment is on the fourteenth floor of a new toothpaste-white high-rise building at the corner of Thirty-fourth Street and Third Avenue. Stepping through the door is like going back into a nineteenth century drawing room. Now about seventy-five, Caroline was born one of the Virginia Randolphs, into great Southern wealth and tradition. As predicted during her honeymoon by a psychic working at Young's Amusement Pier in Atlantic City, she had to become a professional spiritualist reader in 1930 after a series of personal tragedies—her husband lost his Cuban plantation in a change of regimes and went blind and her six-year-old daughter Marjorie died. Marjorie has been her mother's spirit guide ever since. I'd heard about Caroline Chapman from a lady who said the medium had predicted correctly that a man she'd been thinking of moving in with would die violently within a year. Caroline was working under the impression that our interview was supposed to be a reading, and as I found out about her background she told me a number of perfectly accurate things such as the right number of deaths in my immediate family and my unusual family nickname as a child . . . Tanny.

Musical mediumship has been brought back in a big way by Rosemary Brown, a London widow who raised two children on her earnings in a school kitchen job. Rosemary had a bare minimum of piano lessons, and after her husband died in 1961, she didn't have the time or money to go to concerts. She didn't even own a radio till 1965, only an old phonograph and a few 78 rpm records given her by her brother. Rosemary claims to have taken down some four hundred pieces of music from the spirits of the great classical composers since 1964. Her favorite so far is the finish of Schubert's Unfinished Symphony. Some authoritative musicians like Hepzibah Menuhin and composer Richard Rodney Bennett have endorsed the spirit works as genuine, and a

Rosemary Brown recording, *A Musical Seance,* has been released by Mercury. She first displayed her afterlife music at a spiritualist meeting in 1966, and an aristocratic patron organized a $12-weekly fund so she can stay home at the piano with the shades of Liszt, Beethoven, Chopin, and the rest. Rosemary Brown is neither the first nor the only musical medium. In the early 1900's a Frenchman named George Aubert and a three-year-old Spanish boy, Pepito Ariola, produced some astonishingly varied piano works. During the twenties a Negro idiot savant from Georgia—Blind Tom—was a famous concert pianist.

Maxine Bell of Los Angeles had her Beethoven Symphony performed locally in 1945. She says she's got a Brahms Piano Concerto and a Tchaikovsky Ballet ready, as soon as some "rich person who wants to give credit to the earth" pays for the orchestral arrangements. Maxine only gets the melodies from the composers, not the parts written out for each instrument.

Maxine Bell is an astrologer, a medium, and a healer. She lives in a nondescript little house south of UCLA which she says she seldom leaves because strange poltergeist phenomena follow her around. "That's why I had to give up my career as a concert pianist. Every time things would start flying around the auditorium and the audiences would break up laughing."

Professor Thelma Moss, the UCLA parapsychologist, brought a number of well-known psychics to the haunted house of Elke Sommer and Joe Hyams. Maxine scored with most accuracy in describing the ghost that had been seen by the famous tenants. She also predicted correctly that the house was due to burn down soon.

"My doctor says I'm a fool to get myself so sick dehaunting houses for only fifty dollars or so," Maxine says. "He thinks I should charge ten percent of the house's value because they can't sell it without me. When I walked into the home where Karen Kupcinet had been murdered, I started feeling strangled and I had to get out of that atmosphere . . . I guess the doctor will be relieved to know I'm planning from now on to concentrate on healing."

Bishop James Pike had more sittings with George Daisley of Santa Barbara than with any other medium. Transcripts of some of the seance dialogue published in *The Other Side* would seem to be impressive evidence of Daisley's psychic gift. He appeared particularly accurate at describing poltergeist phenomena that Jim, Jr.'s spirit was allegedly causing in order to show his presence, as the bishop resigned his post to take up a new career at the Center for the Study of Democratic Institutions. Pike's very first session with Daisley began as the medium repeated these words supposed to be coming from Jim, "Hello, Dad . . . I was with you recently when you did not think you could find a book in your library that you really wanted to consult. After you left the room and returned, you were startled to find the book on the desk where I had put it in your absence."

George Daisley is a silver-haired, clean-cut Englishman who used to be known as the Boy Wonder Medium when he began performing in London some forty years ago at the age of nineteen. These days Daisley prefers to be called a sensitive rather than a medium and, like Arthur Ford, holds himself aloof from the spiritualist religion. "So much insincerity in a great movement," he sighs. "Spiritualism could no longer give me the high-minded religion I wanted—too much ego and hanky-panky."

Daisley first visited Santa Barbara shortly after World War II, and left England to make his new home there in 1963. "Certainly my exposure in Bishop Pike's book helped establish me," he admits gratefully. He now takes on only two $30 private sittings a day and has a six-month waiting list. It takes the two male roommates he calls his colleagues six hours a day to keep up with the mail. For a recent public demonstration at a Protestant church in Atlanta, 1,500 $3 tickets were sold. When he held his sittings for Bishop Pike, he was living in a small tract house. Daisley has now moved to a $70,000 house which is official headquarters for his Hallowed Grounds Fellowship for Spiritual Healing and Prayer. It's on one of the most tree-lined streets in Santa Barbara's expensive countrified Montecito district. One can only wonder how Daisley's well-to-do neighbors will react to his plans to hold healing services under a particularly majestic oak in his front yard.

When Daisley first settled in the United States arrangements were made to get him on a local Ben Hunter talk show. A bored associate producer came by to audition him muttering, "I can only give you twenty minutes." George Daisley proudly recalls that the producer stayed almost three hours listening to a detailed report about his relatives who'd passed into spirit and when he finally rushed off for another appointment, he commented, "You are either a holy man or the most sophisticated fraud I ever met."

It's almost impossible to understand how Bishop James Pike, whose thinking on the thorniest religious and psychic controversies was so logical and so intelligent, could have thrown his life away by driving out into the Israeli desert to see the Dead Sea Scrolls country in a rented minicar and then, when the auto got stuck on the rutted trail, trying to walk out cross-country in the 130-degree daytime heat instead of waiting in some shade till nightfall.

As the hunt for Pike started, his young, blond, third wife Diane Kennedy Pike—who'd managed to trek out of the desert to bring help after ten grueling hours—could only recall telling the incredulous search party, "My answers were feeble ones, for now that I was riding with the police I could see what a foolish thing we had done."

The night before Pike's body was finally found deep in a canyon, Diane says she had a forty-five-minute vision of the bishop dying, leaving his body in a "filmy cloudlike substance . . . from the base of the neck" and ascending heavenward to a joyous crowd. She recounted the vision to her twenty-year-old brother Scott, as it was happening. Immediately afterward, she sketched a picture of the unusual position in which she'd seen her husband's body lying on an oddly angled rock ledge. Photographs of where the body was actually found several hours later apparently correspond almost exactly to the sketch.

Back in Santa Barbara where she now directs the Bishop Pike Foundation, Diane Kennedy Pike feels her late husband has been in contact with her in "several very vivid dreams" and in her meditations. She has tried two mediums for further communication but feels that the only message unquestionably from James Pike was, "Tell Diane I had an unusual headache about three days before the desert incident." Only she, her brother Scott, and Pike himself would have known about the headache. Diane believes this was a clue that the bishop is trying to speak through mediums with such telling detail that his presence *can't* be disproved.

The approach to a new spiritualism that Bishop Pike had found the most solidly promising is the Spiritual Frontiers Fellowship, which—like England's Church Fellowship for Psychical and Spiritual Studies—is attempting to bring psychic phenomena back into the mainstream of organized religion. SFF was founded in 1956 at a Chicago meeting of psychically oriented clergymen, with Arthur Ford figuring prominently in the proceedings. The fellowship's administrative headquarters is at Evanston, Illinois. SFF spokesman Marcus Bach, a retired University of Iowa professor of comparative religion says, "The Spiritual Frontiers Fellowship holds that the door of revelation is never closed. God still speaks directly to us." SFF points out that the Bible is full of descriptions of classic psychical phenomena presented as miracles . . . prophecy, visions, clairvoyant dreams, prayer fulfilled.

The chairman of SFF in New York City is not exactly one of those stereotype little-old-lady seance-goers in a flowered dress. His name is Bruce Gregory and he's a good-looking twenty-four-year-old financial analyst for one of the TV networks. A soft-spoken native of Atlanta, he began looking into psychic phenomena at the age of eighteen when he first went away to college. "Our family were all staunch Baptists so they always made light of the psychic strain running through us," he says. "I had a grandfather who could do table-rapping and a little healing. My father saw ghosts when he was in his twenties, my mother once felt she'd transcended out of her body while speaking before a church. I started reading about Rhine's ESP research in the college library and gradually things fell into place for me. Somehow I felt I shouldn't go to Harvard Business School even though I was accepted there. So I picked Wharton for my graduate studies and met Arthur Ford, who was still living in Philadelphia then. Also, there's a wonderful occult collection at the University of Pennsylvania Library, lots of Madame Blavatsky's original manuscripts."

The young Ivy League spiritualist is proud of SFF efforts to expose disreputable mediums, as in the study they made of eight mail-order "past life readers" whose fees went as high as $200 and who each produced a completely different previous reincarnation roster for the same client. "But I still think it may be possible to read past lives," says Bruce. "I'm very interested in the work of an independent Methodist minister, Reverend Walker Westcott, who seems to get psychologically significant results by reading the moment of crisis in a person's past existence . . . and he doesn't charge anything for this."

Bruce also enjoys going along to lend a psychic push to SFF Rescue Groups that free ghosts from their earthbound hauntings. The trance medium lets herself get taken over by the ghost, and the rest of the rescuers explain that a discarnate spirit doesn't have to remain on a low material plane. "These are tormented souls," says Bruce, "and you can just see their joy and relief reflecting on the medium's face as they realize they're no longer physically alive and take off into the ether."

He feels that his own experiences in seance have proven to him that communication with the dead exists. "A friend of mine who's developed automatic writing mediumship once brought in my Uncle Claude," says Bruce, "describing him perfectly and capturing all kinds of family details." He's not at all surprised that a midtown Manhattan Methodist church would allow all these goings-on. "It's mostly played down today," he says. "But all his life the founder of Methodism, John Wesley, saw ghosts and had visions."

Chairman of the SFF for metropolitan Los Angeles is Howard Carey, a retired Methodist minister who lives with his wife in an integrated Central LA neighborhood near his last church. Carey's son was one of the first white Freedom Riders and is currently working on the 2,000-acre Soul City industrial community being built by blacks in North Carolina. "I don't think overreliance on psychism is one of the more constructive forms of the Ageless Wisdom," says Carey. "I'm interested in small-group ministry, the Underground Church in living rooms where a few people can meditate together and really relate to a consciousness of being at one with God."

Carey is an admitted latecomer to spiritualistic phenomena. He found himself getting more and more attuned to a psychic approach to religion during his fifties when he opened the doors of his church to SFF meetings. Since reaching the ministerial retirement age, he's been preaching more busily than ever, with one of his living room meditation meetings scheduled somewhere around the LA basin almost nightly.

"My own experiences trying to help people who feel they have become either literally or figuratively possessed by demons after dabbling in black magic," says Carey, "have more than convinced me how powerful and dangerous these forces are. But fortunately this process can sometimes work the other way too. For the past few months I've been working with a seventeen-year-old Cuban boy whose parents thought he was insane when he started showing psychic talents. You'd be surprised how many local clergymen have learned that the Spiritual Frontiers Fellowship is where to call when they find someone in their congregation is having problems of a psychic or demonic nature.

From the first, a very big factor in American spiritualism has been the summer camps where believers spend vacations communicating with their dear departed. The first camp meeting on record was at Lake Pleasant, Massachusetts, in 1873. Most of the major camps still existing today date from the 1890's. Camp Lilly Dale in upstate New York actually had the original Hydesville cabin of the Fox Sisters shipped over and reassembled on its grounds.

The atmosphere at these camps has not always been free of controversy. As recently as 1960, Dr. Andrija Puharich—the MD turned parapsychologist who first brought Peter Hurkos to this country—arrived at Camp Chesterfield in hopes of proving the existence of spirit materializations once and for all. With perfect confidence, the Indiana camp—which had always been known for its flashy physical manifestations—invited Dr. Puharich to photograph the dark room seances with infrared film. Unfortunately, the films seemed clearly to show the medium's confederates moving things about in the darkness. A furious Dr. Puharich published his photos in England's *Psychic News*, the world's biggest spiritualist newspaper. Did this revelation kill Camp Chesterfield? On the contrary, business is better than ever.

Ever since 1895, Harmony Grove Spiritualist Camp has been open between Memorial Day and Labor Day at Escondido, the pleasant little mountain town on the inland route between LA and San Diego. Harmony Grove is the biggest camp on the West Coast. Set in a natural wooded bowl west of the town, it looks like a quaint old bungalow colony. There is, in fact, a permanent community of Harmony Grove members who live there year-round in little cottages tucked among the mighty oaks. Every day during the season there's a breakfast healing service in a special little chapel, followed by morning, afternoon, and evening services in the main chapel. Usually everybody present gets some sort of spirit message. And during the wintertime there's plenty of time for reminiscence among old friends and for showing around photographs in which the shadows through the Grove's huge trees appear to create strange "spirit faces."

Without exception, the elderly residents of Harmony Grove are the friendliest, most giving group you could meet. It's impossible to spend even a day at the camp without feeling you've been adopted by a score of charming grandparents. Their belief in personal immortality—and what they accept as daily proof of it—has given them a truly enviable openness and serenity. They are touchingly eager to share their answers. And Harmony Grove is not there to make anybody a quick fortune; the rental cabins run from $3 to $7 a day and a typical entree at the dining hall sells for $1.10.

The whole area of levitations and materialization seances have had so many seamy exposures that today's spiritualism is nearly all "mental mediumship." But one of the last of the trumpet mediums, Reverend Jim Balcum of Long Beach, was due for a three-day stand at Harmony Grove. Small and white-haired, looking like an ill-at-ease Harry Truman, Balcum has been a medium for fifty years and is said to have done remarkable things in his youth—made up to half a dozen luminous-painted trumpets fly about a dark room simultaneously or produced fantastic materializations of the spirits of loved ones.

Harmony Grove's seances are held during the late afternoons in an air-conditioned concrete blockhouse chapel with heavy doors that ensure that the whole room is in pitch darkness. Chairs are placed in a wide circle, a bit of hymn singing to bring the higher spheres into harmony begins, and the announcement is made that if anybody gets out of his seat or turns on a light the medium will die. Shortly afterward, the spirit trumpet—a lightweight three-section collapsible aluminum megaphone that has been marked with luminous tape—rises from the center of the floor and takes the position it would take if a little old man had slipped out of his chair and placed it over his mouth to speak through. The voices that come through alternate between a little-girl falsetto who calls herself Silver Bell and various basso Heap Big Indian Chiefs whose names keep changing from sentence to sentence.

One wealthy businessman drove over 100 miles here from Santa Barbara and had to rush off to Los Angeles Airport immediately afterward to catch a jet for a Chicago conference. "Are you there, Martha?" he asked as the luminous-banded trumpet floated his way in the darkness. "Yes, I'm here, dear," came the falsetto answer. The businessman began sobbing, "Oh Martha, it's you. I miss you so much, sweetheart." The high-pitched voice from the trumpet at least gave the bereaved widower some good advice, suggesting that he must forget the past and find a new wife.

Arthur Ford has said, "The day of the professional medium is about over. We've been useful as guinea pigs. I have taught a great many groups and I find they all have some spiritual gift. Any group of seven or eight people who takes time to listen and read, to understand the techniques involved, and practice faithfully will generally have some psychic experience within a few months."

My friends, the Denblacker family of Hermosa Beach, have seances at home when they feel moved to it. One evening we were sitting around the massive table where Imy Denblacker works all day sewing custom dresses. The lights were off and we held hands around the tabletop. All we were supposed to do was open ourselves to whatever sensations we felt. "Is something there?" asked Imy's teen-age daughter, Tracy, sitting way across from me. I began to feel an eerie tingle running up both my arms, all the way to the shoulders. I've never felt anything remotely like that pulsation; it's as if I was connected to some vibrating electric current through the hands of the friends sitting on each side of me. "Yes, this means something's there all right," said Imy.

Chapter 16

America's Native Sorcerers

"WHAT everybody seems to forget about the Northeast's great blackout of November 9, 1965, is that it started in a power relay station on land Robert Moses and the New York State Power Authority stole from the Tuscarora Indians," says Craig Carpenter, "and nobody yet has figured out *how* it started."

Craig, at forty-three, looks like an actor on the style of Rory Calhoun made up to play an Indian. He's got hawklike good looks, a wiry outdoorsman physique, long jet-black hair caught in a neat braid behind a red forehead band and a gold ring in his left ear. His normal costume is hiking boots, jeans, and a red-checkered lumberjack shirt. He hit the early euphoric Southern California New Youth culture of the late 1960's like a dashing, with-it combination of the Lone Ranger and Tonto rolled into one. He showed up at all the first love-ins and the Monterey Pop Festival, putting up beautiful tepees and talking quietly with any young people who wanted to know about real Indians. He was one of the most gripping guest speakers during the starting days of FM underground radio. Concerned Southern California students formed the Traditional Indian Land and Life Committee, an Immaculate Heart College began holding annual Traditional Indian conferences largely because of Craig's message.

Craig Carpenter was really the first man to put across to America's counterculture the idea that a significant element in the newly militant Indian Rights movement is the traditional Indian. Traditional Indians couldn't care less about achieving equality within a U.S. melting pot. They want their reservations treated as semi-independent nations, guaranteed as they are by dozens of federal treaties. They want to be left alone to lead an ancient way of life which they call the Creator's Life Plan and which they claim contains secrets that the white man is only now beginning barely to comprehend.

Craig has this very unnerving collection of newspaper clippings about recent "freaks of nature." For example, there was no rain in Washington, D.C., throughout the unusually hot summer of 1966. There had been a three-year drought and the nation's capital was having its worst water shortage in one hundred and seven years. Early in September, the first intertribal national Indian delegation under Traditional leadership came to Washington to try to see the President and the Bureau of Indian Affairs about stopping a Congressional bill which would have disposed of all Indian reservations in the name of equal opportunity. Rachel Welch and Dorothy Orrison, volunteer helpers at the Hopi House Information Office, told their Indian friends how bad things were getting in D.C. "It will rain, don't worry," promised Thomas Banyacya, English-language interpreter for the one-hundred-and-seven-year-old Chief Dan Kachongva. Banyacya and two other Hopis got together with Tuscarora activist Mad Bear, smoked their pipes, and burned some special oatmeal. The rain began that night and continued for twenty hours straight.

From Washington, most of the Indian demonstrators went to the Niagara Falls area for a militant powwow organized by Mad Bear on the Tuscarora Reservation of the six-tribe Iroquois Confederacy. "There," says Banyacya, "we made it known to them that the Great Spirit is about to show us His powers and that we speak the truths." The front-page story in next day's Washington *Post* had this lead: "A flaming meteorite lit up the skies across the north central United States last night, frightening hundreds of persons who saw it before it broke up in bits of smoking debris over northern Indiana. Police departments and newspaper switchboards from the Washington area to Northern Michigan were swamped with calls as witnesses reported everything from flying saucers to airplane crashes . . . Michigan Governor George Romney, flying in his private plane to a convention in St. Clair, Mich., said 'the meteorite almost hit us. It really frightened us—we thought we were under attack. All of a sudden the thing was coming, and it was as bright as noon.' " It was September 17, 1966, New York State's official annual Indian Day.

A *lot* of strange things happened in the Pacific Northwest when Washington State began messing around with the Nisqually Indian fishing-for-food rights guaranteed under the Medicine Creek Treaty of 1855. Black comedian Dick Gregory was sentenced to six months in jail on January 12, 1967, and that same day the same court gave six months to a woman convicted of beating her child to death. Next morning the *Daily Olympian* had a front-page picture story about the Bigfoot monster being sighted and leaving tracks. Five days later an earthquake hit Seattle, and Craig's news file shows that by the end of the month, Washington State had two earthquakes, two mudslides blocking main highways and rail routes, two train wrecks, the second airliner crash on Kit Carson Peak, rain-and-wind storms that closed sheltered Puget Sound to all shipping, and Tacoma's worst fire in history. Also, a few days before the Dick Gregory trial began, on Thanksgiving eve, 1966, Seattle had its first blackout—the whole downtown area including the courthouse, police station, and city hall was without power. According to the Seattle *Post-Intelligencer,* the blackout was set off by a series of mysterious electrical fires near the intersection of Seneca Street and Second Avenue. In 1794 the Seneca Treaty was the second treaty ever negotiated by the United States government.

Craig Carpenter says it was Indians singing something not quite as powerful as their "Last Song" because of the arrest of Indian fishermen in the Trinity River area of northern California which brought on the Great Killer Windstorm of Columbus Day, 1962, that caused fifty deaths in the Pacific Northwest. The first storm victim was millionaire Houston oilman Tom Slick, whose avocation was organizing expeditions to track down both the Abominable Snowman and Bigfoot. The Los Angeles *Times* reported that Slick's private plane "apparently disintegrated in flight . . . struck by lightning or possibly was traveling too fast and tore itself apart" over southwest Montana. "Many of the early victims were killed by falling trees," says Craig, "and that's really unheard of for storm deaths. But it fits with the prophecies about the last days of this world. One man died when a tree fell *in front* of his car and a branch cut his throat. Another woman wouldn't have died if she hadn't run from her tent when she heard a tree outside starting to topple."

According to Craig, eight Indian nations were involved in six months of secret ceremonies that caused the 1964 Christmas Day floods which left all those spectacular high water markers over the Northwest's Redwood country. "They never ask specifically for rain or floods or earthquake or for anybody to get hurt," says Craig. "That's not the way it works at all. They only called the attention of the Unseen Guardians of Land and Life to some gross violations of nature's law and asked for investigation and appropriate action."

The First National Traditional Indian Convention was scheduled for the central Oklahoma town of Henryetta in June, 1968. It rained every day for the last three weeks of May and the worst floods in the state's history crested on May 15, rating federal designation as a "major disaster area." (On that same day there was a tornado in Arkansas, Japan's worst earthquake in forty-five years, and semisecret Congressional hearings on the anti-Indian Omnibus Bill.) "The convention grounds were too muddy for meetings and dancing," says Craig. "It was still raining cats and dogs when the first delegates arrived. But Rolling Thunder was flown in the day before the convention started. He's the most famous medicine man among Traditional Indians, I guess, a Cherokee who's lived in northwest Nevada Shoshone country for twenty years. He's the one who got the prophecy that the hippies were coming to help us. It's like the old Hopi prophecy that in the Last Days of this world will come a new white brother with his own religion, long-haired, peaceful, with his own style of living and dressing, called something like a Hopi but not exactly the same word."

Craig was one of eight witnesses who saw Rolling Thunder "prepare the weather" for the convention. "It happened while he was actually talking to the storm gods and explaining why it was necessary to roll back the clouds and let the sun shine. The fourth time Rolling Thunder asked, the clouds broke. All through the six days of the convention the weather was perfect, even though we were surrounded by continuous storms as close as Tulsa. The day after we left Henryetta it started raining again."

When our Third World began, the Creator's representative in charge—the Great Spirit—appeared in the form of a man to give his primary instructions. But now he and his helpers, the Unseen Guardians, appear only as hairy humanoid giants up to 30 feet tall or else as the "flame which burns, yet does not consume" such as appeared to Moses in the Bible. Craig Carpenter says he's seen both superhuman forms.

"When the Great Spirit begins showing himself in his Bigfoot form, that's one of the signs we must tell all enlightened people it is necessary to get back to the Creator's Life Plan or nature will correct this Third World," Craig says. "Man was given another chance after it became necessary to purify the First and Second Worlds, but all the prophecies agree that next time it will be the turn of the ants . . . When we first made contact with the Mickasuki Seminoles down in the Everglades a few years ago, their old prophecy was the same as all the others across the country—except that instead of red ants taking over, they had it as black ants."

There have been reports of seeing Bigfoot ever since the Pacific Northwest was opened up. Bigfoot descriptions sound remarkably like the Abominable Snowman of the Himalayas and the white-furred Inu of Japan's Mount Fuji. In British Columbia during the 1880's, entire trains and ferries loaded with passengers claimed to have sighted a Bigfoot, known in various Indian languages as the Sasquatch, the Hoopah, or the Ohmah. Modern laboratories have analyzed Bigfoot hair samples, droppings, and plaster casts of footprints—with the current techniques of criminology, footprints are now almost impossible to fake because in any sequence of steps the pressure on different parts of the foot must vary. There are at least two claimed films of the Bigfoot; Robert Patterson has a blurry 29 feet on a northern California female that left 14½-inch footprints, and Ivan Marx has shown 70 feet of a ten-foot-tall orangutan-like creature in northeastern Washington. Stills from these movies have appeared in a number of popular magazines.

"It's important to understand that Bigfoot is not the same as the Primitive Indians who also live in the Northwest," says Craig. "These are like people; they can be killed by bullets. They're not violent, but they're very powerful spiritually, and they can wipe out your whole family if you harm them. Ordinarily, the worst they'd do is scare people away from their fishing grounds or occasionally kidnap somebody for breeding purposes. But there was one group of Primitive Indians in northern Nevada that went haywire and started killing. The Piutes had to corner them in a cave and wipe them out."

Just about three months after this eight-hour interview tape was made with Craig at the beat-up Hollywood office of the Traditional Indian Land and Life Committee, there was a Los Angeles *Times* story: "Scores of red-haired mummies 6½ to 7 feet tall and thousands of artifacts have been discovered in a smoke-coated cave 22 miles southwest of Lovelock, Nevada . . . The Piutes of Lovelock Indian colony called the redheads People Eaters. 'That tribe of barbarians would waylay my people to kill and eat them, they would even eat their own dead,' says an 1883 book by Sarah Winnemuca Hopkins called *Life Among the Piutes*."

There are no more than 3,500 Hopi Indians living today in the high, barren desert of northern Arizona. They believe the Great Spirit meant them to stay in this harsh, inhospitable land because only by keeping faithful to the Creator's Life Plan would their magical ceremonies produce enough rain to water the crops and sheep pastures. They are considered the most spiritually powerful of Traditional Indians. Hopi means Peace and this may well be the only culture in world history that has never made war.

"During the winters, the Hopi men would spin yarn for the women to weave blankets," Craig says. "While they worked, they would talk over the old prophecies. Somebody might say . . . See that flywheel on the spinning wheel? Someday there will be an object that rolls over the ground on something round like that and it will be pulled by an animal. Then there will come an object that rolls without any animal pulling it. These machines will be so popular that there will be two kinds of trails built for them. One trail will be two strips of metal side by side, and when you look down, it will seem the road comes together in the far distance. A machine will come down this trail tied together like a snake and a whole village will ride in it. The other kind of trail is smooth and black and it looks like there's water up ahead on it, but there really isn't. There will be many of these trails and they will cut the land like a cobweb and this will be bad.

Next will come the roadway in the sky; you'll see the machines overhead carrying a whole village. Finally, soon before Purification Day when all wickedness is done away with and the planet returns to the paradise it began, there will be a gourd of ashes. If it is dropped from the roadway in the sky, it will boil water, burn the land, and leave ashes where nothing can grow for many years . . . This will be the sign for Hopis to stand up and declare to the world the message of the Creator's Life Plan."

Isolated as Hopiland is, it happens to be directly below the main transcontinental air route between Chicago and Los Angeles . . . and the first atomic bomb was dropped only a little over 300 miles away at Los Alamos on August 6, 1945.

"A Hopi of the Coyote clan at Oraibi, the Pueblo that's the oldest continually occupied community in North America, thought about the Los Alamos bomb for two years until he was ready to call a meeting of the other village leaders and tell the secret parts of his clan prophecies," says Craig. "When he finished, another man got up and said his clan instructions were to talk when the Coyote talks. There were more meetings among the six Hopi villages until for the first time in history all the secret clan prophecies were combined. By 1949 they were sending out prayers for help. It was about this time I started going buggy as a teen-ager back home in the Great Lakes country. My Dad said I might as well go West and get it out of my system, so I started working my way across the country. I didn't know what I was looking for, and it took me three years till I found Hopiland."

Craig says that his grandparents came from upper New York State to what was then the open countryside beyond Grosse Pointe, Michigan, in order to pass for white. "They thought I was reverting when I started winning trophies as a bow-and-arrow hunter and hanging around with the few Indians left along Lake Michigan. It wasn't till I was about twenty-one and took a trip back to the Mohawk reservation back in New York that I saw people who looked like me and my family, talking and moving fast, sort of tall and thin and with cheekbones like mine." Craig went to forestry school at Michigan State; he was the youngest student on campus and the first ever to attend class in jeans and shoulder-length hair. "I'm the only one in my family who went back to the Indian Way. I have a cousin who's a psychiatrist right in the Sherman Oaks suburb of Los Angeles.

A while back I heard from my parents that his oldest child died of asthma. That made me very sad, because there's a weed growing right alongside the San Bernardino Freeway that will cure asthma in twenty minutes. If my cousin had known about Indian Way or even kept in contact with the black sheep of the family, his son would still be alive . . . There are a lot of other medicinal plants growing all over the place, one that's effective in eighty percent of arthritis cases, others that can help with cancer —Joe Pyne used to do TV shows about one of the less effective ones."

There's a very obvious question that anybody would want to ask about all these supposed Indian wonder-works: If American Indians really have such terrific powers, how is it that they lost to the white invaders and are reduced to such economic deprivation that their average life expectancy is only forty-five years?

"There are several answers that I can see and probably more too," Craig says. "First of all, you don't dare invoke these miracle powers for an improper reason or it will come back and hit you or the weakest member of your family. Indians who can do these things hardly ever talk about it; they're afraid they'll go blind or crazy. I don't have any miracle power myself; I'm not a chief or a medicine man, only a messenger. So I figure it's okay for me to talk about these things . . . I get stopped when I'm saying too much, my throat gets sore or I lose my train of thought. Also, our leaders were warned specifically not to invoke the Unseen Guardians to protect the people during this prophesied period of testing, trial and tribulation. The stories said the test would be four days, a final exam period to see if we could remain faithful to the Great Spirit and use the powers to keep nature in balance. Of course the four days turned out to mean four hundred years. Some of the more warlike Indians had gotten pretty boastful before all this started, and I'm afraid they still may not have learned their lesson. But the powers that the Great Spirit who watches over this world gave to the early people in the name of the Creator have never really been used against the white man. Maybe sometimes they were just *shown* a little bit so that enlightened whites could pick up on what was going on. I guess the biggest demonstration of the powers was Tecumseh's Earthquake . . ."

Tecumseh was a Shawnee who organized an Indian Confederacy during the 1790's aimed at holding back the wave of white settlements at the east bank of the Ohio River. In only sixteen years his Confederacy extended from Hudson Bay to the Gulf of Mexico—covering a lot more land than Alexander the Great ever conquered in his lifetime.

Five thousand Creek Indians gathered at council in 1811 refused to join Tecumseh's Confederacy. "You do not believe the Great Spirit has sent me. You shall know," the history books agree Tecumseh said. "When I return to the Tippecanoe I shall stamp my foot and the very earth will tremble." Exactly two months later, December 16, 1811, came the first of the three great shocks of the New Madrid earthquake. This is very likely the greatest earthquake in the history of man. No other quake is known to have caused so much damage over so many miles—50,000 square miles were torn up, an area the size of New York State. The earthquake was named for a southeast Missouri town at its epicenter, which of course had to be completely rebuilt afterward. Missouri farms were too uneven to be plowed for two years after as the ground rose and fell like ocean waves. The Mississippi River flowed backwards and flooded a 150-by-40 mile area that sank in Tennessee and Arkansas. Even in California, 1,800 miles away, the San Gabriel Mission Tower was knocked down. If an earthquake this size ever happened in a heavily populated urban area, millions would die.

The New Madrid earthquake was "quite unusual" for a number of reasons, Professor Jorj O. Osterberg of Northwestern University has written. It took place almost 2,000 miles from California's San Andreas Fault, the nearest known earthquake fault. Also, "recurrence of quakes in a period of months or even years is quite rare."

The third and strongest New Madrid earthquake was dated February 7, 1812. It was exactly three months to the day after Indiana Governor William Henry Harrison destroyed Tecumseh's capital, Tippecanoe, in a sneak attack. Harrison struck at a time when he knew Tecumseh was still away in the South and the white militia outnumbered the defenders two-to-one. Indian casualties were slightly less than on the white side—and mainly among a suicide squad that covered the evacuation of women and children.

Governor Harrison played up his reputation as a heroic

Indian-fighter to gain election as President of the United States in 1840, campaigning on the slogan "Tippecanoe and Tyler too." But he died within a month after entering the White House. The American President elected every twenty years dating from Harrison's death has likewise died in office. So far the toll is seven, including Lincoln, FDR, and John Kennedy.

Craig Carpenter is perfectly serious about the Creator's Life Plan. "The world *can* go back to a simple, humble, hardworking way of life in self-supporting agro-industrial communities," he says. "The crisis of pollution and the population explosion proves this is necessary. It's the kind of culture Gandhi was trying to lead India to, after the British were driven out. The sweat of hard work is essential to a balanced life, but the main point is that it takes only a half-acre subsistence farm to support one person on a vegetarian diet which can be supplemented with wild game. American commercial farming requires two and a half acres to support one person. You have to grow twelve pounds of feed for every pound of cattle beef. My dean at Michigan State said one-third of a family's income goes for food. So this means a farm worker is putting in four months of the year just to feed his own family. But when I planted an experimental subsistence farm on the Navaho reservation I found it took me only eighty working hours to feed myself for a year—that's about the same time you'd get off your job on a two-week vacation."

Traditional Peoples following local variations of the Creator's Life Plan still exist throughout the world and are beginning to unite toward common goals, Craig believes. "I went to see this Zen Buddhist Roshi teaching in Los Angeles and we found that words in old Japanese are the same as Hopi; they have their own legends of the last days too. There's pretty good evidence that the original Hawaiians came from Japanese and Polynesian stock . . . One thing I can tell you for sure, Oregon logs with the Weyerhaeuser brand have floated all the way down to the South Pacific. What I'm saying is that all the ancient Traditional Peoples were in communication with each other. Indians didn't usually fight among themselves before the whites got here except once in a while when the culture deteriorated someplace temporarily. The Indian Wars began when the whites started pushing tribes west."

Modern archaeology's standard theory of the American Indians' origin is that they were Ice Age Mongolian refugees who crossed the Bering Strait from Siberia to Alaska. But lately a good deal of intriguing evidence has turned up to indicate that many old cultures may have crossed the oceans to the Americas. There are pre-Columbian statues, verified as thousands of years old by Carbon 14 dating, with faces that look remarkably Oriental, Negro, or Egyptian. In 1968 a civilian employee at Fort Benning, Georgia, picked up a stone to build a barbecue pit in his backyard and noticed it had writing-like squiggles all over it. From the Columbus, Georgia, Art Museum, the stone reached Professor Cyrus H. Gordon, Mediterranean studies chairman at Brandeis University. He and Prague University linguist Stanislav Stegert agree that the squiggles are writing from the Greek island civilization of Minoa dating back to about 200 B.C. Professor Gordon also thinks a stone found near Bat Creek, Tennessee, by an 1885 Smithsonian Institute expedition is carved with Bronze Age Hebrew script.

"At Casa Grande National Monument in Utah there's a rock carving . . . a petroglyph . . . that shows a map of the waters made after the Pueblo scouts got back from Egypt," Craig says. "The young men would take the summer route across the Bering Strait to Siberia. They could run two hundred miles in seventeen hours. I'm not in that league myself, but I used to run from Hopiland to Los Angeles in less than a week. There's a man in the Hotevilla Hopi village named Charlie Talwapi who's one hundred and eight years old now, and they say he used to be able to change into a bird or animal. Whether that's literally true or not, the runners in the old days could certainly travel with the endurance of a bird or animal. An Arizona businessman named William Coxon is an expert on these petroglyph trail markers. They're footprints carved in rock, starting at Casa Grande. If you stand at one, you can always see the marker that shows next day's run. He's charted trails to Guadalajara, to the Pacific at Ventura, to the Caribbean along the Azores Islands. The longest trail he charted is across Siberia all the way through Greece and the Negev. He had to stop at the Egyptian border, but any route that's come this far must go all the way down through Africa. And there's no doubt that in the great days of the Six-Nation Iroquois Confederacy they used to send message-runners as far as central Mexico and to the Eskimos at Point Barrow."

Craig feels that in the twenty-odd years since the first atomic bomb went off, his job as a messenger has been accomplished. "We found the key leaders and now I have to assist them the best I can," he says. The Traditional Indian Land and Life Committee keeps track of Craig's mail and phone messages, but though Los Angeles has been more or less his home since the mid fifties, he's on the road half the time. His living expenses are rather low as he travels from one crisis spot to another in various old cars people give him. "I was sent to LA to learn printing so we could get our message out better," he says. "Not that I was given an order, Hopis just explain a situation and if a person feels he should help out, he goes ahead on his own and does it."

It comes as a surprise to find out that Craig Carpenter, the Red Man's Lone Ranger, has been married for fourteen years and has a son. "My wife's place is kind of unhandy for me, but she'd rather I stayed with her than camp out on Kawengna, the magic mountain in Griffith Park. She's an Afro-Indian, brought in from the Oklahoma reservation at eight years old, and strictly a city girl . . . a schoolteacher. Ten years before we met, a medium told me what the woman I married would look like, where she lived, and what her personality would be like. I laughed and said I'd never marry a city girl, especially a beautiful one. They're too much trouble. I met my wife on my thirtieth birthday at a Creek Indian meeting here at the LA Indian Center. I recognized her right off the bat."

When last heard from at the TILL switchboard, Craig was on his way north to help the 529 Pit River Indians of Redding, California, get back 3,000,000 acres the government took away in 1853 and later gave away in large parcels to major corporations like Pacific Gas and Electric. One of the movers in this struggle was Richard Oakes, a twenty-eight-year-old Mohawk student living in San Francisco. Oakes also led the Indian takeover of Alcatraz Island in November, 1969. Then he got hit on the head with a pool cue in a Mission District bar that is the central San Francisco rendezvous for militant Indians and Samoan immigrants. A twenty-six-year-old Samoan was arrested for the crime.

As of June 25, 1970, Richard Oakes had been in a coma for fifteen days. That's when Craig Carpenter's two Traditional leader friends—Thomas Banyacya, the Arizona Hopi, and Mad

Bear, the Tuscarora from New York—showed up at Oakes' bedside in San Francisco General Hospital.

When the hospital administration discovered that these medicine men were not merely here to perform religious rites, but were in fact treating Oakes with some strange Indian herb potion, Banyacya and Mad Bear were thrown out, according to the Associated Press.

Before the Traditional Indian medicine men came, Oakes, unconscious for more than two weeks after a four-hour brain operation that kept him from dying the night he got hit, was still on the critical list, and his family had been told he would probably never regain consciousness.

But by the 1970 Thanksgiving season, fiery Mohawk activist Richard Oakes had recovered completely and was making headlines as he blocked off roads through northern California Indian reservations to collect tolls for the rightful owners.

Chapter 17

Occultism and the Frontiers
of Parapsychology

THE American Association for the Advancement of Science is *the* prestige U.S. research academy, made up of more than three hundred professional societies in science, medicine, and engineering. Since 1957—when the world's approximately one hundred and fifty professional ESP researchers got together to form the Parapsychological Association—the AAAS had turned down three membership applications from parapsychologists.

"We learned a lot from our three failures," says the 1969 PA president, Professor Douglas Dean of the Newark College of Engineering. "It was going to take a great deal of academic lobbying to get past all the red tape involved." When Dean agreed to take on the responsibility of shepherding through a fourth application, he knew it wasn't enough just to send reprints of the best current parapsychology experiments to the AAAS screening committee—previously this evidence had simply gone unread as the committee apparently assumed it was beneath their notice.

Professor Dean began politely pressuring the network of personal contacts he'd built up during more than twenty years in the engineering field. The English-born scientist, ruddy, bespectacled and with a dry donnish wit, is like most other university-affiliated ESP investigators in that he draws his salary for a more "respectable" academic specialty and carries out parapsychology research on his own time, using whatever laboratory equipment he can beg, borrow, or requisition from official school uses. Dean has done more than any other American to demonstrate that telepathy can be picked up subconsciously by a person who isn't even aware of ESP transmissions going on. His most important experiment, reported in the 1966 *International Journal of Neuropsychiatry,* was performed with the plethysmograph, an instrument that measures changes in blood pressure set off by the nervous system. Making plethysmograph readings via a tight rubber cup attached to one of the subject's fingers, Dean found he could measure blood vessel tightenings at the exact same instant a person in another room 250 yards away was concentrating on a card with the name of a person emotionally meaningful to the subject. He later obtained higher-than-chance success in a long-distance plethysmograph ESP experiment between the Jung Institute at Zurich, Switzerland, and a scuba diver 35 feet beneath the surface of the Caribbean Sea. Meanwhile, the Russians were claiming to have succeeded in picking up traces of subconscious telepathy on an EEG over the 1,700 miles between Moscow and Leningrad late in 1966. The clear implication of this line of research is that an ESP telegraphic code system using emotional cues at prearranged time sequences is already possible, making long-distance telepathy a practical method of communication.

Dean attacked the problem of winning membership in the American Association for the Advancement of Science by the Parapsychological Association with the same painstaking thoroughness he would have brought to any scientific project. The application passed all preliminary hurdles and came up for vote at the Boston Statler-Hilton ballroom on December 30, 1969, as the chairman of the screening committee announced, "The committee . . . considered the PA's work for a very long time . . . and came to the conclusion that it is an association investigating controversial or nonexistent phenomena; however, it is open in membership to critics and agnostics, and they were satisfied that it uses scientific methods of inquiry; thus that investigation can be regarded as scientific." But scientists in the audience started leaping up to make outraged speeches about the impossibility of psychic phenomena.

And then Dr. Margaret Mead, probably the most famous and influential anthropologist in the world today, stood up and said, "The whole history of scientific advance is full of scientists investigating phenomena that the establishment did not believe were there. The PA uses standard scientific devices such as statistics, blinds, double blinds, and placeboes. I submit that we vote in favor of this association's work." The Parapsychological Association was voted into AAAS by approximately 170 votes to 30. This is much more than just a bureaucratic paper victory. For the first time in modern history, the organized scientific community has officially recognized the study of extrasensory perception and psychic phenomena.

Perhaps the heart of scientific suspicions against parapsychology is that there isn't any *single repeatable experiment* that proves the existence of ESP beyond a shadow of a doubt under *laboratory test conditions*. In the West, the thrust of modern research into the occult gifts has been to accumulate massive statistics about ESP appearing in large test groups. Dr. Gertrude Schmeidler of the City University of New York has tested thousands of "average" persons at card-guessing since the early 1940's, and her results have been remarkably consistent—relaxed believers in ESP guess cards at higher-than-chance rates while nonbelievers guess significantly below chance. These trends hold up even when other experimenters repeat Schmeidler's procedures. But at best, the weight of statistics constitutes only circumstantial evidence, not the direct, consistent demonstration the disbelievers demand.

In laboratory ESP tests, with their necessary repetitious double-checking, a kind of mental fatigue sets in after a while in the person being tested and his scores drop. This has been a consistent pattern in parapsychological research since Rhine began in the late 1920's—and it has allowed critics like psychology professor C. E. M. Hansel of England's University of Manchester to insist that experimental ESP is no more than a temporary run of gambler's luck. That's why parapsychologists feel that one of the strongest new proofs of ESP is provided by a shy, ultrapatient Czech librarian named Pavel Stepanek. Stepanek is no Edgar Cayce, but he has been guessing the colors of cards sealed in envelopes at a success rate of just under 60 percent since 1961. No gambler in the history of the world has ever had a ten-year winning streak. If Stepanek could have guessed right 60 percent of the time at the roulette tables since 1961, today he'd own every casino on Earth.

Since Pavel speaks English, visiting parapsychologists have

been able to test him in Prague, using their own experimental safeguards—such as three layers of envelopes around the colored cards. But whether the testing is done by Professor Soji Otani of Tokyo or Professor Herbert Keil of Tasmania, Pavel Stepanek still scores just under 60 percent correct. He has even maintained his average during several trips to the United States for tests by Dr. J. G. Pratt at the University of Virginia.

Because a consistent ESP scorer has been sought after for so long by parapsychology, it's understandable that the international experimentation with Pavel Stepanek has concentrated on demonstrating that he maintains his average under the most foolproof conditions. But hopefully the parapsychologists will soon consider this phase closed and shift their efforts to extending Pavel's ESP repertoire and *creating more psychics like him.*

The astonishing truth about Stepanek is that his ESP was brought out from near-zero by biochemist-physicist, Milan Ryzl, the only parapsychology researcher to have worked on both sides of the Iron Curtain. "My working conditions at home were getting too good," Ryzl explains about his defection. "The government became very interested in my results and wanted me to experiment with repressive hypnotic social controls." So he managed to get permission to take his family on an auto vacation to Western Europe and simply kept on going. Ryzl now lives in an all-American tract home in San Jose, located centrally to all the University of California branches he lectures at. In appearance, he is the very model of a Central European professor— stocky and shortish, with gold-rimmed glasses and wavy brown hair brushed straight back. He seems incongruous but happy in his new environment of backyard bicycles and barbecue pits.

"Everybody has latent ESP that can be brought out," says Ryzl in his carefully phrased English. "I found I was able to get significant ESP results in twenty percent of the five hundred persons I worked with in Prague. I prefer to start with people who have no knowledge of, or interest in, psi phenomena so they won't worry if something starts happening. I once had a young man guess all twenty-five colored cards correctly the first time he tried and he got so scared he never came back again."

Ryzl uses hypnosis to lead his subjects to unlock their ESP talents in the most promising directions for them. "Hypnotism probably won't remain the best or the only way to do this, but it's something one can use *now,*" Ryzl says. His process works slowly, first getting the subject used to going under deep hypnosis, then in later sessions inducing visual hallucinations. Ryzl asks them to describe what they see, always praising the description to help build the subjects' confidence. Gradually he switches from suggested hallucinations to genuine psychic exercises, such as telling the subject to leave his body and describe himself.

"Stepanek had no psychic ability or interest when he came to me, he just wanted to earn some extra money when he heard about the experiments from a friend," Ryzl recalls. "But of course as his gift developed, it became very important to his self-image and he took great pride in performing well." The final goal of Ryzl's process is to get the subject to the point where he can use ESP without any hypnosis, though not everybody achieves that.

Pavel Stepanek is by no means the only psychic to have been brought on by Milan Ryzl's hypnotic conditioning. A girl named Josefka was perhaps even more spectacular under hypnosis, once hitting one hundred and twenty-one correct guesses on two hundred and fifty packaged ESP cards when the chance odds should have been fifty—she was exactly average when she tried the same test in a waking state. Another time Josefka, under hypnosis, was able clairvoyantly to envision where Ryzl had mislaid some important documents—in a library book he had returned. But Ryzl lost Josefka when her fiancé forbade her to participate in any more hypnotic ESP experiments. "He seemed to be afraid I was some kind of Svengali," the parapsychologist says, with a sigh.

In 1969 Ryzl taught a parapsychology course at the University of California's San Diego campus. Half of each two-hour session was devoted to experiments with the one hundred and fifty students who signed up. "We tried some group hypnosis, conditioning them toward greater success in clairvoyance," he says. "There were before-and-after tests in clairvoyance, telepathy, and precognition plus a control group of twenty students who weren't hypnotized. All the group results were quite average except for those post-hypnosis clairvoyance tests."

Admittedly, this college classroom test did not allow for as much precision as Ryzl would like for his ESP development programs. "I had an unhappy surprise when I first came to the

United States," he says. "There are few centers, grants, and quality-trained personnel here yet; there's a great deal of suspicion from the public and the sciences. And in Eastern Europe the general opinion is that parapsychology has very wide acceptance in America. Only in the past decade have the socialist countries begun to take parapsychology seriously, but it has already won much more respect there. Throughout Europe, parapsychology is considered an independent science, not a part of psychology. This is a very good thing, because psychology is the branch of science most hostile to us. Psychologists are so worried about psychology's own tenuous acceptance as a science. Another problem in the West is the existence of all these charlatans and fortune-tellers who put the whole field of psychic research into ill-repute with respectable opinion. In the Communist countries there are very strict laws against fortune-telling, and we didn't have constantly to separate ourselves from these things . . . It's a peculiar benefit of censorship."

Ryzl once polled his hypnotized psychics about the right numbers to bet in the Czech lottery. He won a substantial prize with four correct numbers out of the forty-nine on the card—top prize in the lottery is for guessing six numbers. Ryzl used the winnings to improve his laboratory equipment and says that the best way to simulate luck by ESP is to accumulate a lot of precognitive predictions and average them out.

This result is a direct counterattack on the other most common argument against ESP: Why doesn't it work at gambling, where there's such intense motivation to win at each toss of the dice or deal of the cards? Apparently ESP *can* be harnessed for the gambling situation, and recent experiments are zeroing in on the best way to do this.

"Dr. Robert Brier of Rhine's Parapsychology Institute in Durham, North Carolina, has been winning steadily at roulette in Las Vegas and using the money to fund his research," says Professor Thelma Moss of the UCLA Medical School psychology division. "Dr. Brier hasn't published his results yet, but he explained to me that his procedure was to test students for ability to predict red and black on the roulette wheel, until he found some who were consistently a little better than chance and some others who were consistently a little worse than chance. Then he would take a few at a time to Las Vegas and bet with them—or against them if they had been showing psi negative. It only takes a slightly better-than-chance showing to come out ahead of the game, and Dr. Brier was making $100 bets, so profit is quite good."

On her own, Professor Moss has made an informal study of a lady who claimed she attained psychic hunches about horserace winners from running a finger over the track pick columns in the daily newspaper even though she knew nothing about racing. Thelma matched the woman over a two-week period against a UCLA student who claimed to be paying school expenses by his handicapping skills and a graduate assistant who had neither ESP gifts nor any knowledge of horse betting. The psychic bettor was wrong more often than she was right and insisted that her ESP was not working as well as it usually did—but on adding up her hypothetical $2 bets she still came out ahead and won more than the experienced handicapper who had played mostly favorites. The novice who was betting his hunches lost heavily.

Thelma Moss is one of the most articulate parapsychologists researching ESP today and her background clearly explains why. For many years she was a highly successful actress and scriptwriter, appearing on Broadway with such actresses as Ethel Barrymore and writing the Alec Guinness film of G. K. Chesterton's Father Brown stories, The Detective. Her life changed radically when her husband of many years died of cancer and grief drove her to become one of the pioneer LSD therapy patients. Her book about the then-legal psychedelic therapy experience, My Self and I, was written under the pseudonym Constance Newland and sold half a million copies. Then the mother of two went back to UCLA for six years and earned a PhD in clinical psychology. "From the first, I intended to specialize in parapsychology because of the glimpses of psychic phenomena I experienced during the LSD treatments," she says. "But I certainly don't feel the need to use drugs anymore . . . When you've gotten the message, you hang up the phone." Thelma now teaches and conducts psychological testing for UCLA medical students and is allowed—if not particularly encouraged—to use university facilities for ESP research. She is a trim, attractive woman in her early fifties who tends to project the cool authority of a film actress portraying a maturely sexy researcher in a science fiction story. Gradually she has been converting some of the other faculty members to belief in ESP. Psychologist Morris Poulson, a specialist in medical hypnosis, had to admit ESP existed after he helped Thelma hypnotize sender-receiver teams for a telepathy experiment that involved guessing which one of a pair of photographic slides was being shown in another room. Half of the teams that completed the experiment turned out to have statistically significant results, and the best duo connected for twenty-one out of twenty-five slides, at odds of 2,000-to-1.

Thelma Moss' basic experiment is a kind of telepathic isolation-booth slide show. She has assembled a series of two-minute slide projector shows with sound effects, aimed at creating strong emotional feelings—the assassination of President Kennedy, the Watts Riot, nude girls from *Playboy*, Disneyland, or concentration camps. Seventy-five feet away from the soundproof room where the sender is watching the show, another person is lying down in a second isolation booth, talking about whatever impressions he is receiving. Immediately afterward, the receiver is shown two slides, one of which expresses the theme of the full show that the transmitter tried to send telepathically. Guessing the right slide counts as a hit.

Thelma has been able to adapt this setup to a variety of experimental conditions, with all sorts of sender-receiver teams and sometimes over thousands of miles. She has regularly achieved better-than-chance results, finding that in general the best scorers are teams that know each other intimately, believers in the possibility of ESP, and people whose work calls upon the use of creative imagination.

"I have learned to have a great deal of respect for the laws of chance as an indicator of the presence of ESP," she says. "I decided once and for all to find out if I had any ESP myself. So whenever I had a few spare moments I would push the buttons on our new random light generator. This is a wonderful new testing device that works with a geiger counter and a particle of Strontium 90 shielded in lead. The radioactivity turns on one of four different-colored lights in no predictable order. You push a button on the little box to set off the process, and it automatically records the results. Testing ESP with this machine is like playing with a toy. Finally after several weeks I got up to twenty thousand trials. With chance odds of four-to-one I should have guessed right on five thousand—and my total correct guesses were five thousand and one."

Thelma Moss believes that only in the 1960's did Western parapsychology become a major field of study because not until the past decade did ESP research emerge from the spiritual domination of Dr. J. B. Rhine. "I think it will be remembered as one of Dr. Rhine's last great contributions that he refused to accept any active role in the Parapsychological Association even though he was instrumental in getting it started," she says. "Although Rhine still feels personally that the best research strategy is to continue amassing statistics with the ESP cards, he recognized it was time for others to carry out their own ideas without being influenced by his reputation."

The name of Dr. Gardner Murphy is not nearly as well known to the public as that of Dr. Rhine, but within the field of parapsychology he also is regarded as one of the Grand Old Men. Murphy was a founder of American psychology; his book, *Historical Introduction to Modern Psychology,* published in 1925, is still a standard college text in updated editions. He was chairman of the CCNY psychology department from 1940 to 1952, when he moved to the Menninger Foundation in Topeka, Kansas, as research director. Now in his mid-seventies and in uncertain health, he is still one of the most eloquent of scientists and teaches at George Washington University. He has also been the president of the American Society for Psychical Research since 1961. "One of the main questions of psychic research is whether we can give up our precious folklore and intuition about vast regions of the unknown without throwing out the useful data," he says about occultism's relationship to ESP.

Gardner Murphy's openness to paranormal phenomena came in part from his experiences with the unorthodox healing that cured him of near-blindness in 1927 and ended his nine years of semi-invalidism in 1934. His case had been given up for lost by standard medical opinion. Dr. Frank Marlow of Syracuse restored Murphy's sight with eye muscle exercises, and Dr. William H. Hay overcame his long-term influenza aftereffects by a combination of diet and exercise. Murphy calls these some of the "many occasions in which I found a small oasis of personal reality against the monolithic assurance of respectable and organized science . . . It takes an enormous amount of powerful evidence, with a new theory . . . compatible both with the old data and the new data . . . in order to demolish . . . the orderly system."

As keynote speaker at the 1970 University of Maine ESP Seminar, Murphy spoke of the "rubber sheet analogies" which visualize time and space in terms of the flexible field of Einstein's Theory of Relativity instead of Isaac Newton's rigid Law of Gravity. "You can begin to pull and twist and stretch and roll up this rubber sheet until the distance of an inch is an eighth of an inch, and another distance of an inch is three inches and a half," he said. Perhaps the psychic phenomena are "a natural and normal intercommunication" that works by somehow changing the shape of the rubber sheet. "I see ESP as an extended self, an archipelago of mankind." Then, fielding a question from the audience about how much progress in harnessing psychic powers could be expected during the 1970's, he said, "Oh, we'll just keep inching along. I don't think we're ready to put Western Union out of business yet." Murphy also wasn't worried about a time coming when everybody could read each other's minds, pointing out, "Throughout history, mankind has done a pretty good job of shutting out paranormal mental phenomena." That got the biggest laugh of the seminar.

But Dr. Karlis Osis, the man handpicked by Gardner Murphy to be research director of the American Society for Psychical Research in 1962, has a more optimistic timetable. Osis is a long, lean native of Latvia who is one of the handful of men in the world to have been granted a PhD in parapsychology and to have spent an entire career exclusively in ESP studies. He was at Duke University with Rhine from 1951 to 1957 and then took charge of the research program at Eileen Garrett's Parapsychology Foundation for five years until joining the ASPR staff. He received his doctorate from the psychology department of the University of Munich for a thesis that was a critique of all the work then published on the theoretical basis of ESP. Osis still speaks English with a somewhat thick German accent, but it takes only a few minutes of listening to him to realize that his command of the language is really admirably fluent and laced with a salty wit.

"I have two noses," he says. "I have the scientist's hard nose that insists on a rigorously controlled experiment, and I have the soft nose of a seeker who wants to actualize human potential in all its remarkable scope. Why have I done all this research for twenty years? So I can write a paper that fifty other experts will read, and maybe I can find a grant for my next project? No. We are just at the foothills of the Himalayas of the spirit and what we need as human beings, nations need too. The reach of the mind, with its virtual omniscience which has been demonstrated throughout history, gives back to man some of the dignity and grandeur lost in modern scientific concepts of personality. We must be able to change states of consciousness as you can change the program on a television set. There are many ways this can be done. We must find ways to have true, rich relationships again so the young will no longer be right in saying we have lost our humanness."

Under Murphy and Osis, the venerable ASPR has embarked on a newly expanded research program in the society's recently acquired headquarters building, a large, elegant, old townhouse directly behind Manhattan's famous Dakota Apartments, the massive gothic building that was the setting for *Rosemary's Baby*.

"We still investigate spontaneous cases as in the old days, and we're more than happy to open our labs for testing professional psychics," says Osis. "But now it's mostly for a little excitement on the side, like a businessman who goes hunting for kicks. However, we are still coming across cases of hauntings that we can't explain by normal causes, the best-known in recent years being the Seaford, Long Island, poltergeists."

The reactivated ASPR research thrust has become, in effect, one of the most technologically avant-garde investigations of traditional occult theory this side of the Iron Curtain. On one front, Osis is conducting the most extensive research on the relationship between meditation and ESP ever attempted. The experimental design is a mind-boggling combination of traditional consciousness-expansion techniques, advanced electronics, and computerized statistics.

Osis will accept as a volunteer for this study anyone who has had practice in meditation, no matter whether he's learned it through Zen, Quakerism, Yoga, or the Hasidic tradition. "If the altered state of consciousness is achieved properly, it's always the same experience no matter where one approaches it from," he says. On his own, Osis has studied meditation with a Japanese Zen master to the extent of going away on five-day retreats.

ASPR's subjects spend a half hour in a comfortable meditation room before any testing is done. They fill out lengthy before-and-after questionnaires about the mood they are in, and the answers are correlated with test results by the ASPR computer. One of the experiments these subjects participate in after meditation is an improved electronic version of the design Gardner Murphy has called the best ESP experiment ever made.

In 1921 at the University of Groningen in Holland, a team of psychologists under Dr. Brugmans set up a soundproof room with a plate-glass window in the floor that looked down on a blindfolded student enclosed behind a curtain-box in the room below. This receiver was seated at a checkerboard, and his task was to reach through a slit in the curtain and place his finger on a square he felt the senders up above were concentrating on. The squares were picked at random by drawing numbered slips of paper from a bag and of course since the sender could see in which direction the receiver was moving his finger, he could focus his thoughts on the most precisely helpful instructions. Brugmans made one hundred and eighty-seven trials with his receiver. At chance odds there should have been four correct hits. In fact, the experiment resulted in *sixty* squares chosen correctly —at astronomical odds.

The current ASPR version of this classic experiment uses the exact same principle. However, now the sender's room and the receiver's room are on opposite sides of the building as well as on separate floors. The sender keeps track of the blindfolded receiver's hand movements via a closed-circuit video camera. And the squares are chosen from tables of random numbers.

The most universal evidence of a paranormal realm has always been the spontaneous psychic message that flashes between relatives or close friends over long distances at moments of stress. There have been small-scale laboratory attempts to duplicate this historic experience under test conditions, but until the development of the most recent computerized statistical methods it was impossible to test large numbers of people for long-distance ESP.

There were nine hundred volunteers throughout the United

States for an experiment which involved guessing the order of five simple pictures in a one hundred-card deck laid facedown in random order at distances from one-third of a mile to 10,000 miles. The computers are still juggling with the seventy test-control variables involved. Meditation for thirty minutes before each test series was a part of this ground-breaking experiment too. All nine hundred volunteers had mood questionnaires to fill out and were given blank calling cards handled by the sender. These cards were to be held by the receivers during the test period to test whether psychometry helps focus ESP on the distant sender.

Walter Houston Clark, a retired MIT professor of comparative religion and author of *Chemical Ecstasy*, a history of the religious use of hallucinogenics, went around the world with the cards. He laid out the cards at prearranged times in Paris, Sydney, New Delhi, and New York. "My biggest problem was making sure I had the correct local time to correspond with the New York time that had been picked for each three-hour session," says Professor Clark. "In New Delhi, I had to start at four thirty in the morning. Also, most hotel rooms weren't big enough to lay out one hundred cards unless some went under the bed and then I had to try not to walk on them. When I was entering Australia, a pretty blond customs official asked what I was going to do with those strange cards in my luggage, and she became quite nonplussed when I explained I was going to lay them on a hotel-room floor and sit with them for three hours. Fortunately she believed in ESP so I was eventually able to make our purpose clear."

Karlis Osis says, "In general, the results of the long-distance experiment showed ESP was present and declined very slightly, by a factor of about .4, over the ten thousand miles. The moods of both the sender and the receivers were major factors. Our results run counter to the prevailing ESP theory that psychic phenomena aren't affected by distance—but no other experiment has had so much data to work with. So far, our tentative conclusion is that the decline in ESP signal strength over extremely long distances is so small that it has never registered on any test until now. But it is very important to know if distance *is* an ESP factor. After all, this could give us a whole new set of clues to what we're looking for. I'm hoping that the final figures on this experiment may prove to provide a connecting link between ESP and information theory. ESPland is a huge unexplored territory with little roads poking in from the sides. At least we can now be pretty sure the unexplored territory exists. But something very important is still missing, the secret of turning on an average person's psychic abilities at will. When we make that breakthrough, we'll have our superhighway into ESPland!"

Chapter **18**

The Occult Future

HOW likely is it that we will have a major breakthrough in understanding extrasensory perception—today's name for the occult powers—during the 1970's?

The occult explosion itself could make such a step forward far more likely. For the first time a modern industrialized society, contemporary America, has a significantly large occult subculture that is too well-informed about occult and psychic phenomena, too widely exposed to personal paranormal experiences—because of drugs or direct occult experimentation—and simply too well educated and rational to be easily silenced by know-nothing skepticism any longer! This dramatically changed climate of opinion is the vital first step for any expansion of serious efforts to tap the half-hidden powers of the mind and the mysteries of nature hinted at in classic occultism as magic, necromancy, and divination.

As Gardner Murphy pointed out, the sociology of knowledge requires "an enormous amount of powerful evidence, with a new theory . . . compatible both with the old data and the new data" in order to change whatever interpretations of the physical universe are currently taught as facts.

Some lines of research which we have noted as *already showing successful results* might very well lead to evidence so unshakable and so widely publicized that no amount of materialist pooh-poohing would be able to discredit it. And this could happen *within the next few years* with no more than an extension of the current research for which groundwork has been laid. It doesn't depend on the sudden emergence of a contemporary

Edgar Cayce or Nostradamus willing to seek out the ESP laboratories and be tested with the EEG, the plethysmograph, the polygraph, and all the rest of today's instrumentation.

A westward spread of acceptance of Kirlian photography of living auras could be the turning point, or it might be a more widespread confirmation of Cleve Backster's lie detector evidence of cellular intelligence. Perhaps a refinement in the practical uses of bio-feedback brain-wave conditioning will provide that impregnable proof, or it might stem from Milan Ryzl's obtaining the research facilities to train more psychics like Pavel Stepanek and Josefka. Certainly the world would be forced to take a long second look at occult doctrine if Eugen Jonas' astrological method of birth control ultimately proves itself and becomes a universal family planning technique.

And there is virtually no limit to the imaginative new approaches which could be tried if Western governments funded parapsychological research to anything like the extent of $14,000,000 yearly that Russia is spending for psychic research, according to the findings of *Psychic Discoveries Behind the Iron Curtain*.

Just one example of the kind of project which could be attempted: Suppose we took a classroom of children too young to have been conditioned yet to the notion that magic and fantasy don't exist, and, as part of the regular teaching schedule, inserted things like dream recall exercises, psychic practice sessions, meditation periods, and some Human Potential body-awareness techniques? Would it be very surprising to find some high scores on ESP tests given the children at the end of the term? And it certainly couldn't cost a great deal to carry out this kind of an experiment.

A truly moving description of what full utilization of the mind's potential—whether it is called occult powers, mystical illumination, ESP, a psychedelic high, or the altered state of consciousness—could mean to the future of mankind was given at Esalen Institute in introduction to an appearance by Professor Abraham Maslow, researcher of self-actualized man and the peak experience. The speaker was George Leonard, a courtly, native southerner, six feet six, who has written prize-winning articles about race prejudice, flown fighter planes in World War II, is an Esalen board member, a former West Coast editor of *Look* magazine and an educational authority who wrote *Education and Ec-stasy*.

Leonard said, "Ever since the race of man first learned to think and hope, men have been haunted by an irrepressible dream—that the limits of human ability lie beyond the boundaries of the imagination; that every human being uses only a fraction of his abilities; that there must be some way for everyone to achieve far more of what is truly his to achieve. History's greatest prophets, mystics, and saints have dreamed even more boldly, saying that all men are somehow one with God. The dream has survived history's failures, ironies, and uneven triumphs, sustained more by intuition than by facts.

"Now, however, the facts are beginning to come in. Science has at last turned its attention to the central questions of human capabilities. Here is the century's biggest news. What the mystics promised is upon us now, not out on some apocalyptic plain, but in the laboratory, the church, the classroom, the home. We believe that all men somehow possess a divine potentiality; that ways may be worked out—specific, systematic ways—to help, not the few, but the many toward a vastly expanded capacity to learn, to love, to feel deeply, and to create. We believe that most people can best find God and themselves through heightened awareness of the world, increased commitment to the eternal in time.

"But this is not enough. No man can sleep secure while others suffer. If the divine is present in the individual soul, it must be sought and found in men's institutions as well; for people will not readily achieve individual salvation without a saving society. Every one of us must go on working in the usual social and political ways to help reduce the fever that saps men of their natural joy."

There are, however, more ominous visions of what the harnessing of man's psychic powers might bring.

One can't help feeling uneasy about the eerie symbolism behind one of Edgar Cayce's more awesome insights in his psychic history of Atlantis. During a number of his sleep-trance sessions from the 1920's to the 1940's Cayce developed the theme that the technological power of Atlantis was based on Terrible Crystals which functioned by tapping "the oneness of all energy" and could draw force from stars when triggered by psychic concentration. As the culture of Atlantis became more and more decadent, the Terrible Crystals were tuned up to peak power and any excess energy simply ran off into the ground. The greedy Atlanteans didn't realize that the energy was not harmlessly dissipating but instead was accumulating dangerously along a deep underground fissure. And it was this energy pollution which caused the great cataclysm that finally sank Atlantis beneath the oceans.

This story fits into Cayce's general insistence that karma destines us all for whatever our past behavior has caused us to deserve. But it also has disturbing echoes of such contemporary manifestations as atomic energy, laser beams, pollution, and ESP —ideas which barely existed when the Sleeping Prophet began hinting at them as early as fifty years ago. As we have seen, one of the best-understood things about the psychic vision is that it filters up through the subconscious with common patterns of dreamlike distortion. Among the most usual are time distortions, so it could be that what Cayce's sleep-clairvoyance state interpreted as part of the great occult historic cycle—lost ancient civilizations peaking, declining, and mysteriously destroying themselves, to be forgotten along with their secret knowledge—was *really using the Atlantis myth to issue a warning prediction of America's future.*

It is not necessary to cry doom. The point is that it's one thing to finally break through to the ESP potential seemingly locked in every human mind. Learning to use this awesome force for peaceful, constructive, and morally just ends is something else again. Cayce apparently knew this as well as any of the legendary sorcerers of old who were very careful to keep their techniques out of the wrong hands.

At worst, unlocking these occult powers of the mind would simply give man still another dangerously powerful tool with which he must somehow adjust to living. We *already* have a selection of paths leading to the end of the world—atomic war, overpopulation, ecological breakdown—and none of these fearful paths will go away simply because we wish them to. Survival itself dictates that man must try to make himself better than he has been in the past.

And at best, who knows? Maybe the "irrepressible dream . . . that all men somehow possess a divine potentiality," a dream shared alike by "history's greatest prophets, mystics, and saints" will at last come true—and a godlike humanity would become wise enough to be righteous. It's a gamble, but we have no choice but to take it.

Index